The Wrong Man: Who Ordered the Murder of Gambler Herman Rosenthal and Why.

By Joe Bruno

PUBLISHED BY:

Knickerbocker Literary Services

EDITED BY:

Marc A. Maturo and Lawrence Venturato

COVER BY:

Alchemy Covers

Introduction

2012 is the 100-year anniversary of the murder of small-time gambler Herman Rosenthal - the most celebrated murder of its time. Make no mistake, there are no good guys here; no innocent victims. The fact is an offensive and offensive-looking well-known criminal framed a crooked New York City police lieutenant for the killing of an odious stool pigeon. People in the underworld cheered the death of Herman Rosenthal; he was that much disliked. But that doesn't negate the fact that the wrong man sat in Sing Sing's electric chair for ordering Rosenthal's murder, while the man who framed him - and actually ordered the murder of Herman Rosenthal - walked away scot free, content in the knowledge that he was able to fool so many prominent law enforcement officials so easily.

This is how it all happened.

Herman Rosenthal

He was thoroughly unlikeable; mean and snarky, and he would swindle his own mother if it would earn him a few bucks. Yet, the murder of small-time gambler Herman Rosenthal ignited a firestorm in the New York City press, which resulted in New York City Police Lieutenant, Charles Becker, being unjustly fried in Sing Sing's electric chair.

Herman Rosenthal was a runt of a man who was born in Russia and immigrated to the United States with his parents when he was five-years-old. They settled in the Lower East Side of Manhattan, which, in the late 1800s, was a conglomeration of hard-working immigrants, infused with thieves, crooks, cheats, gamblers, and murderers.

Rosenthal's parents were Jewish. But there is no evidence that Rosenthal ever set foot in a Jewish temple after his tumultuous teenage years began. At the age of 14, Rosenthal eschewed school, and he began running with one of the many local street gangs. Rosenthal stole from pushcarts, and picked the pockets of drunks. He perpetrated a myriad of illegal schemes corruptible kids from that era did to amuse and enrich themselves.

Despite his size (he was 5-foot-3-inches), Rosenthal was a competent street fighter, and he gained a reputation as someone who could handle himself in a pinch. (A friend once said of Rosenthal, "He was mighty fast on his feet, and he could hit hard.")

To earn a meager living, Rosenthal sold newspapers on the Manhattan side of the Brooklyn Bridge. However, the money he earned selling newspapers was peanuts compared to what Rosenthal envisioned as proper remuneration for a man of his guile, and what he considered to be his superior intellect. Invariably, Rosenthal gravitated to the money and in the Lower East Side of Manhattan at the turn of the century that usually led to a poolroom. That's where Rosenthal met Big Tim Sullivan, the Political Prince of the Lower East Side, who had as many scruples as a bald-headed eagle has hair.

Because of his spunk and willingness to mix it up when necessary - and also because Sullivan knew that "smart Jew boys" like Rosenthal represented a huge voting block on the Lower East

Side -Big Tim got Little Herman Rosenthal a job as a numbers runner for a downtown poolroom. Rosenthal soon graduated to working inside a secret back room in the poolroom, where he took sporting bets, both in person and by code over the phone.

In 1897, Rosenthal married the lovely Dora Gilbert, and they became partners in the profession of Dora's choice: the back-bruising business of prostitution. Quite simply, Dora did her best work on her knees and on her back in their West 40th Street apartment bedroom, while Rosenthal stood guard outside the bedroom door to make sure the visitors behaved themselves and didn't quibble over the price or the performance. In time, Dora employed two other "working girls," and Rosenthal became their pimp, too.

In the early 1900s, things were going quite well for Rosenthal when Dora decided to give him the gate. Dora divorced Herman, and she used the money she had saved from her sex business to open up a legitimate boardinghouse: no johns need apply. This, in effect, left Rosenthal without a job, and since unemployment insurance had not yet been devised, Rosenthal went back to Big Tim Sullivan with his hat in his hand.

Big Tim, still fond of Little Herman, got Rosenthal a job as the proprietor of a small Lower East Side craps game. Rosenthal did so well for Sullivan in this endeavor, Big Tim procured Rosenthal a prestigious gig as a bookmaker in a storefront in Far Rockaway, Queens, which was the last stop on the New York City subway transit system. Riding the subway daily gave Rosenthal plenty of time to think, and he envisioned the day when he would become a big shot himself.

As a result of Rosenthal's guile and Big Tim's connections, Rosenthal moved up the underworld gambling ladder one step at a time. Rosenthal eventually became the manager at the prestigious Hesper Club, located on 111 Second Avenue and owned by Big Tim Sullivan's brother, Patrick. The private Hesper Club was famous for its full casino. It featured roulette wheel and craps tables, and a back-room poker game which attracted some of the most illustrious gamblers in town. The gamblers included respected judges, assistant district attorneys, and a few mid-to-high-level government employees.

The Hesper Club was a club where you obtained membership only through the recommendation of another member. Big Tim was so intent on his brother Patrick's private club thriving, Big Tim even penned a flowery letter, which was framed and placed inside the club next to the front door.

The letter, dated April 30, 1903, and addressed to then-Hesper president Sam Harris, read:

"Dear Sir: Regarding my election as a life member of the Hesper Club, I keenly appreciate the compliment you pay me, and should it be possible for me at any time to serve you, or any of the members, I would be glad to do so. A simple word from you will command me – Yours truly, TIMOTHY D. SULLIVAN."

This framed letter said reams about the strong connection between the elected politicians of the time and the illegal gambling crowd. Everyone knew Big Tim Sullivan ran the Lower East Side with an iron fist, fitted with a velvet glove. They also knew that Big Tim could provide well-paying jobs, some of them "no-show" jobs, to anyone he desired.

But the implication of the Hesper Club letter was even more sinister than that.

Big Tim basically said in the letter that a simple word from the president of the Hesper Club, and Sullivan would pull whatever strings necessary to keep illegal gambling thriving in the Hesper Club; not to mention giving jobs to whomever the bigwigs at the Hesper Club said needed jobs. This was a classic case of one dirty hand washing the other.

Being the manager of the Hesper club catapulted Rosenthal into the big time. He was raking in so much cash, he was able to rent of suite of rooms at the illustrious Broadway Hotel, which set Rosenthal back more than $1,200 a month; a tidy sum in the first decade of the twentieth century. With his newfound celebrity, Rosenthal decided to take himself a second wife, a chubby bleach-bottled redhead named Lillian, who did not, like Rosenthal's first wife, do business on her back. In fact, Herman was so flush with cash, Lillian had no need, nor any desire, to work at all.

The problem with Rosenthal was that he was not very good at making friends, but quite competent at making enemies; especially those in the New York City police department. While he was manager of the Hesper Club, Rosenthal opened his own gambling operation, with the blessing of Big Tim Sullivan, of course, at 123 Second Avenue, called The Red Raven Club. The Red Raven Club had formerly been a poolroom run by Rosenthal.

It was common knowledge at the time, if you wanted to run an illegal gambling establishment in New York City, you had to pay off the police and pay them good. But giving graft to cops was adverse to Rosenthal's nature. Instead of making his weekly contributions to the "Police Benevolent Association," Rosenthal used that money instead to fortify his gambling houses from unwanted invasion. He installed extra-sturdy doors and employed the most competent doormen, who were experts at sniffing out an undercover cop, or someone from the city who might want to serve the club with a warrant.

This made the New York City police department all the more eager to shut Rosenthal down.

In 1903, New York City Police Captain Charles Kemp spent considerable time devising a way to put Rosenthal out of business. According to Rose Keefe, in her book *The Starker*, Kemp used a dubious "letter of introduction" to gain admittance for one of his operatives to 123 Second Avenue, when it was a tightly run Rosenthal poolroom/illegal gambling house. The letter read:

> *Herman Rosenthal Esq.*
> *This is to introduce my friend, Mr. Ketcham. He is all right.*
>
> *H. Morgan*

The undercover cop gave the letter to the doorman, who in turn, gave the letter to Rosenthal. For some unknown reason, Rosenthal gave the thumbs-up for the visitor to enter. The undercover did so and in the course of an hour, he was able to place bets on several horse races.

This allowed Captain Kemp to get a warrant, and on August 15, 1903, Captain Kemp, five detectives, and 20 policemen broke down the front door of 123 Second Avenue with axes. When they busted inside, they found Rosenthal frantically trying to destroy the day's racing receipts inside a raging fireplace. Rosenthal was cuffed, and along with three of his employees, taken to the police station and charged with "keeping and maintaining a poolroom." Why he was not charged in connection with taking illegal race bets is a testament to Rosenthal's adroitness in pitching papers into the fire.

Rosenthal's rabbi with the law, and his ace-in-the-hole, was always Big Tim Sullivan. However, by the elections of 1908 Sullivan's stronghold on the German and Irish votes had been weakened by the huge influx of Italians below 14th Street and west of Broadway, and Jews east of Broadway. With Sullivan's power waning, Rosenthal, who had an abrasive and defiant attitude when dealing with the legal authorities, had a large target on his back as far as the New York City police department was concerned.

In 1909, New York City District Attorney William Travers Jerome, who had prosecuted Harry Thaw for the murder of famed architect Stanford White, set his sights on police corruption, illegal gambling in general, and on Herman Rosenthal in particular. Jerome had Rosenthal arrested and charged with "running a string of gambling houses." However, as soon as Jerome closed down one of Rosenthal's joints, little Herman just moved his equipment to a similar place nearby and opened again with impunity.

By 1910, the Hesper Club had lost its luster. Due to the decrease in his political power, Big Tim Sullivan and his brother, Patrick, resigned from the club and left its future in the slippery hands of Herman Rosenthal.

With Rosenthal now running the show, instead of the usual politicians and judges spinning the Hesper Club's roulette wheel, shooting craps, and playing poker in the back, they were replaced by neighborhood hooligans, who didn't gamble as much as the previous members and were inclined to cheat a bit on cards, which decreased the Hesper Club's membership even more.

The first blow came on October 28, 1910, when, according to the *New York Times*:

"The Hesper Social and Political Club at 111 Second Avenue was invaded by the police yesterday under orders from Commissioner Cropsey and Police Commissioner Driscoll. The club, which is in Senator Christy Sullivan's district, has long been regarded as one of the most influential East Side organizations, and

the police raid caused considerable consternation in the neighborhood."

Inside the Hesper Club, 250 men were rounded up, and the police found "evidence of gambling" in the form of stuss tables, faro layouts, and blackboards, on which the partially erased words "Track Good" were still visible.

The police let all but two of the men go, but as they were doing so, about 100 or so disappointed gamblers decided to bum-rush past the police officers standing guard at the front door and force their way inside. These men claimed they were members of the private Hesper Club and should not be denied admittance. Seven of those men were also arrested, and the Hesper Club was temporarily shuttered.

Rosenthal, who was not on the premises at the time of the raid, was furious. He immediately sent Matthias Radin, who introduced himself at Police Headquarters as "the lawyer for the Hesper Club," to set the record straight. Radin yelled at Detective Cody, one of the officers involved in the raid, that "Tammany Hall would remember what the police had done and would remember those instrumental in it."

Then Radin tried to push his way into the office of the Police Commissioner. When he was stopped by a phalanx of cops, Radin yelled at them, "You don't know who you're talking to! You're talking in a swell way to a good Tammany man and you'll pay for it, and don't you forget it!"

Newspaper reporters surrounded Rosenthal's mouthpiece, and this was the stage Radin relished.

He told the reporters, "It was an outrage to invade the quarters of the club. It is one of the oldest and respectable clubs on the East Side and had never been interfered with before in history. Those blackboards meant nothing. The police might have written those words 'Track Good' themselves. We hold lectures in the clubhouse regularly and the blackboards were used for illustrating points in these educational lectures. They were for the education and benefit of the members. So far as the stuss tables were concerned, any home might have such tables in it."

The October 27 raid showed how much pull Tammany Hall still had concerning the New York City police department. Due to pressure applied by the aforementioned Matthias Radin, Police Commissioner Driscoll, who had ordered the raid, was relieved of his job and transferred to a local Precinct where his powers were greatly diminished. Also, Detectives Cody and Murphy, who led the raid, were no longer detectives. They were assigned to plain patrol duty, in uniform, in the boondocks of the Bronx.

Through his considerable pull at Tammany Hall, Radin was able to get the Hesper Club reopened. So, the police set their sights on another one of Rosenthal's establishments: the Red Raven Club at 123 Second Ave, right down the street from the Hesper Club. This club was Rosenthal's alone, and it didn't have the protection Big Tim Sullivan had afforded the Hesper Club.

On December 23, 1910, the Red Raven Club was raided by Capt. Kemp's men. It was closed for a while as Rosenthal ordered his man Radin to get a court injunction to reopen the club. That Radin did, but on March 19, 1911, led by District Attorney Jerome himself, the police raided the Red Raven Club again in a rousing midnight invasion.

Seven men were arrested, but the big fish – Rosenthal - was not on the premises at the time. So, Jerome sent his men to the Hesper Club, where there they found Rosenthal and arrested him on the spot. Rosenthal spent the night in Night Court, where his bail was set at $10,000; a tidy sum usually reserved for elite criminals. When the sun rose and the bail bond offices opened, Rosenthal posted bail and was none too happy about it.

He was even less happy, when the police raided the Hesper Club for the final time on April 19, 1911.

The *New York Times* headlines and subsequent article read:

HESPER CLUB RAIDED BY FLYNN'S AXEMEN
Deputy Commissioner Takes the Sullivan Stronghold
By Storm as a Gambling Resort
IT MAY END GAMBLING HERE
Gamblers Thought This Club Immune From Police
Interference on Account of Political Influence.

"The Hesper Club at 111 Second Avenue, generally believed to have the support of political interests allied to those of Big Tim and Christie Sullivan, and known as the gamblers' own club, the

principal citadel in the gambling fortifications throughout the city, was raided by Deputy Police Commissioner William J. Flynn. The raid, the gamblers themselves admitted when they heard of it, may prove to be the last blow necessary to suppress vice in this city."

A known gambler, who frequented the Hesper Club, said, "It will be hard to keep on gambling when every time Flynn gets a man, he is put under a suspended sentence with orders to report to him. Flynn will have a regular roll book, and call roll every time he holds a meeting. It will be fine to hear the roll reading 'Beansie Rosenfeld, Hymie Rosenthal, Bob Kennedy' and so forth. And hear those fellows answer 'Present and voting.' That's what it will come to at this rate, with everyone facing a two-year sentence and a $1,000 fine if he breaks parole."

With both of his money-making gambling joints shut down by the law, Rosenthal was so broke he had to move out of the Broadway Hotel, and he absconded to a flea-bag tenement with his wife, Lillian.

Desperate for a way to make a living, Rosenthal again turned to Big Tim Sullivan for help. Sullivan, whose political power had been seriously diminished and was in the early stages of syphilis dementia, fronted Rosenthal $35,000 to open a posh gambling house, not on the Lower East Side, but in the ritzy "Tenderloin District," which ran from 30th Street to 50th Street, and from Sixth to Eight Avenues. Instead of dealing with the Lower Manhattan mugs, the Tenderloin district was the gambling home of such elegant sporting characters as Richard Canfield, Lou Busteed, Charles Gates, Julius Fleischmann, Henry Sinclair, and Percival Hill.

On November 17, 1911, Rosenthal's gambling den had its grand opening at 104 West 45th Street. This made Bridgey Webber, a former member of the Hesper Club, not too happy. In early 1911, Webber, who had been Rosenthal's archenemy since they were teenagers, had opened his own sporting club at 117 West 45th Street, down the block from Rosenthal's new joint, and he sure didn't like the competition being so close to his lucrative operation.

However, Rosenthal's steadfast insistence not to pay off the local police came back to haunt him. After being open just a few days, Rosenthal was summoned to the offices of Police Inspector Cornelius Hayes, who demanded an immediate payment of $1,000;

to be followed by payments of $1,000 a week. Rosenthal told Hayes to go shit in his hat, which was not such a smart thing do to, because a few days later, Hayes led a contingent of cops to Rosenthal's new club. The police smashed down the doors, then took their axes to every piece of equipment in sight.

Rosenthal borrowed money to purchase new equipment, and he also took in a new partner: New York City Police Lieutenant Charles Becker, who was reputed to have closed down more gambling joints in New York City than any other cop in town.

CHARLES BECKER

In 1870, Charles Becker was born to a German/American family in the tiny town of Calicoon Center, in the Catskill region of upstate New York. Becker's father died when he was seven, and he was raised by his widowed mother. In 1890, when Becker was just 20 years old, he hopped on a train and headed for New York City where he hoped to gain fame and more than his fair share of fortune.

After working at several meaningless jobs, the tall and broad-shouldered Becker took a gig as a bouncer in a German "Biergarten" (beer garden) just off the Bowery. German Biergartens were jovial joints where sometimes an unruly customer, who had one too many brews, needed to get pitched out on his ear. Becker was especially good at this sort of thing, and he got the reputation of someone who could "punch with the kick of a horse." Becker's status as a ruffian grew, and soon he caught the eye of several customers who were politically connected and were in the position to get someone like Becker an appointment in the New York City police department; after he paid them handsomely, of course.

Becker's rabbi was the Republican Police Commissioner John McClave, who had been appointed by Mayor Franklin Edson in 1884 and re-appointed in 1890 by Mayor Hugh Grant. McClave, as was the practice in those days, took the whopping sum of $300 off Becker (nearly six months of a New York City policeman's pay), and in early 1894 Becker became a full-fledged New York City policeman. Soon after he secured Becker his "appointment," McClave was summoned before the Lexow Committee, which was investigating police corruption in New York City. The charge against McClave was "banking the proceeds of bribery," and with his son-in-law Gideon Granger testifying against him, McClave was forced to resign.

There is no record of McClave ever having returned Becker's $300.

After making his bones in several precincts, Becker was given a most enviable post as a vice-stomping uniformed policeman in the Tenderloin, sometimes known as "Satan's Circus." Becker soon learned he could expand his policeman's pay considerably by sticking out his hand whenever he encountered someone breaking the gambling or prostitution laws; both of which abounded in the Tenderloin. Because he was not arresting people who came across with the cash, Becker sometimes had to make a legitimate arrest just to show he was doing his job.

On September 16, 1896, 24-year-old novelist/journalist Stephen Crane was hobnobbing in the Tenderloin, doing research for an article on which he was working. Crane had just received worldwide acclaim for his Civil War novel *Red Badge of Courage* and was looking to add to his reputation by writing a piece about the Tenderloin.

Around 10 p.m., Crane ambled into the Broadway Garden, which was located in the southern tip of the Tenderloin, at the corner of Broadway and Thirty-First Street. There Crane made the acquaintance of three young ladies who called themselves "dancers," which they may have been, but more often they were prostitutes. Crane had finished interviewing these women for his proposed story, and he escorted the three lovelies outside where they intended to go their separate ways.

After Crane had guided one lady to a cable car, he turned back to the other two, just in time to see Patrolman Becker, in his sparkling blue uniform with its shining brass buttons, come out of nowhere and grab both ladies by the wrists. Becker announced he was arresting them for prostitution.

Thinking quickly, one of the ladies pointed at Crane, and she told Becker, "I'm no prostitute. He's my husband!"

Becker turned to Crane and asked him if the lady's statement was true.

Crane said, "Yes, I am. I'm her husband."

Becker let go of the young lady's wrist, but still held tightly onto the other young lady's wrist. "Well, what about this one?" Becker asked Crane.

Crane replied, "I know nothing about her."

Becker smiled. "Well, she's nothing but a common prostitute, and I'm arresting her for soliciting prostitution."

Becker took the girl, real name Ruby Young, but known on the streets as Dora Clark, to the 19th Precinct and locked her up for the night. Crane tagged along, and he found out that first thing in the morning Clark would be arraigned at the Jefferson Court Market, at Tenth Street and Sixth Avenue. Crane decided to show up at her arraignment.

Magistrate Cornell was in charge of the proceedings, and after listening to Becker's charges, Magistrate Cornell turned to Clark and asked what she had to say for herself.

Clark responded with a conspiracy theory she said had started three weeks earlier. Clark stated her arrest was unwarranted, and that she was being persecuted by the police of the 19th Precinct, because she had inadvertently insulted one of them.

Clark told the Magistrate, "I was accosted by a man on Broadway, who because of the poor lighting on the street, I perceived to be a Negro. I told him to go about his business, and that I wanted nothing to do with a Negro."

The only problem was, this man was not a Negro, but a policeman with a swarthy complexion named Rosenberg. Patrolman Rosenberg arrested Clark on the spot, and when she gave her explanation the next day in court, Patrolman Rosenberg was insulted and quite upset. Patrolman Rosenberg got word to Clark that she would be arrested by a 19th Precinct cop every time she set foot in the Tenderloin, whether she had committed a crime or not. Clark told Magistrate Cornell, that since then she has been unjustly arrested several times in the Tenderloin, and the incident last night was just one of her many bogus arrests.

Magistrate Cornell turned to Becker, and he asked if there was any doubt in his mind that Clark was engaged in the solicitation of prostitution on the previous night.

Becker stuck out his chin and puffed out his chest.

"None whatsoever, "Becker said. "She is an old hand at this, and she always lies about it."

Magistrate Cornell asked Clark if it were true that she frequented the streets of the Tenderloin.

Clark, knowing that denying something so provable would do her no good, told the judge that yes, she indeed frequented the Tenderloin, adding, "Why not? This is America. It's a free country."

This cemented in Magistrate Cornell's mind that Clark was indeed a prostitute, since no respectable woman would travel alone in the Tenderloin, especially at midnight. But before he could proclaim his decision, Stephen Crane jumped to his feet near the back of the courtroom.

As was reported in the *New York Sun*, Crane said, "Just a word, Your Honor. I know this girl to be innocent. I only know that while with me she acted respectably and that the policeman's charge was false."

Crane went on to delineate the reasons why Becker had made an improper arrest of Clark. Then he added, "If the girl will have the officer prosecuted for perjury, I will gladly support her."

Since Magistrate Cornell was aware of Crane's fame and could not imagine such an illustrious writer lying in court, he dismissed the charges against Clark. This did not please Becker too much. He was even more irritated, when Clark, three weeks later, marched into Police Headquarters at 300 Mulberry Street, and pressed charges against Becker and against Patrolman Rosenberg for "continued harassment."

Clark's chief witness was Stephen Crane, which caused Becker more than a few bouts of agita. So much so, a few days after Clark brought charges against Becker, he accosted her on the street at three in the morning and beat her unmercifully in front of witnesses; none of whom would come to her aid because of their fear of Becker and his methods. When Becker was finished pummeling Clark, a husky hooker named "Chicago May," who was alleged to be one of Becker's paramours, landed a few kicks and punches of her own on the fallen Clark.

Because of Crane's fame, for the next several weeks the Becker/Crane/Clark case made national news. It was spread across the front page of newspapers in big cities like Philadelphia and Boston. It even made headlines as far west as Chicago, where the *Chicago Dispatch* made the snide observation that "Stephen Crane is respectfully informed that association with women in scarlet is not necessarily a 'Red Badge of Courage.'"

While Becker was waiting for his police trial to take place, he ordered his pals in the department to do everything possible to make Crane's life miserable. First, they raided Crane's apartment, looking for anything that might discredit Crane. Then they interviewed Crane's friends and acquaintances, digging for more dirt. By pounding the pavement and knocking on doors, Becker's pals discovered that Crane frequented brothels and that he had more than a casual relationship with opium dens. Future United States President Theodore Roosevelt, who was the New York City Police Commissioner at the time and casually acquainted with Crane, advised Crane not to testify at Becker's trial, or suffer ruin to his reputation.

Crane decided to testify anyway.

At Becker's October 16 trial, every police officer in the 19th Precinct who was not on duty at the time showed up in court to support Becker. Before the four judges, who were comprised of the city's four deputy police commissioners, Becker's lawyer, Louis Grant, was relentless in trying to discredit Crane's testimony.

Grant painted Crane as a man who not only frequently smoked in opium dens and took solace in the company of prostitutes, but also as a man who lived off the ill-gotten gains of those poor girls' debaucheries.

On the witness stand, with Grant in Crane's face, Crane meekly denied Grant's accusations, saying his presence in opium dens and brothels were solely for the purpose of doing research for his writings.

At one point, Grant was so venomous is his conduct toward Crane one newspaperman wrote, "Crane appeared to not know where he was at. At one time the questions were so severe as to cause the young author to place his hands to his face with the apparent desire to shut out the questions from his mind."

Things got so sticky for Crane on the witness stand, he refused to answer several of Grant's questions on the grounds that "they would tend to degrade and incriminate him."

After the humiliation of Crane was complete, the four deputy police commissioners, led by Fredrick Grant - the son of United States President Ulysses Grant - found Charles Becker innocent of all charges.

After the verdict was rendered, Stephen Crane skulked from New York City; his reputation in ruins.

Crane would never again garner acclaim as a writer; either of fiction, or nonfiction. Disgraced in the Northeast, Crane absconded to Key West; then to Jacksonville, Florida, where he met his true love, Cora Taylor, the owner of a house of ill-repute named *Hotel De Dream*.

Unable to make a decent living off his writings, Crane took a war assignment from *Blackwood's Magazine*, which sent Crane to Cuba to report on the Spanish-American War. In Cuba, Crane contracted yellow fever and malaria, worsening his already tenuous health. In late 1899, his work in Cuba complete, Crane journeyed to England where he continued his love affair with Cora Taylor, whom he finally married.

In England, Crane's health continued to deteriorate, and after he suffered a severe hemorrhage of his lungs, he decided to enter a health resort in Badenweiler, Germany. Crane lingered in ill health for several months before he passed away on June 5, 1900, at the age of 28.

Charles Becker didn't kill Stephen Crane, but he certainly was instrumental in quickening the young writer's demise.

With the Crane/Clark matter behind him, Becker became more resolute in working the Tenderloin for his personal profit. Becker made a career out of shaking down prostitutes and gambling houses, making the occasional sensational arrest, so that his name would be firmly entrenched on the front page of the New York City daily newspapers.

After his first wife, Mary, died from tuberculosis, he married a Canadian lass named Letitia Stensen, with whom he had a son, Howard Paul. This marriage lasted less than a year, mostly because Becker had been unfaithful to his wife; fooling with a string of Tenderloin hookers, from whom he accepted sexual favors, in addition to the shakedown money they paid Becker to keep operating without fear of arrest. Letitia sued for divorce on the grounds of infidelity. She won her divorce, and then scurried off to Reno, Nevada where she married Becker's older brother Paul.

Go figure.

In 1902 Becker met his third and final wife - Helen Lynch, a teacher in the New York City Public School System. This marriage lasted as long as Becker did, and Helen would play a major part in the melodrama that followed the death of Herman Rosenthal.

THE SECRET (STRONG ARM) SQUAD

In 1911, Police Commissioner Rhinelander Waldo appointed Becker to head an elite group of police strongmen which Waldo proudly called "The Special Squad," but christened in the press as "The Strong Arm Squad."

In a *New York Times* article dated August 13, 1911, the headline read:

THE STRONG ARM SQUAD – A TERROR TO THE GANGS

"Lieut. Charles Becker was picked to be in command of the Strong Arm Squad. He looks the part, standing over six feet in his socks, tipping the scale over 200 pounds, broad-shouldered, with eyes, jaw, and fists of a fighter."

The Strong Arm Squad was right up Becker's alley, because it gave him and his boys carte blanche to crack heads whenever they deemed it necessary, and that was often. The Strong Arm Squad was comprised of, according to the *Times*, "twenty huskies whose sole duty is to travel around the city and hand out generous doses of strong-arm medicine to any and all who showed unmistakable signs of being in need of it."

The Strong Arm Squad wore no police uniforms, nor did they dress like police detectives. The Strong Arm Squad wore the attire of the times associated with ruffians, longshoremen, and the rabble in the streets who were committing mayhem on the general public. In other words, the Strong Arm Squad dressed to blend in with the crowd they were looking to beat up, then arrest; in either order, as they saw fit. These 20 men were plucked from various precincts because "they had earned the reputation for their fighting capacity, for their judgment in making arrests, and for their ability to back up their arrests."

In fact, the last two criteria had nothing to do with the selection of the Strong Arm Squad. The first criteria was all that was required to be given the opportunity to legally crack heads.

According to the *Times* article,

"The Strong Arm Squad consisted of such thugs as Alex Whitman, the 'strong man' of the Police Department, and his brother Nathan Whitman, who has been dubbed the 'Yiddish Irishman.' Then there was Conlon, the 'strong arm dude.' 'Old Sleuth' Faubel, Joe McLaughlin, known as 'Eat 'Em Up Alive,' and finally 'Boots Trojan,' who knows all the gangs and whom Becker described as 'good as four ordinary men to go into a muss with.'"

Becker's squad of thugs knew what Waldo wanted, and they provided it in spades. Waldo was interested in arrests all right, but that was secondary to beating the crap out of whomever Becker deemed worthy of such actions. Waldo's thinking was - strike fear in the hearts of the underworld element and they will stop doing whatever they are doing. Of course, this tactic never works and only makes the hard men harder when they finally are released from prison.

Whenever arrests were made, the New York City's Magistrates were regaled by the prisoners' tales of "cruel and abusive" treatment by Becker and his gang. However, Becker always denied these claims, and thanks to the interference of Police Commissioner Waldo, no charges were ever brought against Becker and his thugs.

With his ruthless reputation flaunted frequently in the press, Becker was in an even better position than he was before to do what he did best: shake down prostitutes and known New York City gamblers, especially in the Tenderloin. In fact, Becker was such a commanding presence in the Tenderloin; he was christened "The Czar of the Tenderloin."

With his squad of goons behind him, Becker went on a rampage, closing down 100 gambling joints in the period of nine months. Of course, Becker took care of those who took care of him. If the proprietor of a gambling house came across with the proper amount of cash, Becker would ignore the gambling house's existence. And if that were not possible – if Waldo issued a direct order to close down that particular dive – Becker would tip off the gambling house owners in advance, so that when Becker finally did axe down the front door of the gambling den, all of the establishment's best gambling paraphernalia had been secreted away, and only decrepit tables and gambling wheels would be axed or confiscated. Big-shot gamblers were also tipped off, so when Becker's men made their arrests in their favored gambling houses, the arrestees were nonentities, with no bucks to back up their play with Becker.

According to Mike Dash's fine tome *Satan's Circus*, Becker was raking in so much cash that he personally banked, between October 1911 and July 1912, an average of $10,000 a month. Becker had 15 bank accounts dotted throughout the five boroughs of New York City. Some were solely in his name; some in joint accounts with his wife, and others under fictitious names. Becker also had safe deposit boxes in several banks filled with cold, hard cash; sometimes as much as $2,000 in one box.

This brings us back to Herman Rosenthal.

A PARTNERSHIP MADE IN HELL

In November of 1911, after Inspector Cornelius Hayes led his raid on Rosenthal's West Forty-Fifth Street gambling house, Rosenthal was basically broke, and he needed a partner to reopen his gambling house. Since Becker was in the newspapers so often and was such a big shot when it came to destroying or allowing gambling houses to prosper, Rosenthal thought Becker would be a perfect mate to partner with.

Rosenthal said in the July 14, 1912 edition of the *New York World*, "The first time I met Charles Becker was at a ball given by the Order of the Elks on 43rd Street near Sixth Avenue, and we had a very good evening, and drank freely, and became very good friends. Our next meeting was by appointment on New Year's Eve, 1912, at the Elks Club.

"We drank a lot of champagne that night and later in the morning we were all pretty under the weather. Becker put his arms around me and kissed me. He said, 'Anything in the world for you Herman. I'll get up at three o'clock in the morning to do you a favor. You can have anything I've got.'"

Knowing Becker's reputation as a cad, it's hard to believe Becker used exactly those words.

Rosenthal was a well-known bullshit artist. So it's safe to assume they probably met for the first time at the Elks Club, and at their second meeting at the Elks Club's New Year's Eve celebration, they most likely came to an agreement as to how much cash Rosenthal needed to cough up not to have his joint raided on a regular basis (Rosenthal said he had to give 20 percent of his profits to Becker).

Rosenthal also claimed, as one of the conditions for taking in Becker as a partner, Becker had to loan Rosenthal $1,500 for operating expenses and to spruce up the gambling hall. Rosenthal said that to receive the $1,500, he had to sign legal papers putting up his house furniture, or chattel, as collateral in case he reneged on the loan.

However, Becker denied he had any financial arrangements with Rosenthal.

On July 13, 1912, Becker told the *New York Times*, "I have never been connected with him in any way, either in business, or friendship. He tried hard to make it seem I was by inviting me to dinner in public places, but I always declined."

So it's clear, one of them was lying; or they both were lying. The latter seems most likely.

What we do know is this: Becker and Rosenthal came to some sort of agreement that either Rosenthal would pay Becker a flat sum per week to keep his joint open, or a percentage of the profits (most likely a flat sum, since Becker could not prevent Rosenthal from cooking the books). That was all well and good for Becker; he was shaking down so many gambling establishments in town, one more trophy in his case could do him no harm.

Or could it?

The problem was that Police Commissioner Waldo was getting letters complaining about Rosenthal's establishment being allowed to operate. The rumor was that old archenemy Bridgey Webber, whose gambling joint was just down the block from Rosenthal's, was the author of these letters. As a result, Waldo put the pressure on Becker to raid Rosenthal's place, and Becker told his "partner" Rosenthal that he had no choice but to follow the police commissioner's demands.

Becker told Rosenthal something like, "What's the big deal? I'll give you advance notice of the raid so that you can hide all your valuable equipment. Plus, you can make yourself scarce on the night of the raid so you won't have to spend the night in jail. Then in a few days, you'll put your best stuff back in the joint and we'll be back in business like before."

Rosenthal told Becker something like, "Go shit in your hat! You're my partner and if my joint gets axed, I'll make your life miserable!"

It was not such a great idea for a little nobody like Rosenthal to dictate to big, bad Lieutenant Becker what he could do and what he could not do.

At around 10 p.m., April 17, 1912, Becker, along with his Special (Strong Arm) Squad plus a battalion of policemen, raided Rosenthal's 45th Street "sporting club." As a favor, Becker did warn

Rosenthal in advance, so little Herman hid in a hallway down the block and waited for the raid to reach its conclusion.

Rosenthal said Becker contacted him the next day and told him not to worry; that Becker himself would fork over the money caused by his men's action.

"Five hundred bucks should do the trick," Becker allegedly told Rosenthal.

There is no proof this money actually changed hands. But what is known is that Rosenthal's club remained closed for weeks, and that one of the people arrested in the raid was Rosenthal's favorite nephew, Herbert Hull, a 17-year-old with no criminal record.

When Rosenthal's nephew was indicted a few weeks later, Rosenthal demanded and received a private summit with Becker. The two men, acting like Russian spies, held a clandestine meeting; reportedly in a New York City taxi cab. Nothing was accomplished at this meeting, and according to Rosenthal, the two men left on very bad terms.

ROSENTHAL BECOMES A RAT

Feeling like he was the odd man out, and being persecuted by the police, especially Lieutenant Becker, Rosenthal decided to take his case directly to Mayor William J. Gaynor. A man of Gaynor's exalted stature wouldn't be caught dead in the same room with a weasel like Rosenthal, so Gaynor's secretary told Rosenthal's to take a hike, or something similar.

Rosenthal then figured, "If the Mayor won't see me, I'll go straight to Police Commissioner Waldo."

This was not a very bright idea, since it was Waldo who had ordered Becker to raid Rosenthal's joint in the first place. It was no surprise that Waldo also refused to see Rosenthal.

Two strikes against him and tired of whiffing, Rosenthal took another swing, and he wound up in the office of New York City District Attorney Charles S. Whitman, a confirmed alcoholic, who was often drunk on the job and sometimes even in court. Despite his frequently inebriated condition, Whitman had ambitions to become Governor of New York State, which he accomplished in 1914. Presumably sober at the time of their meeting, Whitman gave the pudgy gambler an extended audience, where Rosenthal laid out his terrible tale concerning the conduct of Lieutenant Becker towards him.

However, after hearing Rosenthal's account, Whitman told Rosenthal there was nothing he could do on Rosenthal's word alone. Whitman said he would need corroboration from someone else; someone who could verify Becker was indeed shaking down gambling halls.

"Find me another gambling-house owner who would squeal on Becker," Whitman told Rosenthal. "Then I can pursue a case against him."

Rosenthal knew getting corroborating evidence against Becker was impossible, since all the gambling-house owners, who were paying Becker and knew Rosenthal was paying Becker, hated Rosenthal more than they hated Becker. So, Rosenthal played his final card, his ace in the hole. He decided to bring his story to the New York City press.

Enter *New York World* columnist Herbert Bayard Swope.

Swope was a tall, red-headed whirlwind, whose ambition matched that of Whitman's, a New York City District Attorney, who loved seeing his name in the newspapers, preferably on the front page. Swope and Whitman made a perfect team. The boozy Whitman made and sometimes contrived headline news, and Swope reported Whitman's achievements in his columns with a flourish. It was a win-win situation for both men.

After being shot down by Mayor Gaynor, Police Commissioner Waldo, and D.A. Whitman, Rosenthal asked around as to who might listen to his terrible tale of woe. With Big Tim Sullivan now in a mental institution and in no condition to help anyone, including himself, Rosenthal decided on Swope, who was known for throwing huge amounts of shit against the wall and hoping some of it stuck.

Knowing the ways of the Tenderloin, Swope bought Rosenthal's story, and he figured the best way to make Becker's actions known publically was to have Rosenthal write up two lengthy affidavits (with Swope's help of course), and run the affidavits verbatim in the Saturday and Sunday editions (July 14 and 15) of the *New York World*. And that's what that two men did, which immediately thrust smoke out of Lieutenant Charles Becker's ears.

In the affidavits, Rosenthal said because Becker was his partner and had a piece of the joint, Becker had warned him about the impending the raid on the gambling house (Police Commissioner Waldo had insisted on the raid, Becker had told Rosenthal). In addition, since they were partners, Becker had the good grace to tip off Rosenthal in advance about the impending raid, so that Rosenthal could make himself scarce and not spend the night in the slammer. And, there was the also the little problem of the squad of policemen Rosenthal claimed were now basically living in his house since the raid (the gambling house and Rosenthal's home were in the same building).

Rosenthal whined to the *New York Times*, who picked up on the story after it had been released by the *New York World*, "I won't stand for it! There are no other policemen living in other houses that

I know of. My lawyer has advised me to throw them out. District Attorney Whitman has advised me to throw them out!"

According to Rose Keefe's excellent book *The Starker*, Rosenthal went so far as to invite reporters to take a tour of his house. Unfortunately for Little Herman, when the press arrived, not a policeman was in sight.

Still, Herman persevered, and while Rosenthal gave the reporters the grand tour, his chubby wife Lillian whined to the press, "It's very annoying, as I do want my home to myself. There they sit and read newspapers or books all day long, and night too. They smoke cigars and leave butts around. It's very annoying. They're better now, but we would like to lock them out, only we're afraid they'd knock down the door."

At this moment, on the afternoon of July 15, 1912, if Rosenthal had half-a-brain in his head, he would have known his life was in imminent danger. Rosenthal was an unlikable nobody; Becker was a big-shot police lieutenant. And most importantly, Rosenthal had several fellow gamblers who would like nothing better than seeing Rosenthal six-feet under. One was the aforementioned Bridgey Webber, and another was a contemptuous, toadyish, vile-looking individual named Bald Jack Rose.

We'll get to Bald Jack Rose later.

With the New York City newspapers heavy on the case, Whitman heeded Swope's advice, and he decided to pursue a criminal indictment against Becker. But to do so, Whitman needed Rosenthal's testimony on the official record, not in the newspapers. Whitman told Swope to tell Rosenthal to meet Whitman at Whitman's uptown home on Sunday night.

After the Saturday (July 14) Rosenthal affidavit (No. 1) was published in the *New York World*, Becker and his lawyer, John W. Hart, stampeded into the offices of the newspaper and began throwing words around like "libel" and "lawsuit," and other words not printable in a family newspaper. Becker and Hart met with Isaac White, the legal counsel for the newspaper, and although White told them a second installment of Rosenthal's two affidavits was due to be published on Sunday, he would do them the courtesy of releasing the original affidavits to them after the second one was published (July 15).

Becker and Hart told White thanks for nothing, and they immediately informed every newspaperman in town that they were going to sue Rosenthal and the *New York World* for libel, defamation of character, slander, or any possible combination of the three. Rosenthal must have laughed when he heard that, since he was now flat broke and totally bullet-proof from civil lawsuits.

Enter "The Brain" – Arnold Rothstein.

The son of a rabbi, Rothstein was the most famous gambler in New York City and the acknowledged "King of the Tenderloin." Rothstein once said he'd bet on anything, except the weather - the reason being the weather was the only thing he couldn't fix. Making strange bedfellows indeed, Rothstein and Swope were fast pals, and in fact, when Rothstein married actress Carolyn Greene in 1914, Swope served as his best man.

On Sunday morning July 15, after Rothstein got wind of what Rosenthal was doing, which threatened the very fabric of the Tenderloin, Rothstein called Swope, wanting to know exactly how far Rosenthal was willing to go with his insubordination. When Swope told Rothstein that Rosenthal was ready to go all the way to the United States Supreme Court if necessary, on the afternoon of July 15, Rothstein summoned Rosenthal to his palatial home in uptown Manhattan. At this meeting, Rothstein laid down the law to Rosenthal; even offering Rosenthal $500 to get out of town immediately and more money if he needed it later. Rosenthal turned Rothstein's offer down, and by doing so he basically put a bullet in his own head.

On the same day, four known gamblers and all-around-bad-guys - Bridgey Webber, Bald Jack Rose, Harry Vallon, and Sam Schepps - got together to discuss the Rosenthal situation. On a boozed-up boat trip around Manhattan Island, they were overheard saying that if Rosenthal did not stop his yapping, "someone would get him and get him for keeps."

HELLO HERMAN; GOODBYE HERMAN

On Sunday night July 15, Lieutenant Charles Becker made himself visible at the prize fights at Madison Square Garden, for the reason, it was said later, to give himself an alibi when Herman Rosenthal was aerated with bullets.

At the same time, Rosenthal was at the home of Charles Whitman, making a verbal agreement that he would be in Whitman's office at 8 a.m. sharp the next morning to get the ball rolling (give sworn evidence) against Becker for a slew of crimes Rosenthal said Becker had perpetrated against him.

Right around midnight, a visual monstrosity named Bald Jack Rose was seen in a rented, gray Packard, accompanied by several unsavory characters. The car was registered to William Libby and driven by Louis Shapiro, who thought he was out for a nice drive around town, followed by a fat payday, including tip.

It was just after midnight, when Herman Rosenthal wobbled like a penguin through the front door of the Hotel Metropole, on 43rd Street near Broadway. The Hotel Metropole was owned by brothers Jim and George Considine, who had as their silent partner Big Tim Sullivan, now a ward of the state in a loony bin in Westchester, New York. However, when Big Tim still had all his marbles, he had used his influence at Tammany Hall to get a much-sought-after 24-hour liquor license for the Café Metropole, which sat to the right of the lobby in the hotel.

The hotel and the café had seen better days, but never a night like it was about to see.

Whistling and happy as a lark, Rosenthal waddled through the lobby of the hotel and into the café. As soon as Rosenthal's feet hit the floor inside the café, the usual patter of patrons turned to stone silence.

It was as if Herman Rosenthal had sucked all the air out of the room.

Still, Rosenthal looked quite jolly and did not display the countenance of a man who in just a few hours would be spilling his guts to District Attorney Whitman. Newspaper accounts later speculated that Rosenthal had come to the Café Metropole not for a few drinks, but for a nice payoff to get out of town before he met Whitman. Rosenthal was expecting someone to give him, not the $500 that Rothstein had promised, but as much as $15,000; chipped in by all the gamblers he could hurt with his testimony. And there were dozens. With the cash safely in his pocket, Rosenthal would then board a train at Grand Central Station for parts unknown. He could always send for his bottled-redheaded wife later, if that's what he desired.

Rosenthal sat at a table and was soon joined by a gaggle of other gamblers, with names like Fat Moe Brown and "Boob" Walker, who was a strong-arm man for Bridgey Webber. Foregoing any food, Rosenthal ordered a concoction consisting of bourbon, ginger ale, and bitters, which was called a "Horse's Head."

Most of Rosenthal's acquaintances would agree Rosenthal was the opposite end of the horse.

A few minutes after Rosenthal entered the Café Metropole, an old foe entered the cafe. It was none other than Bridgey Webber. After making the rounds of the other tables teeming with gamblers, Webber approached Rosenthal's table.

Webber said, "Hello Herman."

Rosenthal returned the greeting, and when Webber left the table and exited the café, Rosenthal turned to his companions and said, "See, Bridgey's all right. I'll get my money."

If this conversation occurred, and there's no reason to believe it didn't, it was another indication that Rosenthal had no intention of going to Whitman's office in a few hours. Rosenthal was going to take the money and run.

At about 1:20 a.m., Rosenthal exited the Hotel Metropole, and from a newsboy out front he bought seven copies of the morning edition of the *New York World*, in which Rosenthal's story was splattered across the front page. He went back into the Café Metropole, sat at his table, and his shirt buttons bursting with pride, Rosenthal showed his pals the front page of the newspaper.

"How's that for a headline?" Rosenthal said to anyone who'd listen.

Right about then, a strange thing happened outside the Hotel Metropole.

For no apparent reason, a police lieutenant, not named Becker, started shooing people away from the entrance of the hotel, including cars that were in the vicinity of the hotel's entrance. In several of these cars were cabbies waiting for a late-night fare, and they protested some, but not much.

About 1:30 a.m., a New York City newspaper received an anonymous phone call, asking, "Is Rosenthal dead yet?"

The person was never identified, but at 10 minutes before two, a well-dressed man entered the Café Metropole and told Rosenthal that someone was waiting for him outside the hotel. Without question and with a huge smile on his face, Rosenthal immediately departed the hotel, as if he had expected such a request.

As soon as his feet hit the pavement outside, four men (later identified by Bald Jack Rose as "Big Jack" Zelig's henchmen Harry "Gyp the Blood" Horowitz, Frank "Whitey Lewis" Muller, Lewis "Lefty" Rosenberg, and Frank "Dago Frank" Ciroficci) rushed up to Rosenthal and opened fire. Five shots blasted into Rosenthal, all which could have been fatal. But the one that hit him over the bridge of his nose and entered his brain killed Rosenthal instantly.

A comedy of errors ensued, as it was obvious to all in the vicinity of the Hotel Metropole that a murder had been committed.

The four shooters jumped back into the gray Packard, and they ordered the driver, Louis Shapiro, to hightail it out of there quick or suffer the same fate as Rosenthal. Shapiro did as he was told, and the killers escaped down 43rd Street.

Even though there were five policemen within a few yards of where Rosenthal lay dead, not one of them attempted to stop the getaway car. In fact, all five policemen later gave a different license plate number for the car. And oddly, none of the policemen immediately went over to where Rosenthal was lying dead to determine the identity of the victim.

The first responding officer was Policeman William J. File, who was off-duty at the time and drinking with friends at the Café Metropole when he heard the shots. As Policeman File ascertained that Rosenthal was indeed dead, a known gambler pushed his way through the crowd surrounding Rosenthal's body. The man bent down, stared into Rosenthal's unseeing eyes, and said, "Hello

Herman." Then the man straightened up, smiled, and said, "Goodbye Herman."

Just as quickly as the man appeared, he disappeared into the crowd.

The news of Rosenthal's murder spread like wildfire throughout New York City. At 2:30 a.m., Police Commissioner Waldo was awaken at home and told Rosenthal had been murdered. Waldo briefly entertained the thought of waking Mayor Gaynor and telling him the bad news, but then he decided a good night's sleep was more important, and he went back to bed.

Herbert Bayard Swope was up and about when he heard the news about Rosenthal. Swope immediately rushed to the 16th Precinct on West 47th Street to find out the details. He was not too shocked to discover that the police were bumbling along, not even being able to agree on the license plate number of the getaway car. At 3 a.m., Swope rushed to a telephone, and he called District Attorney Whitman, who was fast asleep. Swope screamed into the phone that Rosenthal had been shot dead. Whitman pulled a Waldo, and said he'd see to it in the morning. By this time Rosenthal's body had been transported to the 16th Precinct.

Swope would have none of that. He yelled into the phone at Whitman, "No, you have to come right now to the 16th Precinct!"

"No, I'm in bed. I have my pajamas on," Whitman said.

None too happy, Swope jumped into a cab and hurried to Whitman's East 26th Street apartment. Swope practically dressed Whitman, and then he pushed him into the waiting cab. They arrived back at the 16th Precinct, where Whitman, with much help from Swope, tried to get a firm grip on the situation.

At about this time, a friend of the family phoned Lillian Rosenthal and told her about her husband's demise.

Lillian screamed into the phone, "I told him to stay home tonight! I had a premonition something bad was going to happen! It was that man he was going to see! I told him not to keep that appointment!"

Lieutenant Becker had enjoyed a fine time at Madison Square Garden on Sunday night. After the fights, he went for drinks with friends, before driving to his house in the Bronx. Becker got home at about 2:15 a.m., and the phone rang a few minutes later. It was a newspaper reporter telling Becker about Rosenthal's little accident. Becker mulled over what to do, and then, probably figuring he was the main suspect anyway, he took the subway back to the city and walked over to the 16th Precinct.

Becker went directly to Captain Day's office expecting to see the captain, but instead came face-to-face with District Attorney Whitman and his sidekick Herbert Bayard Swope.

This was the beginning of a very bad time for Lieutenant Charles Becker.

By some stroke of luck (or more likely a tip was phoned in), at around 6 a.m. the police found the gray Packard in a downtown garage rented by William Libby. The owner of the garage told the police that Libby and Louis Shapiro lived in the same boarding house a few blocks away from the garage. The cops dragged Libby and Shapiro out of bed and herded them up to the 16th Precinct. It didn't take the two men long to cough up the name of the man who had rented the car - Bald Jack Rose.

On Tuesday afternoon, Bald Jack Rose strolled into police headquarters. Rose admitted to the police he helped orchestrate the murder of Herman Rosenthal, and he said he had done so at the direction of Lieutenant Charles Becker. Rose said he had to do what Becker demanded, or Becker said he would make life miserable for Rose and for several of his gambler friends. Rose said Becker promised Rose if he didn't do as Becker demanded, Becker would send the gamblers up the river on a trumped-up charge, and then kill Rosenthal himself. Rose said Becker also promised him that after Rose had Rosenthal whacked, Becker would use his police influence to make sure nothing happened to Rose or the killers.

Within hours of Rose's appearance at Police Headquarters, the police arrested Bridgey Webber. Harry Vallon turned himself in two days later. Fellow gambler Harry Schepps was arrested on August 10, in Hot Springs, Arkansas.

With the arrest of Bald Jack Rose and his boys, Swope went into full attack mode, and his prey was the New York City police department.

The day after Rosenthal's murder, Swope wrote in the *New York World*:

"Herman Rosenthal was murdered in cold blood by the System. The System is the partnership between the police of New

York City and the criminals of New York City. The System murdered Rosenthal because he threatened to expose it. It murdered him because he came to the World offices Saturday night and made affidavits as to the System's activities."

Of course, this was typical Swope. He had made himself and his newspaper part of the story, and to a certain extent, they were. But by doing this, Swope forced his puppet Whitman to concentrate solely on the New York City police department, and specifically Lieutenant Becker, when the more likely suspects were the dozens of gamblers whose livelihoods were at stake because of Rosenthal's intended actions. Bald Jack Rose, Harry Vallon, Sam Schepps, and Bridgey Webber, for instance, had much to gain if Rosenthal was eliminated. First, because of the intense scrutiny he was bringing to their operations, Rosenthal's babbling was hurting them in their pockets. And second, Rosenthal was a direct competitor, whose elimination would send Rosenthal's clientele into their own gambling joints.

Rose, Webber, Schepps, and Vallon were the more likely suspects, but all Swope and Whitman could see was Lieutenant Charles Becker.

Another reason why Swope and Whitman were so hot for Becker was that the arrest and conviction of lowly gamblers like Rose, Webber, Schepps, and Vallon was small-time news. But the arrest and conviction of a New York City police lieutenant was just what Swope and Whitman needed to further their careers.

While Rose, Webber, and Vallon stewed in the sweltering and decrepit Tombs Prison (Schepps was still in Hot Springs, Ark.), they got together and decided if they gave Whitman Becker as a scapegoat, they might be able to escape prison altogether, not to mention avoid the possibility of frying in Sing Sing's electric chair.

On Sunday July 28, the three gamblers asked for an audience with Whitman. Whitman agreed to the meeting, and at this meeting, which took place in a room at a midtown hotel, Rose, who was well-known as a stool pigeon and collection man for Becker, told Whitman that Becker had given him $1,000 to disperse to Rosenthal's four killers. Rose also told Whitman that he had first approached the killers' boss - Big Jack Zelig - who was known at the time as "The Toughest Man in New York City."

However, Zelig turned down Rose's proposition, and he wasn't too nice about it either. It seemed that when Zelig had been arrested recently by Becker's men, it was for carrying a gun, which Zelig said Becker's men had planted on him. Zelig also blamed his set-up arrest on Rose, who was notorious for doing this sort of thing to people he didn't like or felt threatened by.

However, Rose said Zelig's four hatchet men - "Gyp the Blood" Horowitz, "Whitey Lewis" Muller, Louis "Lefty" Rosenberg, and "Dago Frank" Ciroficci - seemed quite interested in whacking Rosenthal. And although Zelig didn't tell them explicitly not to get involved, he didn't forbid them to whack Rosenthal either (coincidentally, Zelig was on the lam at the time of Rosenthal's murder; ducking the law on the illegal-gun charge).

The following morning, Whitman convened a grand jury to hear evidence from Rose, Webber, and Vallon concerning the murder of Herman Rosenthal. Becker, along with his attorney, John Hart, was summoned to the grand jury meeting in the evening. But Becker's fate had already been sealed.

Becker sat there stoically; befuddled by what he heard coming out of the mouths of the three gamblers. Rose did most of the talking, and Webber and Vallon each parroted the main parts of Rose's story. At the meeting's end (around 9:20 p.m. that night), the indictment was immediately read to Becker, charging him with arranging the murder of Herman Rosenthal. After attorney Hart entered a not-guilty plea, Becker was led to his cell on the bottom floor of the Tombs, never again to be a free man.

Before he pinned the rap on Becker, if Whitman had been thinking straight, he would have realized that Becker, considering Rosenthal's conduct of the past two days, would have been the last person in the world to want Rosenthal murdered in such a public fashion. The reason being: Becker would be the prime suspect in Rosenthal's murder and the perfect patsy for a frame. But Whitman wanted a big trophy over his mantelpiece: the head of a New York City police lieutenant, Charles Becker. Innocent or guilty, Whitman wanted Becker to go down for the murder of Herman Rosenthal. For his career's sake, Whitman felt this was the right thing to do.

The four shooters in Rosenthal's murder were rounded up in the weeks that followed. "Dago" Frank Ciroficci was captured first, at a boarding house at West 154 Street; and then Whitey Lewis was nailed in the upstate Catskill Mountains. "Lefty" Rosenberg and "Gyp the Blood" Horowitz were found hiding in a Brooklyn apartment with their wives.

THE "TOUGHEST MAN IN NEW YORK CITY" GETS WHACKED

Big Jack Zelig returned to New York City in early August to discover he was wanted by a grand jury to testify as to his involvement in Rosenthal's murder. This was in addition to the concealed-gun charge Zelig had been wanted on since June.

Zelig had an axe to grind with Bald Jack Rose, since it was Rose who had approached him with the idea of the Rosenthal hit in the first place; which Zelig had turned down flat. Zelig was certain it was Rose who had told Whitman that Zelig was somehow involved in Rosenthal's murder. And even though it was Becker's men who had planted the gun on Zelig, Zelig figured it was done without Becker's knowledge and by the direction of Bald Jack Rose, who for some reason envisioned Zelig as a threat to him personally. This made Big Jack Zelig quite angry indeed; not a good thing for Bald Jack Rose, if and when he hit the streets of New York City.

Rose had to figure out what to do about Zelig, and do it quickly.

On August 22, Zelig marched into the Criminal Court Building on Center Street to testify in the concealed gun charge against him. Before testifying before the grand jury, Zelig was greeted by a group of reporters outside the courtroom. Zelig told them, as far as the concealed gun charge was concerned, it was Bald Jack Rose who had framed him; not Becker.

As for the Herman Rosenthal murder, Zelig said, "Herman was my friend. If I were not in the predicament I am at the present, I would make it a point to find out who did the killing and break his leg for him."

When Bald Jack Rose read Zelig's comments in the next day's papers his head began to hurt.

However, Rose was nothing if not diabolically brilliant. When he learned that Zelig was scheduled to testify for the prosecution at Becker's trial, which was set for October 7, Rose figured a way to eliminate Zelig, and then have the blame put on Becker; the proverbial gambler's daily double. Rose found his Lee

Harvey Oswald-like patsy in the name of "Red Phil" Davidson, a degenerate gambler and part-time pimp, who, because of his gambling habit, never had two nickels in his pocket at the same time to rub together. How the connection was made and what the payoff was are all conjecture, but the facts are the following:

Around 8 p. m., on Saturday, October 5, a little less than two days before Becker's trial was set to begin, Zelig was sitting in his usual hangout - Segal's National Café, on Second Avenue - when the phone rang, and a woman asked for Zelig. Apparently, it was a paramour of Zelig's; a manicurist who owned an uptown salon. Even though Zelig was married, he had a weakness for members of the opposite sex, and that became his undoing. Zelig agreed to meet this pretty young thing, and after bragging to a few pals what he had in store for the evening, Zelig left Segal's, hopped on the Second Avenue Streetcar, and headed for the girl's uptown apartment.

Zelig was in such a jovial mood, he didn't notice "Red Phil" Davidson slip out of a doorway near Segal's and jump onto the trolley behind him. Davidson was the perfect man for the job, since just two days earlier, the big, burly Zelig had knocked out Davidson with one punch, after the two men had argued about a gambling debt.

As the street car neared 14th Street, Davidson pulled out a police-issued .38 caliber Smith and Weston revolver, snuck up behind the seated Zelig, pressed the gun against the back of Zelig's right ear, and blew "The Toughest Man in New York City" into the hereafter. The fact that it was a stolen police gun pointed the finger at Becker and his boys more strongly.

Davdison jumped off the trolley, but he was so inept a killer, he was arrested minutes later on 14th by a passing policeman, who just happened to be in the right spot at the right time.

At his arraignment later that night, Davidson said he killed Zelig because earlier that evening Zelig had robbed him at gunpoint of over $400. However, Davidson's acquaintances all agreed Davidson never had $400 at one time in his entire life; so Davidson had no real motive to kill Zelig, unless he was paid to kill him.

As noted before – Bald Jack Rose was diabolically brilliant.

When the news of Zelig's demise was related to Whitman, he admitted it would be a minor setback to his prosecution. However, Whitman said he certainly had enough evidence to convict Becker, especially with Rose's testimony and the presiding judge, John William Goff, in Whitman's back pocket.

CHARLES BECKER'S TRIAL No. 1

From the first day of the trial, which commenced on October 5, 1912 at 1 p.m. sharp, Becker's attorney, John McIntire, was constantly harassed by Judge Goff. It was as if Judge Goff, and not District Attorney Whitman, were prosecuting the case against Becker. Goff was obviously anti-police, and he was especially annoyed that he had to cancel a planned vacation in order to preside over the Becker trial. Goff insisted that this trial would be over in two weeks, even though most experienced court observers thought that task would be almost impossible.

During the trial, when Whitman objected to McIntire's line of questioning, Goff sustained the objection every time. And on the occasions when McIntire asked a question of a witness that Goff did not approve of, he would not even wait for Whitman to object. Goff would strike McIntire's question from the record himself. Even when assistant D.A. Frank Moss took over from Whitman, Goff was decidedly pro-prosecution. It was obvious to all seasoned court observers, that Goff had already found Becker guilty and that a jury "guilty" verdict was just a formality.

The key witness against Becker was, of course, Bald Jack Rose, who during the trial was referred to in the newspapers as "Cue Ball" Jack Rose, because his shiny bald dome resembled the cue ball in the game of pool.

On October 14, Whitman's questions to Rose were obviously well-rehearsed. Rose stated on the stand that he had no choice but to arrange the killing of Rosenthal for Becker, otherwise Becker, whom Rose seemed to believe ran the entire city of New York, including the court system, would find a way to have Rose incarcerated for a very long time.

Rose said he tried to talk Becker out of having Rosenthal killed, and he offered to have Rosenthal beaten instead.

Rose said Becker told him, "If I wanted Herman beaten, I'd do it myself. I'd just raid his place and beat him up during the raid. No, I want him croaked. Cut his throat. Dynamite him. Anything."

Rose also said he and Becker had met with Bridgey Webber and Harry Vallon in a Harlem gambling house on June 27, three weeks before Rosenthal's murder. Rose testified it was outside this Harlem gambling house that the four men had first planned the murder of Herman Rosenthal. Rose's testimony about the "Harlem Conference" was also verified later by Bridgey Webber and Harry Vallon. Sam Schepps also testified, and even though he admitted to being in the murder car with Rose the night of the murder (but not at the time of the actual shooting), most of Schepps's testimony was hearsay evidence, because he had not actually participated in the planning of Rosenthal's murder.

When it was McIntire's turn to cross-examine Rose, Judge Goff outdid himself in his efforts to railroad Becker.

McIntire's strategy was to have Rose admit on the witness stand that he was a ruthless criminal himself and was looking to involve Becker in Rosenthal's murder in order to save his own hairless skin. But whenever McIntire tried this line of questioning, he was cut off by Judge Goff, who then told Rose to plead the Fifth Amendment against self-incrimination.

It was obvious to those in court that McIntire, overweight and 57-years-old, was not in the best of health. This was compounded by the fact that the courtroom was stifling hot (unusual for early October), and the windows had been ordered closed by Judge Goff just before McIntire started his cross-examination of Rose.

McIntire began his questioning of Rose at around 2:45 p.m. At 8 p.m. McIntire was near exhaustion, and he asked Judge Goff if he could resume his cross-examination on the following day.

Judge Goff adamantly said no.

McIntire tried to keep questioning Rose, but as the clock was nearing 9 p.m., McIntire nearly fainted. Wiping his brow, he told Judge Goff he could no longer continue with his cross examination. Instead of allowing McIntire to resume his cross-examination of Rose the following day, Judge Goff declared the cross-examination of Rose over, and he dismissed Rose from the witness stand.

Judge Goff also insisted that the final summations by the defense and the prosecution were to take place on the same day. On Oct. 22, at approximately 3 p.m., Judge Goff asked McIntire how long his summation to the jury would take. McIntire said he was not certain, but said it could take as long as four hours. And besides, McIntire said he was overcome by the heat again and would rather give his summation the following day. Caught between a rock and a hard place, Judge Goff agreed that McIntire would be allowed to start his summation the following morning at 10 a.m., but it could not run longer than 2 p.m. At that time, they would take a recess until 3:30 p.m., when Assistant D.A. Moss would start his summation, which also could not run longer than four hours. Both McIntire and Moss agreed with the judge's decision, and Judge Goff dismissed court for the day.

As Becker was led from the courtroom, reporters asked him why he did not take the stand in his own defense.

Becker said, "It has been my desire all along to tell my story to the jury, confident that I could sweep aside every particle of seeming evidence brought against me. But my lawyers have advised against it, and I have yielded to their advice."

His lawyer's advice was on the mark. Since if Becker had taken the stand, Whitman could have introduced tons of evidence that Becker was a crooked cop; taking graft with both hands. And this would have undoubtedly prejudiced the jury against Becker.

Becker was also asked by the press what verdict he expected the next day.

"What can they do but acquit me?" Becker said. "What evidence has been brought against me other than that of crooks and thugs? I am confident of complete vindication."

However, after the summations by the prosecution and the defense were completed the following day, Judge Goff decided he needed more time before he gave his charge to the jury. And that he did, not on October 23, but on the morning of October 24.

It was apparent to all: Judge Goff's instructions to the jury stuck a proverbial knife in Becker's back.

As Judge Goff went over point after point concerning the evidence, he presented the prosecution and their witnesses' statements as if they were the gospel truth. There was never any question of Judge Goff being fair. Any testimony made by Bald Jack Rose on the witness stand, Judge Goff accepted in his charge to the jury as absolute fact. And if Rose was telling the truth, of course Lieutenant Charles Becker was guilty as charged for ordering the murder of Herman Rosenthal.

At 4:30 p.m., the jury started its deliberations. By 10 p.m., no verdict had been reached and there was speculation in the press that this was good news for Becker, since it usually took a jury longer to find a man not guilty than guilty. However, that speculation evaporated around 11:30 p.m., when the jury announced it had come to a decision.

At exactly 11:54 p.m., Becker was seated and awaiting his fate.

Clerk Penny rose, and after he gave his roll call to the jury, he spoke directly to jury foreman, Mr. Skinner, "You have reached a verdict, gentlemen?"

Skinner and the other 11 jurors rose to their feet. Skinner said, "Yes, we have."

"How do you find?" Clerk Penny said.

Mr. Skinner said, "We find the defendant guilty as charged in the indictment."

The room became quiet as a tomb; all eyes concentrated on Becker.

Becker's face turned red and his mouth opened in a silent scream. He tried to say something, but the words stuck in his throat.

Clerk Penny said to the jury, "You find the defendant guilty of murder in the first degree, and so say you all?"

All 12 jurors said "Yes" in unison.

Clerk Penny read the names of each juror individually, and he said to each one, "Is that your verdict?"

One by one, the jurors all responded "Yes."

While Clerk Penny was verifying the jurors' verdicts individually, twice Becker appeared as if he were about to faint. Finally, two court officers rushed to his side and held him upright.

Judge Goff, a look of satisfaction on his face, said that he would administer sentencing on October 30.

As Judge Goff exited the courtroom, two court officers took Becker by each arm and led him from the courtroom. They crossed a bridge separating the courtroom and the Tombs prison called "The Bridge of Sighs," and they took Becker back into his cell in the Tombs.

After the verdict was announced, there was bedlam outside the courtroom door.

Helen Becker was not in the courtroom to hear her husband's verdict. The courtroom had been so packed, she was stuck outside; her face pressed against the courtroom door. When the door was finally flung open and the cry of "Guilty!" permeated the air, Helen Becker hit the floor in a faint. She was picked up and carried to a bench, where she was attended to by friends, one of whom was McIntire, who assured her there would be a successful appeal and a new trial.

McIntire repeated this statement to a group of newspapermen, and when they asked him his basis for an appeal, McIntire said, "I can tell you no more."

It wasn't until 12:55 a.m. that Helen Becker was able to walk out of the courthouse. She was whisked away in a car by her relatives. But not before she released a statement to the press, which was relayed by her brother-in-law, saying, "I was so shocked. I could not believe it. To think that this thing could happen to my husband, it seems impossible."

Despite the fact that the Becker family was now devastated, things looked quite rosy for Bald Jack Rose, and his fellow gamblers Bridgey Webber and Harry Vallon. As per their agreement with Whitman, after the trial of the four actual shooters was completed, all three gamblers were to be set free from their cells in the Tombs. Sam Schepps, because he did not participate in the planning of Rosenthal's murder, was immediately set free after Becker was found guilty.

As for Whitman, it's safe to say he put on a big bender after Becker's conviction. The word quickly spread around town that Whitman would become the next mayor of New York City.

However, Whitman had set his sights much higher than that.

He announced to the *Saturday Evening Post*, "I'd like to become Governor of New York State instead!"

On October 30, 1912, Judge Goff sentenced Becker to death in the Sing Sing electric chair, during the week that started on Monday, December 9, 1912.

The following day, Becker was taken from the Tombs, and, handcuffed to a sheriff, he boarded a train to Sing Sing Prison in Ossining, New York. While at Sing Sing, Becker hired attorney Joseph Shay, to represent him for his appeal.

The four killers, who actually shot Rosenthal, went on trial before Judge Goff on December 8, 1912. Originally, through their lawyer, Charles Wahle, all four men had requested separate trials. But at the last moment, Wahle convinced "Gyp the Blood" Horowitz, "Whitey Lewis" Muller, "Lefty" Rosenberg, and "Dago Frank" Ciroficci that it was in their best interest to be tried together. Whether this was the right course of action, or not, is hard to determine. But the results speak volumes. (Wahle must have figured he had four losers, so why go through the task of four time-consuming trials for one payday?)

The trial of the four killers lasted a week, and the same cast of characters who had testified at Becker's trial, especially Bald Jack Rose, were called to the stand by District Attorney Whitman, who tried this case himself without any help from Assistant D.A. Moss.

Predictably, the results were the same as in the Becker trial.

This time it took only one ballot and a mere 25 minutes for the jury to come back with a guilty verdict.

As he was led from the courtroom, "Whitey Lewis" Muller complained to the press, "When I heard Goff make the charge to the jury, I knew we was dead. The jury would have convicted a priest after listening to that charge."

After various appeals were denied, all four killers were executed in Sing Sing Prison in April of 1914.

The day after the four Rosenthal killers were convicted, as per their arrangement with Whitman, Bald Jack Rose, Bridgey Webber, and Harry Vallon were released from the Tombs prison. They were soon seen circulating in the Tenderloin, doing what they had been doing before they had been arrested. So much for justice.

But all three men had targets on their back, since it was well-known in the underworld that all three were rats. And rats don't have a long life expectancy in the mean streets of New York City.

Attorney Shay was able to obtain several delays to Becker's execution, and Charles Becker was still alive in the spring of 1913. However, Shay, who had never handled a criminal case before (his specialty was personal injury), resigned and was replaced by Marion Manton; a bulldog of a criminal attorney, who had been given the moniker of "Praying Manton," because of his ability to trap people on the witness stand into saying things other than what they had intended to say. Manton also was a bigwig at Tammany Hall, and Becker needed all the help he could get.

The only problem was – Shay worked cheap and Manton commanded big bucks. Not having the money to pay Manton, Helen Becker signed over the deed of the Becker's Bronx house to Manton as payment for his services.

Becker got a tease in early 1913, when New York State Gov. William Sulzer, a longtime pal of Big Tim Sullivan (and close to Manton too), said that documents that had been submitted to him proved Becker's innocence. Sulzer said that after the appeal decision came back from the Court of Appeals, and if Becker was not given a second trial, Sulzer would use his powers as governor to commute Becker's sentence.

However, Sulzer, who took over as governor on January 1, 1913, had difficulties of his own, and he never got his chance to help Becker.

Sulzer's first setback came when it was uncovered that he had diverted campaign contributions into his own personal coffers, and then, when confronted with the evidence - he lied about it. However, Sulzer's biggest blunder was not playing ball with the head of Tammany Hall: Charles "Boss" Murphy.

Murphy, as payback for getting Sulzer elected, wanted certain men appointed to prestigious positions in Sulzer's administration. The biggest fish Sulzer turned down for Murphy was James E. Gaffney, the owner of the "Miracle" Boston Braves. Murphy wanted Sulzer to appoint Gaffney to the State Commission of Highways, but Sulzer told Murphy to take a flying leap. Sulzer said, instead of appointing a man to that position, he would put the plum appointment up for a vote.

This was not a smart thing to do to the man (Boss Murphy) who just got you elected governor.

Murphy then used his powers at Tammany Hall to induce the New York State Assembly to impeach Sulzer, which they did on August 13, 1913, by a vote of 79-45. Sulzer was replaced by Lieutenant Gov. Martin H. Glynn, who acted as if he didn't know Charles Becker ever existed.

Becker always had a big ally in Big Tim Sullivan. However, as early as the beginning of 1912, Sullivan had begun experiencing extreme bouts of dementia. Big Tim escaped from his upstate asylum several times, but he was always found at one of his New York City haunts, playing cards and drinking like a fish.

The last time Sullivan escaped was on August 31, 1912, and he did so after waiting for his guards to fall asleep after an all-night card game. Two weeks later, an unidentified body turned up in an Bronx morgue. The man had apparently been run over by a freight train in Pelham, New York. No one claimed the body, but before the body was buried in Potter's Field, a policeman recognized it as the body of Big Tim Sullivan.

Big Tim was given a proper sendoff, as 25,000 people followed his casket from a downtown funeral home to his funeral mass at old St. Patrick's Church on Mulberry Street, just south of Houston Street.

Despite the setbacks of Sulzer's impeachment and Big Tim Sullivan's demise, Becker finally got a lucky break.

On Feb. 24, 1914, the New York State Appeals Court, by an overwhelming 6-1 majority, ruled that Becker's first trial had been grossly improper. The main reasons given by the appeals court were the dubious actions in the courtroom by Whitman and his staff; statements presented to the jury that were certainly prejudicial against Becker and should have been objected to by Judge Goff. As for Judge Goff, the appeals court cited his obvious one-sided performance in the courtroom; favoring the prosecution and constantly lambasting the defense. Judge Goff was also taken to task for dismissing Bald Jack Rose from the witness stand when McIntyre could no longer physically function in court because of heat exhaustion.

There was also the problem of the so-called "Harlem Conference," which was alluded to by Rose, Bridgey Webber, and Harry Vallon; all co-conspirators in the plot to kill Herman Rosenthal. Rose, Webber, and Vallon said the plot to kill Rosenthal was hatched by Becker in front of a Harlem gambling house three weeks before Rosenthal's murder. The appeals court ruled that since all three men admitted they were in on the plot to kill Rosenthal, there was no independent corroboration that this meeting actually took place.

The appeals court also stated that Judge Goff's charge to the jury was so contemptibly prejudicial to Becker, only a guilty verdict was possible. Also, new evidence had been uncovered that was not available in Becker's first trial.

Justice Nathan Miller wrote in his ruling: "In my opinion a new trial should be granted because the newly discovered evidence imperatively demands it in the interest of justice, because the verdict is shockingly against the weight of the evidence, and because the trial was so conducted as to insure a verdict of guilty, regardless of the evidence."

Judge Frank Hiscock was particularly forceful in his denunciation of Judge Goff.

Hiscock wrote: "On some occasions, the ruling of the trial judge passed beyond the limits of digression and were erroneous as a matter of law."

CHARLES BECKER'S TRIAL No. 2

Becker's second trial started on May 5, 1914, at the New York City Courthouse. The day
before the trial Becker was taken from his cell in Sing Sing Prison and plunked back into his old digs at the Tombs.

The judge in the second trial was Samuel Seabury, who had once been the youngest judge in New York State, but was now a very ambitious 41-year-old with political ambitions. Although Seabury did not act as outlandishly prejudicial against Becker as Judge Goff had done at Becker's first trial, he was decidedly pro-prosecution and anti-police.

The same cast of characters from the first trial took the stand in the second trial. The prosecution was directed by District Attorney Charles Whitman, who had thrust himself back into the Becker case, instead of letting his subordinate, Assistant District Attorney Moss, do all the heavy lifting. Whitman's re-involvement in the Becker case occurred despite common knowledge Whitman was in campaign mode and actively running for governor of New York State. Whitman correctly deduced if he prosecuted another conviction of Becker this would certainly earn Whitman enough brownie points to propel him into the Executive Mansion in Albany.

After a few top-of-the-order witnesses were put on the stand by Whitman to set the table, the cleanup hitter for the prosecution was Bald Jack Rose.

The *New York Times* described Bald Jack Rose's unusual physical appearance on the witness stand as such:

"Rose looked prosperous, well-dressed and in good health. His head is still without a single hair and as shiny as it was two years ago. His chin was just as peaked and his widespread ears finished the picture of one of the most eccentric figures that ever walked into a courtroom."

However, eccentric and duplicitous are two different things, and Rose certainly was both.

On the witness stand, Rose told the sorrowful tale of how he was a reformed gambler just trying to get on with his life. As Rose related his sad narrative to the court, tears welled up in his eyes and cascaded down both sides of his waxen face. He made no attempt to wipe away the tears, but instead let them dry on his cheeks, making his face shine like a fishbowl.

Rose's tears came in a torrential downpour when he told the jury of a meeting between himself, Bridgey Webber, Harry Vallon, and Charles Becker in a darkened doorway near Sixth Avenue and 43rd Street soon after Rosenthal's murder. Rose said it was at this meeting that Becker assured the three men that he would use his commanding police powers to make sure none of the three gamblers or the four shooters would be hurt by the law.

Outside the courtroom, after his command performance on the witness stand, Rose was asked about his crying.

Rose shuddered and said, "Yes, I guess I did cry. Like a flash, the whole scene came to me again! The scene after the murder! Oh…!"

Like in the first trial, Rose said Rosenthal told him more than once that Rosenthal and Becker were partners. Then Rose dropped a bombshell, when he intimated that Rosenthal was a "spy" and a "stool pigeon" for Becker (although he did not use those exact words on the witness stand, they were in the headlines in the following day's newspapers). This is something Rose had not mentioned in Becker's first trial. This statement led credence to the defense's contention that Rosenthal was killed by other gamblers in retaliation for Rosenthal giving up the location of their gambling houses to Becker.

Rose said that on one occasion Becker had sent Rose to ask Rosenthal for $500 to help one of Becker's underlings who might be indicted on a murder charge (we'll meet Charles Plitt later).

Rose said Rosenthal told him, "No, I can't do it. Tell Becker there isn't a chance in the world. And I will let him raid me if he can get the evidence legitimately. But there will be no friendly raiding around my place."

Rose said he felt Rosenthal's attitude was very disturbing, so he said to Rosenthal, "There's no use you talking that way; he started you, why don't you do this and save everybody a lot of trouble?"

Rose testified Rosenthal then told him, "You don't know what I've been doing for that fellow Becker. I've been doing things I would have never done for anyone else on earth. It was me who made it possible for him to raid every place on the avenue so as to help him make a show. If Becker couldn't get the goods on a place, I would go in for him and get the layout. I would get a couple of fellows from the gambling house and parade them on the sidewalk. You know Detective Foye on the Strong Arm Squad? It was me who placed him on the squad, and he's Becker's best man. Why only last week, Becker collected $1,000 on a place that I wised him up on."

With Whitman's prodding, Rose fully explained the details of the Becker-led conspiracy to murder Rosenthal. Rose told the court that he had enlisted the gunmen at Becker's urging, and that Becker had told him that if the gunmen balked at doing the job, Becker would frame them on trumped-up charges that would put the four men behind bars for a very long time. Rose also told the court the details of how he obtained an affidavit on the Sunday night before Rosenthal's murder from Dora Gilbert, Rosenthal's first wife, which would "blacken Herman's character" as nothing but a cheap pimp who forced his first wife to sell her sexual favors for a few bucks.

Rose said when he informed Becker that he had obtained Dora Gilbert's affidavit, Becker told him, "I'm glad you got it. Now get Rosenthal off the earth and everything will be alright."

The next day, Rose said Becker was not so keen on the affidavit. Rose said Becker told him, "We won't be needing it now."

Author's note: Why would Becker tell Rose to get an affidavit from Dora Gilbert if he were planning to kill Rosenthal anyway?)

Concerning the night of Rosenthal's murder, Rose told the court how an automobile containing himself, San Schepps, and Harry Vallon had broken down in front of Tom "Sailor Tom" Sharkey's Café (Sharkey was a world-class heavyweight boxer who had unsuccessfully fought twice for the heavyweight title).

From Tom Sharkey's, Rose had phoned for "Shapiro's machine." When Shapiro arrived, he took Rose, Schepps, and Vallon to Harlem to pick up "Dago Frank." Then they drove downtown to

Webber's poker rooms, where they met up with "Gyp the Blood," "Whitey Lewis," and "Lefty Louie." Rose left Schepps, Webber, and Vallon behind, and he accompanied the four killers in Shapiro's car to the Metropole Hotel where Rosenthal was killed.

Rose said after the murder he went back to Webber's poker rooms and phoned Becker. Upon hearing about Rosenthal's demise, Rose testified Becker said, "Good boy. That's fine work. You wait for me. I'll be downtown as soon as I can get there."

On cross-examination, Becker's attorney, Manton, bitterly fighting for his client's life, tried to get Rose to slip up and make a mistake. Time after time Manton would barrage Rose with a verbal assault, but whatever Manton asked, Rose deftly evaded the question. Manton produced transcripts from Becker's first trial showing discrepancies concerning the meetings between Becker and Rose. Rose simply admitted the discrepancies and offered no explanation. Then he slumped back in his chair, with a satisfied smile on his face, knowing he had survived Manton's attack unscathed.

The next person on the witness stand was Bridgey Webber, who was described by the press as "extremely nervous" and "teary eyed." Under questioning by Whitman, Webber said he had been a collection agent for Bald Jack Rose and that he had met Becker through Rose. Webber also said he had been present at a conference outside a Harlem gambling house where Becker had discussed with him and Rose the plot to murder Rosenthal.

Webber testified, "Becker told me of Rosenthal's threat to squeal to the district attorney. Then Becker called me aside and told me he wanted the boys to croak Rosenthal. I said there would be a lot of trouble if that were done, and Becker replied, 'I'll fix everything. There will be no trouble. I will see to that.' So I agreed to have Rosenthal croaked."

Webber then described how the four gunman met in one of Webber's poker rooms on the night of the murder. Webber said he then went out and succeeded in finding Rosenthal in the Hotel Metropole. Soon afterwards, the four killers gunned Rosenthal down. Later that morning, Webber said he and Rose met with Becker. Webber said, "Becker congratulated Rose and then borrowed $1,000 from me to get the gunmen out of town."

Upon cross-examination, Becker's attorney, Manton, tore Webber's testimony to shreds. Manton got Webber to admit that he had lied to Deputy Police Commissioner Dougherty after Rosenthal's murder about his whereabouts on the night of the crime. Manton also pried out of Webber the fact Webber had said things during his direct examination by Whitman earlier in the day that he had omitted in Becker's first trial. Manton also got Webber to confess that in Becker's first trial Webber had made affidavits that he swore today were false.

While Manton spat out his forceful cross-examination, Webber trembled in the witness chair. Sometimes his mouth quivered, and sometimes his lips curled into a snarl. At times, Webber tried to defy Manton to get him to contradict himself. In other instances, he gave way to despair when Manton was easily able to do so. When Manton mentioned the executions of the four gunmen in the electric chair, Webber, as Rose had done in the same witness chair before him, broke into tears. Webber gripped the arms of the witness chair to steady himself, and then he continued with his testimony.

Outside the courtroom later that day, Manton told the press, "I'm gratified I made Webber admit he lied in the first trial."

However, it was Charles B. Plitt, who had been Becker's right-hand man in the Secret (Strong Arm) Squad for two years, whose surprise testimony was the most damaging to Becker in his second trial. For those people who were convinced of Becker's guilt, Plitt's testimony nailed it to the wall. There is no question - if Plitt was telling the truth on the stand – then Becker was certainly guilty. But if Plitt was telling a pack of lies, the question is why?

Was Plitt paid a handsome sum of money by someone to do so? Was he involved in the Rosenthal murder himself, and by pinning the murder on Becker, it would remove all suspicion from himself. Or was there some other crime that Plitt wanted to be absolved from?

That's all speculation, but Plitt's testimony had a ring of insincerity to it: the stink of rancid fish.

On the morning of May 18, 1914, Plitt took the witness stand, and he told Whitman that on July 15, 1912, the night before Rosenthal's murder, Becker had told him, "Keep a memorandum of your movements tonight, so you can have an alibi. And above all things, keep away from Times Square tonight."

Then the following morning, after Rosenthal was dead, Plitt said Becker said to him concerning the owner and driver of the murder car, "What in the hell was the matter with that bunch? Were they all cock-eyed drunk? From the way they acted in pulling off that trick, you would think they were setting the stage for a motion picture show."

Plitt also said that, while Becker was imprisoned in the Tombs before his first trial, an emissary from the gunmen approached Becker, through Plitt, asking for $500. Plitt said Becker told him, "Tell them I'll pay them the money as soon as I can get it."

However, the most incriminating evidence against Becker supplied by Plitt was when Plitt testified that after Becker's first trial, while Becker was en route to Sing Sing prison on a train, he told Plitt, "If anything happens to me, I want you to kill that squealing Rose."

Even though almost everything Plitt said in court could be categorized as sensational, the man himself was decidedly not. According to newspaper reports, "Plitt looked insignificant in the witness chair, and he spoke so low the jury could hardly hear him. His eyes seemed gazing at something far away; his face was devoid of expression and his body almost inert."

In addition to speaking with unusual slowness, Plitt also took a long time between answers. Often Plitt waited between five and 10 seconds before replying to one of Mr. Whitman's questions. Mr. Manton timed him once or twice waiting for an answer, and complained to Judge Seabury of the long silences. Judge Seabury ignored Manton's pleas and told Whitman to get on with his questioning of Plitt.

The press said Becker seemed confused during Plitt's testimony. At times, Becker would smile sarcastically and whisper something into his lawyer's ear. At other times, his face was a mask of apprehension. Once, Becker slid down the entire length of the defendant's table, so he could look Plitt straight in the eye. However, Plitt just stared at the ceiling and refused to return Becker's gaze.

Becker's wife, Helen, sat through Plitt's testimony with her hand on her chin. Her eyes seemed to bore a hole right through Plitt's forehead. Helen Becker stared at Plitt, a man she knew quite well through her husband, with a mixture of contempt and downright hatred.

After a 1½-hour lunch break, Becker's attorney, Manton, attacked Plitt like a piranha would devour a school of angel fish. Manton spat seemingly innocuous questions at Plitt designed to make Plitt look like a moron.

Manton asked, "How old are you Mr. Plitt?"

Plitt hemmed and hawed, and after a few moments, interrupted by blocks of complete silence, he finally answered, "26 or 27."

Manton ridiculed Plitt's answer and forced him to make a decision.

Manton said, "Well sir, can't you make up your mind? Are you 26, or 27. Surely you must know."

Plitt was forced to admit he really didn't know his exact age.

Smelling blood in the water, Manton said, "Well Mr. Plitt, where were you born?"

Plitt answered, "The U.S."

Manton sneered, "What's that?"

Plitt squirmed, "The United States."

His voice dripping with sarcasm, Manton asked, "Can't you give us any more definite place than that?"

Finally, Plitt narrowed down his birthplace to New York City; then he narrowed it down even further to Allen Street on the Lower East Side of Manhattan. Plitt then reiterated he was not sure exactly what year he had been born.

Manton inquired if Plitt had ever been in an institution "for the feeble minded," or had ever been "examined as to his sanity."

Plitt rolled his eyes upward and waited for what seemed like an eternity before he finally replied, "Not that I can remember."

Manton asked Plitt about his arrest for the murder of a Negro while accompanying Becker on the raid of a gambling house. District Attorney Whitman jumped to his feet and objected. Judge Seabury sustained that objection. Not realizing he didn't have to answer the question, Plitt admitted he had been a joint defendant with Becker concerning the shooting Manton had alluded to.

Judge Seabury angrily told the jury to ignore Plitt's remarks. But the damage had already been done.

Manton then asked Plitt, "Did you ever write to Becker in Sing Sing about that?"

"I don't remember," Plitt said.

Manton would not let go of his line of questioning. "Don't you remember writing to Becker that he must get a lawyer to defend you?"

"I don't remember what I wrote," Plitt said.

"Did you ever put your alleged conversations with Becker in writing?" Manton asked.

Plitt replied that he had certainly not done so.

Manton pounced. "Yet, you recalled those conversations for Mr. Whitman this morning. The things you never wrote are clearer in your mind than things you wrote."

Plitt did what he did best. He played dumb and said not another word about the subject.

Suddenly, Manton surprised Plitt, Whitman, and the court by producing a piece of paper and having Plitt write down the words "opportunity," "sticky," "expense," "minute," "consult," and "involuntary." Plitt did as he was told, and when Plitt was finished, Manton asked that the court summit Plitt's handwriting into evidence. Manton didn't explain why, but soon it became evident.

Manton then produced letters that were allegedly sent by Plitt to Becker after Becker's first trial, while Becker was incarcerated in Sing Sing Prison. The letters were addressed to "My Dear Friend Charles," and signed by "Hiram Charles." These letters contained numerous declarations that Becker was innocent of the murder of Herman Rosenthal.

Manton asked Plitt if he was the author of those letters. After dawdling and staring at the ceiling, and after Manton reminded Plitt that he had just given his handwriting samples to the court, which had been introduced into evidence, Plitt finally admitted that he was indeed the author of those letters.

At this point, Manton read to the jury a copy of the testimony to the grand jury that indicted Becker. In this testimony, Plitt had sworn that Becker was innocent and that Becker had been framed by Whitman.

Even though Manton had punched holes in Plitt's credibility, he could not get Plitt to retract his statement that he had given that morning under questioning by Whitman. Plitt insisted that after

Becker's first trial, while Becker was being taken on the train from the Tombs to Sing Sing Prison, Becker had asked Plitt to kill Bald Jack Rose.

After Plitt's testimony was completed, Whitman produced a surprise witness: a Negro named James Marshall. Whitman claimed Marshall was the missing link to the "Harlem Conference" alluded to in Becker's first trial. One of the reasons Becker had won his appeal for a second trial was because the appeals court had ruled that there had been no independent corroboration, aside from Bald Jack Rose, Bridgey Webber, and Harry Vallon, that this meeting had ever taken place.

Mr. Marshall was an actor and a tap dancer who had appeared around the country in theatrical reviews. Whitman claimed the reason Marshall did not testify during Becker's first trial was because Marshall was out of town and could not be located. As soon as Marshall sat in the witness stand, Whitman cemented the link between Becker and Marshall.

Whitman said, "Do you know the defendant Becker."

"Yes sir, I do," Marshall replied.

Marshall went on to testify that he first met Becker when Becker's Strong Arm Squad raided a café on Twenty-Eight Street. When Marshall, along with several other Negros who were arrested, was brought to Police Headquarters, Marshall met Becker. Becker proposed to Marshall that he would be released if Marshall began working for Becker as a "stool pigeon"; getting evidence for Becker on Negro gambling houses.

On the night of June 27, 1912, Marshall said that Becker ordered him to infiltrate a Negro gambling house on 124th Street and Seventh Avenue, which Becker planned to raid later that night. After the raid was completed, Marshall said he saw Becker standing on the street corner conversing with three men. One of the men Marshall positively identified as Bald Jack Rose.

"How did you know it was Mr. Rose?" Whitman asked Marshall.

"I've seen his pictures," Marshall said.

Manton jumped to his feet and said, "I object."

Judge Seabury overruled Manton's objection.

Whitman asked Marshall, "Have you seen the man you refer to as Mr. Rose after that meeting on the Harlem street corner?"

"Yes sir," Marshall said. "I saw him a few weeks ago in a theatrical agency owned by Mr. Robinson. The man I saw there was the man I saw that night with Mr. Becker. I have since learned that it was Mr. Rose."

After his questioning of Marshall, Whitman turned to Manton with a satisfied smile on his face, knowing he had now proven the existence of the "Harlem Conference" which the appeals court said Whitman had not done in Becker's first trial.

When it was Manton's turn to cross-examine Marshall, his tactic was to try to trip up Marshall into contradicting parts of his testimony. But Marshall was a rock on the stand, and in fact, Marshall turned out to be one of Whitman's most believable witnesses.

Becker's second trial lasted 17 days. On the final day, Judge Seabury made his charge to the jury, and it was just as one-sided as Judge Goff's had been in the first trial. It was said later, that Judge Seabury was aware that the New York press, especially the *World*, had been hostile to Becker. Judge Seabury was also aware that he needed that same press to further his political ambitions. As a result, Judge Seabury gave a detailed charge to the jury that almost exactly parroted the one District Attorney Whitman had given in his summation to the jury.

As soon as Judge Seabury finished his charge, one of Manton's co-counsels, John B. Johnson, jumped to his feet and said, "I object to the whole charge on the grounds that is it an animated argument for the prosecution."

On the day before the verdict was rendered and both the prosecution and the defense had finished their summations, Mrs. Helen Becker spoke to the press.

She said, "I cannot believe that any 12 sensible men can give credence to such cooked-up stories as those told by Rose, Webber, and Plitt. I don't expect a conviction. The worst that can happen is a disagreement. Charles is innocent and he will be exonerated."

On Friday, May 22, 1914, the jury took only one ballot and less than two hours to find Charles Becker guilty for the second time of the first-degree murder of Herman Rosenthal.

As Becker was led from the courtroom, his wife Helen threw her arms around his neck. She cried, "Oh, Charlie I'm so sorry, I didn't expect it."

As soon as he left his wife's embrace, Becker was led out of the courtroom, around the corridor, and to the other side of the courthouse.

There he issued a brief statement, "I am very sorry for myself," Becker said. "That is all I have to say."

Then, after chains were attached around both ankles, Becker crossed the Bridge of Sighs for the final time, and he plodded back to his Tomb's prison cell.

Helen Becker stood in the sheriff's office for some time after her husband was led back to his cell. Relatives said she was too overcome with grief to leave immediately; and when she did, she had to be assisted out of the building and into a waiting car.

After the verdict, several people connected with the trial made statements to the press.

District Attorney Whitman puffed out his chest and said, "The verdict speaks for itself. Becker is guilty. It was proven. Now he must pay for his crimes."

Becker's attorney Manton had a totally different take.

Manton said, "The verdict was a complete surprise to me and my co-counsels in the case. We are all astounded. So is Becker. We were all confident of an acquittal. And of course we will file an appeal."

Manton's co-counsel Johnson simply said, "I am surprised."

In front of his adoring press, Judge Seabury stuck his chin out and opined on the courtroom proceedings.

"I am not to be interviewed on the verdict," Judge Seabury said. "But I may say that the conduct of those having business at the trial was exemplary and an aid to the dignified administration of justice."

Even chubby and flush-faced Lillian Rosenthal offered a statement.

"The verdict was a just one and I expected it," she told the *New York Times*. "I wish to thank the people of the State of New York for what they have done in repairing my heart in a small way. I wish to thank the jurors and the friends of the jurors who have stood behind them in this trying ordeal. I'm thankful it is all over."

Then, Lillian Rosenthal issued a sincere shout-out to Helen Becker.

She said, "My heart goes out to Mrs. Becker for her trust and loyalty to her husband during the hours of the trial. My heart goes out to her, for she feels like I felt at the time of the trouble which caused the death of my dear husband."

Then she added, "I live for only one thing: to see the day that Becker pays the penalty."

As several New York City daily newspapers pointed out in the following day's dailies, it was almost unprecedented for a second trial to render the same verdict of "guilty in the first degree" as had the first trial. Only once before, in the entire history of the state of New York, had this anomaly taken place.

As was pointed out in the *New York Sun*, "The jury could have saved Becker's life even in finding him guilty if they had wanted to show mercy. Justice Seabury had told them they could choose among three degrees of murder, and two of those degrees could have meant imprisonment. But like the 24 men who had come before, the first Becker jury and the gunmen's jury, they believed Jack Rose told the truth. Becker and his counsel never thought there was a chance in the world that 12 men, after the Court of Appeals' decision to grant Becker a new trial, would send Becker to the chair."

Despite the great disappointment of being found guilty a second time of the murder of Herman Rosenthal, Becker, who had not yet been sent back to Sing Sing Prison, had no trouble sleeping in his cell at the Tombs. According to a Tombs' keeper, after the second guilty verdict, "Becker jumped into his bed and slept like a baby until 7 a.m. the following morning."

"That man is no longer like other men," the keeper told the *New York Times*. "He is calloused by his experience. He saw 13 men go to the electric chair and what happened on Friday hasn't wrecked his nerve. He is pinning his hope on the Court of Appeals and is not worrying about himself. But he grieves for his wife, and he can't conceal that fact when she is near him."

Some jurors spoke quite freely to the press after the verdict. There had been erroneous reports circulating in the courtroom that there had been five separate ballots, and the jurors were quite divided as to the verdict. To dispel any false rumors, the jurors released an account of their deliberations, noting which witnesses' testimony they believed and which witnesses' testimony they totally disregarded.

The jurors' statement said that after Judge Seabury's charge to the jury, the jurors went into the jury room, and a ballot immediately was taken. Seven jurors voted for murder in the first degree, three for murder in lessor degrees, one was blank, and one voted not guilty. Then the jury went to lunch and not a word was spoken about the case.

When they returned, the real deliberations began. While one juror smoked, another juror detailed the entire story put forth by the prosecution. The discussions were informal and never heated.

The jurors first discussed the testimony of Charles Plitt, who had once worked under Becker and had said, after Becker's first conviction, Becker had told him to murder Jack Rose. The jury totally disregarded Plitt's testimony as an unbelievable tale told by a man with limited intelligence.

The "Harlem Conference" and the testimony of James Marshall was discussed next. To a man, every juror said Marshall's testimony was quite believable, and it had confirmed the testimony of Jack Rose that he, Bridgey Webber, Harry Vallon, and Becker had met in Harlem to discuss Rosenthal's murder.

Then the jurors discussed the testimony of Bald Jack Rose. One juror said that after Rose's testimony, "I was convinced that Becker's relationship with Rose was more than the relationship of a police lieutenant with a stool pigeon. Rose was not a mere acquaintance of the underworld. He was a big factor in Becker's relations with Rosenthal."

The jury bought Rose's main contentions that not only did Becker order Rosenthal killed, but Becker was also in constant contact with Rose soon after the murder, trying to aid and abet a cover-up.

At the end of about 40 minutes, jury foreman F. Meredith Blagden walked over to each juror one by one and looked them in the eye. Each juror nodded in the affirmative that Becker was indeed guilty of first degree murder.

Blagden then said, "I think we are all agreed. Aren't we?"

None of the jurors dissented.

However, Blagden was concerned he and his fellow jurors had not taken long enough to come to a decision. He stepped out of the jury room and asked one of the courtroom attendants how long the first Becker jury had been out. He was told that the first jury took eight hours to find Becker guilty. This confirmed in Blagden's mind that maybe, not to appear like they had come to a hasty decision, the jurors should stay in the jury room somewhat longer. So Blagden and his 11 fellow jurors sat in the jury room for one more hour without saying another word about the case. One juror smoked, while several of the other jurors closed their eyes and tried to take a nap.

When Blagden thought the time was right, he sent a message to Judge Seabury that they had reached their decision. Ten minutes later, the 12 jurors filed into the courtroom.

So, in fact, it did not take nearly two hours and five ballots to convict Becker; there was only one ballot and the entire deliberations took a mere 40 minutes.

Several of the jurors, who were approached by the press in the following days, refused to discuss their deliberations, but some were quite chatty. One juror, who asked that his name not be revealed in the newspapers, said, "I was astonished when I read in the newspapers that we had cast five ballots. That might create the impression that there was a wide difference of opinion. As a matter of fact, we were practically of one mind from the beginning."

This same juror was asked if the summation of any of the lawyers had influenced the jury. The anonymous juror said, "I can't answer positively for anyone but myself, but I believe District Attorney Whitman's brilliant summing up wholly convinced one of the jurors. He came into the jury room a changed man after that speech."

Then came the million-dollar question: did this juror think Becker had received a fair trial?

"I certainly do," he said. "And I include in this the care and attention in the jury room."

The anonymous juror then added something that gave credence to Becker's co-counsel, John B. Johnson's, strenuous objection to Judge Seabury's charge to the jury.

"Justice Seabury's charge helped a great deal," the anonymous juror said. "It put the case in sequence that made everything clear and distinct."

Unfortunately, that was not the role of Judge Seabury, but instead of District Attorney Whitman. So there can be no doubt Judge Seabury's inclination to side with the prosecution played a huge part in Becker's second conviction.

Juror No. 6 was Walter Goodyear, the owner of a bookstore on Fifth Avenue and someone who considered himself an amateur psychologist. When a reporter asked if he could interview him about the Becker trial, Goodyear readily agreed.

At this interview, which took place in Goodyear's bookstore, Goodyear surrounded himself with numerous books on psychology, to make himself appear an expert on the subject. Without much prodding from the reporter, Goodyear admitted he had applied his method of psychological analysis to Rose, Vallon, Becker, and others during the trial, which helped him reach the guilty verdict.

Goodyear categorized Rose, Webber, and Becker in the same class, which he called, "The Underworld." Goodyear said his study of these men in the courtroom revealed to him "common motives, common ideas, and common avenues of thinking and acting."

"My placing Becker in the same class with men like Rose, put Becker into the same groove in which these men found themselves," Goodyear said. "Thus parallel lines of thought of Becker and Rose could easily be explained."

The reporter asked Goodyear if he had considered Mrs. Helen Becker in reaching a verdict.

"She added sympathy in the case, of course," Goodyear said. "I saw her every day, but she did not weigh in the evidence. You can well believe that the verdict was a strain on all of us. This is reflected in the fact that some of the jurors at first favored a lesser degree of punishment. But sympathy could not modify the verdict justified by facts, could it?"

After his second Becker win, District Attorney Charles Whitman was the "toast of the town." In just the two days after the verdict had been rendered, Whitman received hundreds of congratulatory letters and telegrams. One man sent Whitman a long letter (which Whitman released to his adoring press) that referred to Whitman's victory as the "triumph of the right." The letter ended with the man saying that he would immediately send Whitman a rug "on which you can place your feet and rest."

The Mayor of New York City, John Purroy Mitchel, also got into the act.

Mitchel sent Whitman a letter (which again Whitman released to the press) that said, "I have just heard of the outcome of the Becker case. The whole community is under obligations to you. Your work has been splendid."

Whitman did a few victory laps in certain New York City bars and restaurants, strutting his success in prosecuting Becker twice and winning twice. Then he easily took the Republican nomination for Governor, winning the primary against Harvey D. Hineman by the lopsided vote of 120,073 to 61,952.

In November, the Governor's race also went easily to Whitman. He defeated the incumbent acting-governor Martin Glynn by a vote of 686,701 to 412,252. On Jan. 1, 1915, Charles Whitman was sworn in as the 41st Governor of New York State.

This did not bode well for Charles Becker.

JAMES MARSHALL TAP DANCES AROUND THE TRUTH - TWICE

On February 13, 1915 a series of events occurred concerning James Marshall, the Negro who had testified at Becker's second trial. These events resembled a comedy of errors viewed in a funhouse mirror.

First, Marshall, a professional tap dancer, who was then living in Philadelphia, gave his wife an early Valentine's present by beating the crap out of her while he was in a drunken stupor. Marshall's wife called the police to make a formal complaint, and both husband and wife were hustled down to the police station. While Mrs. Marshall was giving her statement to the police, she happened to mention, that in addition to being a brute, her husband was also an habitual liar. In fact, Mrs. Marshall said Mr. Marshall had lied under oath in Becker's second trial when he said that he had seen Becker with Jack Rose on a Harlem street corner – the infamous "Harlem Conference."

Two Philadelphia scribes overheard Mrs. Marshall's rantings, and after putting two and two together, they figured they had a hell of a story.

The two scribes hurried to Marshall's cell where Marshall was trying to sleep off his inebriation, and woke him. Marshall, still very drunk, admitted that he had committed perjury at Becker's trial. Marshall said he had done so because he had been threatened with prosecution by Whitman's assistant Fredrick Groehl. Marshall also said he had been paid to lie on the witness stand by Groehl.

The newspapermen wrote their stories and the following day, Becker's attorney Manton heard about Marshall's flip-flop. He sent his assistant John Johnson to Philadelphia, where Johnson met with Marshall in the offices of the *Philadelphia Daily Ledger*. In front of Johnson and several of the newspaper's staff, Johnson swore an affidavit, that according to the *Ledger*, "repudiating his words (at the

Becker trial) and accusing an Assistant District Attorney (Groehl) of forcing him to testify under threat of arrest."

To add more grist to the mill, Marshall said Groehl had put an earlier affidavit before him where he (Marshall) had sworn false information about a raid made by Becker. Marshall admitted he had done so under the fictitious name of "Moore." Marshall said this false affidavit was used as a lever by District Attorney Whitman to force him to testify for the prosecution at Becker's second trial.

Marshall said in his Philadelphia affidavit, "I met District Attorney Groehl who asked me at once what I knew about a meeting between Becker and Rose. I explained to him that I didn't know Jack Rose and had never seen him.

"I was then asked, 'Did you see Becker, Jack Rose, and Bridgey Webber talking at the corner of 124th Street and Seventh Avenue,' and I said I did not. I said I knew Becker, but I did not know the other men and can't say I saw them talking with Becker."

Marshall said that Groehl had told him he could be arrested immediately and held as a material witness for Becker's trial. Marshall said he told Groehl that he had several theatrical engagements (as a tap dancer) in Washington, D.C. Marshall said that, with Groehl's permission, he went to Washington, D.C. and an "attaché" from Whitman's office accompanied him on the trip. During this trip, Marshall admitted that Whitman's offices gave him three separate checks for his expenses: two for $70, and one for $150.

"Life was very pleasant for me there," Marshall said. "It was nothing but theaters and auto rides through the park all day long. I went to the theater almost every afternoon and never got up before 11 in the morning."

Marshall then added, "I never knew Jack Rose. My only knowledge of Rose was what Mr. Groehl told me and what I read in the papers."

At this point, Marshall was interrupted by Becker's co-counsel Johnson, who said to Marshall, "So you say now that you don't know whether or not it was Rose who met Becker that night, but you testified it was Rose because the prosecution told you to do so, is that right?"

Marshall said, "Yes sir. That was it."

As soon as the ink was dry on Marshall's affidavit, Johnson hustled Marshall to New York City to see Becker's chief counsel Manton, in Manton's offices at 31 Nassau Street. There, Marshall confirmed everything he had sworn to in Philadelphia.

Then Marshall decided to call his mother, which led to another sequence of astounding events.

At the precise time Marshall was phoning his mother from Manton's office, Assistant District Attorney Groehl, angry as hell at what Marshall had done in Philadelphia, was entering the basement apartment of Marshall's mother, at 129 East Seventy-Sixth Street, where Mrs. Marshall was the janitor. When Groehl heard it was Marshall on the phone, he grabbed the receiver from Marshall's mother.

Groehl growled into the phone, "Did you make a statement or an affidavit in Philadelphia as the papers this morning said you did?"

Marshall, a professional tap dancer, did a little two-step. "No sir, I did not."

Within an hour, Marshall was with Groehl in Marshall's mother's apartment. There, Marshall told Groehl that he had been drunk in Philadelphia, and that it was John Johnson who had dictated the affidavit, then paid him $2,500 to sign it.

Groehl had Marshall sign a second affidavit denying everything in the Philadelphia affidavit he had signed the day before. This effectively ended Marshall as a credible witness, either against Becker or for Becker in Becker's upcoming appeal.

The day after Marshall's monumental turnabout, new District Attorney Charles A. Perkins, who had been appointed by Governor Whitman the day Whitman morphed from D.A. to Governor, told the press he doubted Marshall would be indicted for perjury, "because the contradicting affidavits Marshall signed on two consecutive days were signed in different states."

When Manton was told about Marshall's about-face, he said, "My opinion is that the Negro's word is no good. I am independently convinced that he did not see Becker and Jack Rose talking on 124th and Seventh Avenue, and in admitting this in Philadelphia he was telling the truth. But I wouldn't count on him sticking to the truth. Nothing he says can be counted on without corroboration."

Manton did say he was in the process of filing an appeal, without Marshall's cooperation. Manton didn't go into explicit detail, but he did say, "In regard to the testimony of Mr. Rose, there are more than 60 contradictions in what he said at the first trial, compared to what he said at the second trial. Most of these contradictions are about his conversations with Becker."

CHARLES BECKER'S FINAL APPEALS

Manton went ahead and filed his appeal, but it was to no avail. Part of Manton's written appeal pointed out the unreliability of Marshall as to being a witness to the "Harlem Conference." However, the Court of Appeals accepted Marshall's testimony in the Becker trial to be true, and not the affidavit Marshall signed in Philadelphia.

In opposition to Manton's motion, New York City Assistant District Attorney Groehl had filed another affidavit signed by Marshall to the Court of Appeals, which said: "I testified to the truth in everything that I said at the Becker trial, and I do not want to change or take back anything that I have said, and if I am called upon as a witness again, I will tell the same things because they are true."

Justice Weeks, to whom Manton filed his appeal in court, was unimpressed with Manton's argument. Justice Weeks told Manton, "My first impression is that the affidavit is manifestly an ingenious invasion of Marshall's testimony and does not come within the legal provisions for granting a new trial."

Justice Weeks then took Manton to task.

He said, "Does Marshall say he did not see Becker talking to one of two men at the corner of 124th Street and Seventh Avenue?"

"He does not," Manton admitted.

"Why does not your affidavit set forth its contents in language that cannot be misunderstood?" Justice Weeks said. "An affidavit bearing on an important fact can be made in a few clear words without circumvention. The affidavit of Marshall said that he did see Becker speak to a man. It says that he later identified that man as Jack Rose. Where an affidavit is produced to interfere with the orderly process of an appeal, it should be so clear as to be impossible to be misunderstood."

A second part of Manton's appeal questioned Judge Seabury's impartiality in Becker's second trial. Manton's appeal stated that, "The facts and law were arrayed and marshaled by Judge

Seabury in a way highly inimicable to defendant's rights and wholly devoid of any serious and anxious desire to their preservation."

However, the Court of Appeals did not buy Manton's argument concerning Judge Seabury's conduct in the trial (by this time, Judge Seabury was a member of the Court of Appeals himself, but he recused himself from reviewing Manton's appeal). In the end, for some baffling reason, the Court of Appeals somehow found Judge Seabury's conduct to be exemplary.

The Court of Appeals said: "The most sedulous care to preserve the rights of the defendant was manifested, not only in the charge, but throughout the whole trial, and the assertion seems both unwarranted and underserved."

The final vote from the Court of Appeals was 5-1 in favor of denying Becker's appeal. Justice William Bartlett wrote the majority decision. The lone dissenter was Justice John Hogan.

At this point in time, there were only four means available for Becker to escape the death penalty. They were:

1. A plea for Executive Clemency from Governor Whitman, the very man who twice successfully prosecuted Becker. (Fat chance)
2. An application for a new trial based on new-found evidence. (There was none)
3. An application for writ of habeas Corpus in Federal District court, based on an allegation of violation of Becker's constitutional rights. (Longer than a longshot)
4. An application directly to the Supreme Court. (Worth a shot)

On July 9, 1915, just days before Becker's execution (scheduled for July 15), his new high-powered co-counsel, Bourke Cockran, made an impassioned plea to United States Supreme Court Justice Charles E. Hughes at Hughes' summer home on a lake in Maine.

Winston Churchill had once said of Cockran, "I have never seen his like, or in some respects his equal."

In his request for a "writ of error," Cochran argued that the agreement made by then-New York City Assistant District Attorney Frank Moss with Harry Vallon, Jack Rose, and Bridgey Webber, "practically demanded that the three informants, in order to avoid prosecution, should tie Becker up to the murder of Herman Rosenthal."

The second point on which Cockran sought the writ of error was that the defendant Becker was denied a change of venue. This had been requested on the grounds that, even before the trial started, District Attorney Whitman had released statements to the press which could influence possible jurors against Becker.

The third point Cockran argued to Justice Hughes, was that Governor Whitman, the man to whom Becker would have to make his plea for Executive Clemency, was not the unbiased person the Constitution holds should pass on this plea.

A week later, Cockran's three pleas were shot down by United States Supreme Court Justice Hughes. However, Cockran was able to get Becker's execution date pushed back two weeks to July 30, 1915. During this time, Cockran said he would prepare a new affidavit to the New York Supreme Court asking for a new trial.

On the same day Cochran saw Justice Hughes, Charles Plitt visited Governor Whitman in Whitman's Executive Chamber in Albany. Plitt told the press he supplied Whitman with new evidence of police graft in connection with Becker's case. According to a report in the *Washington Post*, "The Governor did examine the statement Plitt gave him, but gave Plitt little encouragement. Governor Whitman told Plitt to put the statement in legal form and that then he would examine it."

However, Plitt felt his statement was of great importance; much greater importance than Whitman had indicated to him. Plitt told the press that his statement, which was prepared with Becker's knowledge, would "prove sensational and save Becker's life."

As he left the Executive Chamber in Albany, Plitt said, "Charles Becker will never go to the chair."

At that point in time, the only way for Becker to be spared from the electric chair was for Governor Whitman to grant Becker clemency. Doing so was not unprecedented for a United States Governor. In fact, this is exactly what had happened on July 19, 1915, less than two weeks before Becker's execution.

Leo Frank, a manager in a pencil factory in Georgia, was convicted of killing a 14-year-old girl named Mary Phagan. The chief witness against Frank was an ex-convict named Jim Conley, who some people, including ex-Georgia congressman W.M. Howard, thought was the murderer himself. Thanks to Howard's pleas to Georgia Governor John M. Slaton, and the aggressive intervention by a Chicago group called the "Chicago Anti-Capital Punishment Society," the night before Frank was scheduled to be executed, Governor Slaton commuted Frank's sentence from death to life imprisonment (the Chicago Anti-Capital Punishment Society also collected signatures on petitions to induce Governor Whitman to commute Charles Becker's death sentence, but to no avail).

Of course, some people in Georgia were outraged at the murder of Mary Phagan and not too happy with the Governor for cancelling Frank's execution. Although Slaton's actions were praised by the *Atlanta Journal Constitution*, an angry mob charged the Governor's mansion, forcing Governor Slaton to call out the National Guard. A few days later, Governor Slaton slithered out of Georgia and absconded with his wife to New York City, where they stayed at the tony Waldorf Astoria Hotel, before departing on a tour of New York State, as well as Canada, and the Northern Pacific states (it seemed like Georgia Governor Slaton wanted to be anyplace but in Georgia).

When New York City reporters asked him if he "had slipped out of Georgia" to avoid the angry mobs, Governor Slaton bristled, "I am incapable of slipping out of Georgia, or anywhere else."

Slaton was then asked if he thought Frank was guilty, and he gave an answer that played more to his ideology than to Frank's innocence or guilt.

"I do not know if Frank was guilty," Slaton said. "I was simply asked to commute his sentence. And if I had done otherwise, I would have felt like an assassin. As it was, I went six nights without sleep. But I'd rather go without sleep than to go 40 years, if I live that long, with the blood of that man on my hands."

Governor Whitman, on the other hand, did not complain about missing any night's sleep, when within hours of Becker's appeal being turned down again by the New York Court of Appeals, Whitman refused to commute Becker's sentence.

BECKER'S FINAL DAYS

On July 29, the day before Becker's scheduled execution, Becker was awakened at 7 a.m. He was taken from his cell, given a bath and a brand-new set of underwear. At 8 a.m., Becker was taken to the prison barber and administered a close-cropped haircut, so the metal helmet he'd wear in the electric chair would make close contact with the electrodes.

When Becker returned to his cell, he was dismayed to discover that all of his personal belongings, including his clothes, a few articles of furniture, and most importantly – a picture of his wife - had been removed from his cell. On a new cot lay a heavy black suit, white shirt, and a black felt slippers; the clothing he would wear when he was executed.

On that same morning, John Ford, the Chief Justice of the New York Supreme Court, issued a statement denying Becker's last bid to stay alive. This appeal had been presented to him in an affidavit written by Becker's lawyer Bourke Cockran, after Cockran's appeal had been turned down by United States Supreme Court Justice Charles E. Hughes. Cockran tried throwing a last-second "Hail Mary" to Justice Ford, but the pass fell incomplete.

Justice Ford said he had "labored for several days and several nights on briefs for and against the application of a new trial." He then called the newspapermen into his chamber, and as his secretary handed them his written decision, Justice Ford said, "I have denied the motion for a new trial. And this is my birthday. It's a pretty rough way to spend your birthday, isn't it?"

Upon hearing about Justice Ford's decision, Governor Whitman released a statement saying, "Justice Ford did the only thing he could do. The evidence was conclusive. If I had any doubt to Becker's guilt, I would pardon him."

When Becker was informed that his last appeal had been denied, and that Governor Whitman had refused to commute his sentence, he told Sing Sing Warden Osborne, "Well, I'll die like a man anyhow."

Becker also spoke to prison chaplain Father Cashin, who was spending Becker's last day with him in order to get Becker's spiritual affairs in order.

"There is no justice here," Becker told Father Cashin. "I am confident, however, that I will get it in the next world. I know that the truth will come out, and that the world will know that Becker told the truth and is not the murderer he is accused of being."

These are hardly the words of a guilty man speaking to a man of God shortly before he's about to be put to death.

Becker also told Father Cashin, "I do not fear death, but I feel the stigma attached to the name Becker, and I feel the distress and sorrow it will cause my wife."

Helen Becker Tries to Save Her Husband's Life

Even though all methods to save Charles Becker's life had been exhausted, Helen Becker would not give up without a fight.

On July 29, Helen Becker arrived at the Governor's mansion at 11:30 a.m., accompanied by Becker's co-counsel, John Johnson. When she arrived, Mrs. Becker was dismayed to discover Governor Whitman had left Albany and had traveled to Camp Whitman, near Fishkill, New York. The Governor did receive a telegram in advance notifying him about Mrs. Becker's arrival, but he left her a letter saying that he had been summoned away from Albany (no reason was given) and would meet her at 6:30 p.m. in the Governor's mansion.

That didn't happen either, and it appeared as if Governor Whitman was ducking Helen Becker at all costs.

When she learned the Governor was not in Albany, Helen Becker was crestfallen. She had planned not to ask the Governor to commute her husband's sentence, but on the advice of her attorneys, instead to reprieve her husband's sentence until October, when the New York Court of Appeals convened again. At that time, Becker's attorneys would put in an appeal for a new trial based on new evidence. Becker's attorneys did not disclose what that new evidence was, and they seemed just to be stalling for time.

However, there had been some speculation, that in order to save his own life, Becker was willing to plead guilty to second-degree murder.

This notion was struck down when Becker's chief counsel Manton said from his office in New York City, "There is absolutely no truth in the statement that Becker offered to plead guilty to murder in the second degree, or to any degree, so far as I know. Certainly no such offer was made while I was counsel. Becker will go to the chair with a dying declaration of innocence."

With his execution less than 24 hours away, Becker asked for a copy of the daily newspaper. Ignoring the pleas of Father Cashin that he no longer be concerned about worldly things, Becker devoured every word in the newspaper concerning his present predicament. He became outraged when he read that he had agreed to plead guilty to murder in the second degree. Becker became even further unhinged when he read that someone in Albany had released a statement that Becker's first wife's death was "suspicious."

Becker was trembling when he told the priest, "I want to deny those falsehoods. I want to set myself right in the eyes of the world."

Becker asked for a stenographer, and with the help of Father Cashin, he penned a scathing report to the press, denying any plea to a lesser degree. He also vigorously castigated Governor Whitman for allowing the statement to be published that Becker's first wife's death was somehow suspicious. Becker insisted his first wife died of consumption after a long bout with tuberculosis.

Becker spent the rest of the daylight hours writing a series of letters to friends and relatives that he did not want mailed until after his death. The bulkiest letter he wrote was to Governor Whitman.

This scathing letter, which was released to the press after Becker's execution said, in part:

> "I am as innocent as you of having murdered Herman Rosenthal, or having counseled, procured, or aided his murder, or of having any knowledge of that dreadful crime. Mark well, sir, these words of mine. When your power passes, then the truth of Rosenthal's murder will become known. But not while your nominees remain District Attorneys and can hold the club over these persons. With the aid of judges who were misled into misconceiving the testimony offered on my trial and into misstating it both to the jury and on appeal, you have proved yourself able to destroy my life. But believe me; I will surrender it without rancor. Not all the judges in this state, nor in this country, nor the Governor of this state, nor the District Attorney, nor all of them combined, can destroy permanently the character of an innocent man."

CHARLES BECKER

It wasn't until 9 p.m. on the night before her husband's execution that Helen Becker was finally able to receive an audience with Governor Whitman. However, the meeting wasn't in the Executive Mansion, but in a room in the Nelson House in Poughkeepsie, where the Governor had decided to spend the night. (The governor, probably trying to duck the press until after Becker was dead, never returned to the Executive Mansion that night.) Mrs. Becker was still accompanied by her husband's co-counsel, John Johnson.

Johnson entered Whitman's room first, while Mrs. Becker waited in an adjoining room. Johnson extended his hand to the Whitman. Whitman took it and said to Johnson, "Mr. Johnson, I am here to do whatever I can, as a governor and a citizen, for your client."

Johnson pleaded with Whitman to give Becker a stay of execution until October, when the New York State Court of Appeals came back into session. Johnson said he believed he could convince the appellate division that Justice Ford had erred in refusing to grant Becker a new trial. Johnson spoke for about 15 minutes, but Whitman overruled every plea from Johnson, saying he could do nothing.

When he was finished listening to Johnson, Whitman told him, "I am now ready to see Mrs. Becker."

Whitman entered the adjoining room and Helen Becker rose to greet him. No handshake was offered by either person.

Whitman told Mrs. Becker, "Mrs. Becker I am now ready to hear anything you have to offer new in this case. I will consider any confidence you wish to make at this time."

Mrs. Becker was distraught. She tried to stand straight, but her shoulders slumped in exhaustion.

"There is nothing new and I have nothing to tell you in confidence," she said. "But I do ask for sufficient delay to provide a review of Justice Ford's decision."

The governor shook his head. "That is impossible. I'm sorry, but I can take no action."

Mrs. Becker started sobbing softly.

"But surely a delay will not defeat the ends of justice," she said.

Then without warning, Mrs. Becker's soft sobs transformed into a convulsion of wails. Unable to catch her breath, and with walls of tears cascading down both sides of her face, she fell face-forward in a faint towards the governor. Governor Whitman caught her against his chest and laid her gently on the floor. A doctor had to be called in to revive Mrs. Becker.

After she regained consciousness, and before she and Mr. Johnson left the hotel, Governor Whitman did throw a small bone to Mrs. Becker. He ordered his aide, Major Moore, to telephone Sing Sing Prison to tell Warden Osborne that the rule a condemned man cannot have any visitors after 12 a.m. be done away with in the case of Mrs. Becker. And that she should be allowed to stay with her husband as long as the warden deemed proper.

Mrs. Becker thanked Whitman for his small kindness, but before she left she told him, "I know my husband is no saint, but he is not as black as he's been branded."

CHARLES BECKER'S FINAL HOURS

Throughout the day of July 29, Becker inquired about the whereabouts of his wife. He knew she was trying to track down Governor Whitman; but he also realized there was no chance the man who had successfully prosecuted him twice, would ever allow himself to commute Becker's death sentence to life imprisonment.

However, Becker did receive courtesies on July 29 that no condemned man had ever been afforded in Sing Sing Prison. Becker was permitted to receive visitors, not in the usual visitor's room, but in the office of Warden Osborne - a room usually reserved for prisoners meeting with their counsels. With a prison keeper standing guard, Becker was allowed to grasp the hands of loved ones and even embrace them if he wished. While meeting with his brother John and his brother-in-law John Lynch, Becker suddenly inquired as to what time it was.

When he was told it was 20 minutes past nine, Becker said. "This is remarkable! To the minute, it is now three years since I've been arrested."

It wasn't until 11:30 p.m. that Helen Becker finally arrived at Sing Sing Prison to see her husband. Helen was with Charles for one hour, alone in the warden's office; except for the two guards present in the room, under orders not to take their eyes off the married couple. Both guards disobeyed that order and diverted their eyes, while Becker and his wife embraced their last embrace.

It wasn't until 12:30 a.m. that Helen Becker tore herself loose from her husband and bid him her last goodbye. She was led from the room sobbing heavily and in the state of collapse by her husband's co-counsel, John Johnson.

Charles Becker was led back to his cell, where he paced the room the entire night. In his company was Deputy Warden Johnson, who had promised Mrs. Becker her husband would not be alone in his final hours.

Mrs. Helen Becker arrived at her home at 2291 University Avenue in the Bronx at about 3 a.m. She was so worn out with grief, she had to be carried up the steps to the entrance of her home. There she stayed with family and close friends to await the news that her husband was indeed dead.

BECKER'S EXECUTION

At 5:41 a.m., Charles Becker, accompanied by Father Cashin and Father James B. Curry, entered the execution room at Sing Sing Prison. Becker, dressed entirely in black except for a white shirt, held a black crucifix about ten inches long in his left hand.

The members of the press in the adjacent room, who had known Becker since his days with the Special (Strong Arm) Squad, were shocked by his appearance. Instead of the big, broad-shouldered and strapping man they were accustomed to seeing, the man who was minutes from his death was now the shell of his former self. Becker's shoulders slumped forward, the cheeks of his face were creased with thick lines, and his eyes looked like black, hollow sockets.

The two priests began intonating the *Litany of the Holy Name* as Becker approached the electric chair - the machine of death the guards had christened "Old Sparky."

As soon as Becker, in response to the priests' prayers, uttered the words "Lord have mercy on us," five burly guards seized Becker and sat him in the electric chair. They immediately tossed heavy straps around his knees, ankles, wrists, elbows and chest, and tightly secured them with buckles. Not able to move anymore, Becker mouthed the words, "Oh Lord, assist me in my last agony. I give you my heart and soul."

Two guards slapped a leather cap down on Becker's head and began screwing in the electrodes on the front and back of Becker's head and over his temples.

Standing behind and slightly to the right of Becker was the official executioner; a grim, shaven man, dressed in gray and about 30-years-old, whose name was not released to the press. The executioner was to be paid $100 - $50 for executing Becker and $50 to execute a Negro named Sam Hayne, who was to follow Becker into the electric chair.

At 5:43 a.m., Dr. Charles Farr, the doctor in charge of the execution, motioned to the executioner. The grim man dressed in gray pulled down the electricity lever, which thrust 1,850 volts and

10 amps into Becker's body. Becker stiffened straight from the initial shock, and the crucifix slipped out of his hand. A guard caught the crucifix before it hit the ground. The muscles of Becker's head and neck swelled outward, as Father Cashin and Dr. Farr stood solemnly on rubber mat just feet away from the electric chair. The doctor stood quiet and grim, but Father Cashin's lips moved precipitously in prayer.

The first shock lasted about a minute. Dr. Farr then stepped forward, ripped open Becker's coat and tore open his shirt. Exposed for all to see was a picture of Helen Becker, pinned to the inside of Becker's shirt and close to his heart. Dr. Farr applied his stethoscope to the middle of Becker's chest.

Becker's heart still beat strongly.

The executioner pulled the lever down a second time. This shock lasted only 10 seconds - five seconds longer than is usually required for a man's second jolt. Dr. Farr moved forward again, this time removing Becker's leather cap.

His second stethoscope examination revealed a slight heartbeat.

A third shock was administered; Becker's body heaved forward and then fell limp. Dr. Farr made his third examination, and at exactly 5:55 a.m., he said in a loud voice, "I pronounce this man dead."

Immediately after Becker's execution, the press assembled outside the execution room. Warden Osborne then proceeded to read a statement by Becker that Becker was not allowed to say in the execution room. It read.

Gentlemen: My dying declaration:

I stand before you in my full senses, knowing that no power on earth can save me from the grave that is about to receive me. In the face of that, in the teeth of those who condemn me, and in the presence of my God and your God, I proclaim my absolute innocence for the crime of which I must die. You are now about to witness my destruction by the State, which is organized to protect the lives of the innocent.

May Almighty God pardon everyone who has contributed in any degree to my untimely death. And now, on the brink of my grave,

I declare to the world that I am proud to have been the husband of the noblest woman who has ever lived – Helen Becker. This acknowledgement is the only legacy I can leave her.

I bid you all goodbye; Father I am ready to go. Amen.

CHARLES BECKER

After Warden Osborne finished reading Becker's dying declaration, Father Cashin was asked by the press, "From your experience with condemned men, isn't it your belief that a condemned man always confesses in the hours before his execution?"

"Invariably," Father Cashin said. "Usually the confession comes after the sacrament has been given. Becker maintained his innocence to the end."

Father Cashin said after he had administered the holy sacrament of Extreme Unction (the Last Rites) to Becker, he had asked Becker, "Are you guilty by word, or deed or by any manner whatsoever of this crime?"

Becker firmly answered, "Father, as I stand on the brink of the grave, I am not."

CHARLES BECKER'S FUNERAL

Charles Becker's body was transported to his home in the Bronx and arrived later that same afternoon. His coffin was carried up the steps of the apartment building and laid to rest in the living room for one day of viewing.

Helen Becker, her rage for Governor Whitman, his actions and his inactions, still stewing, commissioned a local engraver to construct a five-by-seven-inch silver plaque for her husband's coffin. She took full responsibility for this herself, and she made it clear her husband had not requested such a plaque be placed on his coffin.

The plaque read:

CHARLES BECKER
MURDERED JULY 30, 1915
BY GOVERNOR WHITMAN

District Attorney Francis Martin of the Bronx read about the plaque in the newspapers. He immediately rushed to police headquarters, where he met with Inspector Joseph Faurot and first Deputy Commissioner Leon Godley. They determined that this plaque was illegal, and as a result, Inspector Faurot and Captain Wines rushed to the Becker residence to see if such a plaque actually existed. When they saw the plaque for themselves, they informed Helen Becker that the plaque was criminally libelous and had to be removed immediately. When Helen Becker refused, Inspector Faurot unscrewed the plaque himself, put it into his pocket, and he and Captain Wines exited the premises.

District Attorney Martin explained his actions to the press, "While I have sympathy for Mrs. Becker, as I would for anyone in trouble," Martin said, "I could not, as District Attorney, permit the Governor to be libeled."

District Attorney Martin insisted he had not been given any direct orders from Governor Whitman to remove the plaque.

From the moment Becker's body was returned to his home, a curious crowd began forming outside. On August 2, when Becker's coffin was being transported from Becker's home to St. Nicholas of Tollentine Church three blocks away, there was an estimated three thousand people gathered around the cordoned-off area from Becker's home to the church. Becker's pallbearers were five members of the police department: Lieutenant James Brady, Captain John Bourke, Lieutenant Patrick Shea, patrolmen John O'Connor and John Ferrick; and former police officer Joseph Shepard.

As the pallbearers carried Becker's coffin toward the church, scores of people broke through the barricade. Policemen used their clubs to beat back the rioters, and it took five minutes for order to be restored so the pallbearers could continue their journey.

After Becker's coffin reached the church and his funeral mass began, an estimated 10,000 people surrounded the area near the church. There were seats for 700 people inside the church, but it was estimated at least twice as many had piled inside.

Outside the church during the service, battles ensued between the police and a belligerent crowd, and more police enforcements from the High Bridge Police Station were summoned to the scene. In front of the church, people were jammed so close together, women began to faint.

While the funeral services were taking place, a wagon containing floral tributes pulled up in front of the church. One large floral arrangement was a large cross made of lilies, bay leaves, and asters. Large purple lettering across it said: "Sacrificed for Politics." On the cross was pinned a large envelope with the inscription, "From a Friend."

Another large floral arrangement had the words, "To the Martyr, with sincere sympathies." A third floral arrangement, sent by former inspector Alexander "Clubber" Williams, who had instructed Becker in Becker's early years as a policeman on the proper use of the billy club, read, "In sympathy and respect to Charlie."

When the funeral mass ended, the long trip to Woodlawn Cemetery began. The hearse that contained Becker's coffin was pulled by two black horses and followed by five black carriages; the first of which carried Helen Becker and her brother. They arrived at Woodlawn Cemetery at 11 a.m.

As the flowers were taken off the wagon to be placed near Becker's grave, cemetery officials were ordered by the police to pull letters off the floral arrangement which said "Sacrificed for Politics."

When they had finished their task, all that read was "S O P." The floral arrangement that read "To the Martyr, with sincere sympathies" was also altered as to make it meaningless.

Immediately after Charles Becker's body was buried, Mrs. Becker told the press she had nothing to say today, but would issue a statement in a few days.

That statement never came.

Helen Becker returned home after her husband's funeral, not only heartbroken, but dead broke. She had used up all her husband's ill-gotten gains to pay for his numerous defense lawyers, who did not work cheaply.

Helen Becker continued to live on her meager teacher's salary, and she eventually became an assistant principle in a northern Manhattan public school. She retired in the mid-1940s and lived until 1962 - 50 years after her husband's conviction for the murder of Herman Rosenthal.

Although she had been proposed to many times, Helen Becker never remarried. As to why she never accepted any future proposals of marriage, she often said, "I prefer to remain a widow in memory of a man who was put to death by the great state of New York for a crime he did not commit. He was not an angel; he never made a pretense of being one. He was just an ordinary human being, and that is why I loved him so."

CONCLUSION

The $64,000 question is: Did Lieutenant Charles Becker order the murder of Herman Rosenthal? Or was he framed? And if Becker was framed, who did the framing, and why?

The answer to the first question, to me, is self-evident. Charles Becker did not order the murder of Herman Rosenthal. Yes, Becker was a lout, a ruffian, a crooked cop, and much worse, and he certainly had the makeup to be a murderer if that's what Becker thought was in his best interest. But that doesn't mean Becker ordered Rosenthal's murder.

As for the motive, some people might say Becker had plenty of reasons to want Rosenthal dead. I say it was in Becker's best interest to keep Rosenthal alive.

Let's examine the facts as we know them.

It was obvious that Becker and Rosenthal were partners in an illegal gambling house, and at the time of his death, Rosenthal had already informed on Becker in the most open of forums – the New York City press. Killing Rosenthal would not have undone the damage Rosenthal had already wreaked on Becker and his career. Keeping Rosenthal alive was the best thing for Becker, since it would give Becker a chance to discredit the gambler and possibly clear his own name in the process. Becker had a lot of pull in law enforcement and in Tammany Hall. It is not inconceivable that Becker could have walked away from Rosenthal's accusations unscathed.

And surely, Becker was not a stupid man. If Rosenthal were to be killed just hours before he was to visit District Attorney Whitman's office to make a formal affidavit against Becker, Becker would be the first person to come under suspicion. This fact made Becker the perfect pigeon for a frame.

Who else who stood to gain if Rosenthal were croaked?

Bald Jack Rose certainly fits that description. With Rosenthal out of the way, Rose, and his pals Harry Vallon and Bridgey Webber assumed they would be standing pretty in the Tenderloin. With the competition from Rosenthal's gambling house out of the way, these three creeps probably figured they would rake in the fallen crumbs from Rosenthal's gambling residue. As events further unfolded, they were chased from the Tenderloin instead, by irate members of the underworld, who, by nature, despised informers.

Let's assume for a moment that Rose arranged Rosenthal's murder without Becker's knowledge. It could have been the perfect crime if Rose and his pals weren't so stupid.

Why rent a car for the murder; a car that could be traced back to Rose? Efficient killers would have stolen a car to do the dirty deed. And surely, if Becker were arranging Rosenthal's murder he would have been intelligent enough to make sure the killers didn't use a rented car. Once the owner and the driver of the murder car (William Libby and Louis Shapiro) were caught, and they were caught quickly, the entire scheme fell apart.

This is where Rose used his ingenuity; his ability to survive. As soon as Libby and Shapiro were arrested, Rose knew he was in deep unless he came up with a plan. Rose decided to turn chicken shit into chicken salad by first turning himself in. Soon, Webber and Vallon were sitting in the same Tombs prison cell next to Rose, so they could plan and scheme to their heart's delight.

Behind bars was where Rose transformed himself from a dumb murderer into a smart witness; a witness against Becker, who was dumfounded; first when Rosenthal was killed, and again when he was arrested for Rosenthal's murder. Bridgey Webber, Sam Schepps, and Harry Vallon, out to save their own skins, backed up Rose's play, and this was the start of the demise of Lieutenant Charles Becker.

Rose also knew he had two aces in the hole; two men who wanted Rose's story to be true for their own personal ambitions - District Attorney Charles Whitman and newspaper columnist Herbert Bayard Swope.

Whitman wanted to be Governor of the state of New York, and then President of the United States of America. The best way to accomplish this exacta was to successfully prosecute a highly visible case; especially one where the accused was a decorated New York City police lieutenant (a variation of this same strategy was later employed by New York City Special Prosecutor Thomas E. Dewey and U.S. Attorney for the Southern District Rudolph Giuliani, amongst others).

Whitman didn't want to know the truth, and like Jack Nicholson once said in a movie, "He couldn't handle the truth."

The truth was three lowlife gamblers arranged the killing of another lowlife gambler. This was not the stuff dreams were made of; at least not Whitman's dreams. Whitman needed a big splash to further his political career, and his two successful prosecutions of Becker were the right ticket Whitman needed to propel him upward politically; the truth be damned.

As for Swope, he was just a huckster who knew a good story when he saw it, even if the story lacked the ingredients of the truth. Swope, who later won the first Pulitzer Prize in 1917 for his reporting on *Inside the German Empire*, once said, "It occurred to me that nothing is more interesting than opinion when opinion is interesting, so I devised a method of cleaning off the page opposite the editorial, which became the most important in America. And thereon I decided to print opinions, ignoring facts."

And that's exactly what Swope did concerning the murder of Herman Rosenthal. Swope knew the most sensational "opinion" to have was that a corrupt police lieutenant had ordered the killing of Rosenthal. Swope, like Whitman, saw no career advantage in stating the truth, so he tilted his reporting in a manner that would assure a guilty verdict for Becker.

AFTERMATH

When Bridgey Webber was released from the Tombs prison (after the trial of the four killers), he found out the hard way that the underworld of New York City does not like informers, rats, and canaries. In June of 1913, while exiting a Second Avenue gambling den, someone rushed up behind Webber and stabbed him in the back.

Knowing a second Becker trial was coming soon and not wanting to lose one of his star witnesses, District Attorney Whitman rushed to Polyclinic Hospital to make sure Webber was not in any danger of dying. After being told by hospital personnel that Webber's wound was a superficial one, Whitman asked Webber if he could identify his assailant. Webber clammed up this time, saying only that a kid had stabbed him; he did not know the kid and couldn't even identify him even if he saw him again.

Then, figuring New York City was no longer a safe place for him, Webber hightailed it to South Fallsburg, New York, where he bought a farm under his brother Charles Webber's name. Bridgey Webber returned to New York City only to testify at Becker's second trial.

Harry Vallon, knowing what happed to Webber could soon happen to him, trekked over to Pittsburgh, Pa., where he lived in a swanky hotel under an assumed name. It was reported that Vallon had relatives in Pittsburgh and friends of the most dubious character. On July 28, 1915, just two days before Becker's execution, Vallon's identity was unearthed by a member of the press.

Vallon told this reporter, "I feel compelled to talk before it's too late."

When Vallon was asked if that meant that he had evidence Becker was innocent and that Vallon was ready to come clean, Vallon answered, "Yes, if I get a chance."

The Pittsburgh reporter also noted that Vallon was in the charge of a rather large man, who was said to be a detective in the employ of New York Governor Whitman. Vallon told the reporter that he had great animosity against the New York City police department, saying, "They are hounding me to the nut factory by hanging a perjury charge against me."

Vallon also said that the New York City police had "frightened his girl" away from him by threatening to prosecute him.

Two days later, Becker was executed, and there is no indication that Vallon ever returned to New York City, or that "his girl" ever returned to him.

As for Sam Schepps, he opened a successful jewelry store called the *Maison Cluny* with his brother Nathan at 437 Madison Avenue. On March 30, 1918, a man named Henry Cohen, better known as "Harry the Yot," was shot and killed in Schepps's jewelry store, hours before Cohen was set to squeal to the District Attorney about a gambling swindle Cohen said was perpetrated against him by Schepps. Schepps and two other men were arrested for Cohen's murder, but they all beat the case due to lack of evidence.

In 1921, Schepps was arrested again and charged with usury, because he refused to return two diamonds worth $80,000 to famed opera singer Lydia Lipkowska, after she had pawned the diamonds to Schepps in order to borrow $12,000. According to Lipkowska, Schepps said he would not return the diamonds unless Lipkowska forked over another five grand.

In October of 1933, Schepps was arrested a third time, this time with his brother Nathan, and charged with forging more than $10,000 worth of bank checks, which the Schepps brothers had foolishly deposited in their own business account.

There are no accounts of Schepps having any more run-ins with the law before he died on January 26, 1936 in the Fifth Avenue Hospital.

Bald Jack Rose reinvented himself after Becker's convictions. Knowing he was marked as a rat throughout the New York City underworld, and also not wanting to get stabbed like Webber did, Rose donned a black wig and bought a farm in Newport, Conn. Rose, capitalizing on his newfound fame, first made a living writing "true crime" books. When his literary talents were exposed as less than ordinary, Rose toured churches in the Northeast, making compelling sermons about the evils of gambling and other vices. When that gig ran its course, Rose set up a movie production company with the intention of making short films on the subjects of his sermons: gambling is bad; mother and apple pie are good.

This scheme of Rose's didn't go over too well, either.

Highlighting the notion that only the good die young, Bald Jack Rose lived until the ripe old age of 72. On Oct. 8, 1947, Rose expired in the arms of his loving wife, Hilda, in New York City's Roosevelt Hospital from an "internal disorder."

According to newspaper reports, unlike Charles Becker, Rose's funeral service at Riverside Chapel on Amsterdam Avenue and Seventy-Sixth Street attracted no public attention. By that time, 35 years after the murder of Herman Rosenthal, most New Yorkers had never heard of Bald Jack Rose, and those who did would rather forget him.

It might be whimsy, but it would have been incredibly nice if when Bald Jack Rose entered into the afterlife, he was met by Charles Becker and his billy club, in a hot place with no cold-running water and no air conditioning.

That would only be right.

The End

MOBSTERS, GANGS, CROOKS, AND OTHER CREEPS – VOLUME 1 – NEW YORK CITY

By Joe Bruno

PUBLISHED BY:
Knickerbocker Literary Services

EDITED BY:
Marc A. Maturo and Lawrence Venturato

Ah Hoon - The Murder of Chinese Comedian Ah Hoon

Sometimes a comedian can be dead funny, but after one of his onstage performances, Chinese comedian Ah Hoon turned up quite dead instead.

The Tong Wars started in Chinatown in 1899, with the powerful On Leong Tong dominating the gambling and drug interests in downtown Manhattan. The smaller Hip Sing and the Four Brothers Tongs joined forces and engaged in violent confrontations with the On Leong Tong, over the rights to control Chinatown's illegal activities. Almost daily, dead bodies littered the streets of Chinatown, which at the time only consisted of Mott Street, Pell Street, Chatham Square, and Doyers Street.

Ah Hoon was a famous Chinese comedian, who was featured often at the Chinese Theater at 5-7 Doyers Street, right in the middle of the Tong War Zone. The Chinese Theater was a venue, not only for the Chinese, but for English speaking audiences who were brave enough to venture into an area where gunpowder permeated the air. Ah Hoon was an associate of the On Leong Tong, and the content of his jokes, in which he constantly disparaged the Hip Sing and Four Brothers Tongs, made it seem like he thought he was bullet-proof.

Things started to get hairy for Ah Hoon, when the Reverend Huie Kim, the pastor of the Christian Morning Star Mission on Doyers Street, warned Ah Hoon that his jokes were not too funny with certain people. The good reverend also told Ah Hoon that Ah Hoon could get badly hurt if he kept telling his jokes on stage, where hundreds of people could hear the many indignities he spewed disparaging the Hip Sing and Four Brothers Tongs.

Ah Hoon thumbed his nose at the Reverend Huie Kim, and as a result, the Hip Sing and Four Brothers Tongs formerly declared war on the On Leong Tong. Instead of holding back, Ah Hoon stepped up the frequency and the ferocity of his jokes on stage. This thoroughly annoyed the Hip Sing and Four Brothers Tongs, so they announced publicly that they were going to kill Ah Hoon. To make sure Ah Hoon got the message, they sent an emissary to Ah Hoon, giving him the exact time and date he was going to be murdered.

Ah Hoon took the threat with a shrug. But it was Hoochy-Coochy Mary, who lived on the floor below Ah Hoon, in a boarding house on Chatham Square, who ran to the police and begged them to protect the comedian. On December 30, 1909, Police Sergeant John D. Coughlin and two patrolmen accompanied Ah Hoon to his performance at the Chinese Theater. Word had spread quickly on the streets of Chinatown that Ah Hoon was scheduled to be murdered, and as a result, the theater was packed with people hoping to see a live execution for the price of a simple theater admission. Standing-room-only tickets were also sold out, and there was a huge crowd outside, not too happy at being turned away from witnessing Ah Hoon's dramatic demise.

Seeing the police presence, inside and outside the theater, the Hip Sing Tong decided to back away from their word, and at the end of the show, Ah Hoon, to the chagrin of the crowd, was still alive and joking. Sergeant Coughlin and his two underlings hustled Ah Hoon out of the theater, though a hidden underground tunnel, to his dwelling on Chatham Square. Ah Hoon climbed the stairs of his building, entered his room and locked the door. A group of heavily-armed On Leong bodyguards stood guard outside Ah Hoon's door, while dozens milled in the street outside his building looking for any impending attack. Ah Hoon went to sleep that night, but he did not wake up the following morning.

Hoochy-Coochy Mary heard a shot in the middle of the night, and she ran upstairs to alert the On Leong bodyguards. When they broke through the door, they found Ah Hoon dead on his bed with a bullet hole in his chest. What made the matter all the more vexing was that there was only one window in Ah Hoon's room and it faced a blank building wall five feet away.

The solution to Ah Hoon's death was quite simple and complicated at the same time.

So they wouldn't be seen by the On Leong bodyguards, the Hip Sing assassins had slipped into a tenement several buildings down from Ah Hoon's building. They climbed the stairs to the roof, then they jumped across three roofs to the roof of the building next to Ah Hoon's building. There they lowered the killer on a boatswain's chair tied to a rope, down the narrow alley, until he was parallel to Ah Hoon's window. The killer then quietly entered Ah Hoon's room and shot the Chinese comedian right through the heart. The deed being done, the killer exited the room in the same manner in which he had entered.

The Hip Sing Tong was so overjoyed at the success of their mission, they held a parade the next day in the streets of Chinatown, complete with fireworks, ancestral music, and the dancing of the mythical Chinese dragons.

On New Year's night 1910, two days after the murder of Ah Hoon, the Chinese Theater was packed to the rafters again. In the middle of the performance, someone threw several packs of lit firecrackers into the air. People panicked, and they fled the theater quickly; except for five On Leong Tong members, who were shot dead during the distraction of the fireworks.

No one was arrested for their murders, and the Tong Wars continued for another generation.

Allen, John

He was a con artist, a drunk, a murderer, and a pimp, and he ran one of the most obscene dance halls in the history of New York City. For all his vast transgressions, John Allen was dubbed "The Wickedest Man in New York City."

John Allen, the youngest of eight sons, was born in 1823 in upstate New York. His father was a prominent Presbyterian minister, and two of Allen's brothers became Presbyterian ministers too, while a third became a Baptist minister. The rest of his brothers absconded to New York City and became burglars, crooks, and confidence men.

Allen's father sent him to the Union Theological Seminary, hoping young John would pick the righteous path rather than the wicked road his brothers had traveled in New York City. Allen studied religion for a few months. But wanting more out of life, he packed his bags and joined his evil siblings in downtown Manhattan.

Allen's brothers showed him the tricks of their trade, and in no time Allen became proficient at the crimes his brothers had taught him. One day, one of his brothers became suspicious of Allen, when he realized the police in the area seemed to know, in advance, what crime they were going to commit, and where and when they were going to commit it. His brothers accused Allen of being a stool-pigeon. Allen reluctantly admitted they were right, which induced his brothers to beat him to a pulp, then cast him out into the street, never again to return.

In 1855, after freelance thievery earned him a significant sum of cash, Allen met and married a known criminal named Little Suzie. Little Suzie's specialty was rolling drunks, after she seduced them with sex, and then put knockout drops in their drinks. While Little Suzie plied her trade in the waterfront district of the 4th Ward, which included Cherry, Water, Dover, and Catherine Streets, Allen got a job working for a waterfront crimp who ran a boarding house for sailors.

Allen's job was to entice sailors into the crimp's establishment, where they would get the sailor drunk, then drug his drink. When their mark was out cold, they robbed him of all his possessions. Then Allen and his boss would carry the unconscious sailor to an outgoing vessel, in which the sailor was shanghaied to faraway places, where he would spend several months, if not several years, in servitude.

One day, Allen was dumb enough to have a drink with his boss. And the next thing he knew, Allen was on a ship to South America, not to return to New York City for six months. After Allen's return, his former boss was soon found beaten to death, courtesy of an iron belaying-pin, which was a device used on ships to secure lines of rigging. Allen was the obvious suspect, but since the cops had no evidence, and also because the dead man was so intensely disliked by everyone on both sides of the law, no charges were ever brought against Allen.

Allen reconnected with Little Suzie, and they went to work for Hester Jane Haskins, called "Jane the Grabber," a monster-of-a-woman, who ran several houses of ill-repute in the area surrounding Sixth Avenue and 30th Street, in the middle of what was called Satan's Circus.

Allen's and Suzie's gig was to travel throughout the northeastern states and fetch young girls, with the promise of getting them well-paying jobs in New York City. Of course, when these poor girls were introduced to "Jane the Grabber," Jane immediately beat them and drugged them, then forced them to work as prostitutes in her brothels.

This all went fine for Allen and Little Suzy until "Jane the Grabber" got greedy and started abducting women from prominent families, including the daughter of the Lieutenant-Governor of a New England state. Knowing heat from the police was inevitable, Allen and Little Suzie quit their jobs for "Jane the Grabber," and headed back to the confines of the 4th Ward. That turned out to be good timing for them, since "Jane the Grabber" was soon arrested for her crimes and sent to prison for a very long time.

In 1858, the Allens opened John Allen's Dance Hall, at 304 Water Street, which became known as one of the most licentious establishments in New York City. Allen dressed his 20 or so "dance hall girls" in short skirts and red-topped boots, with sleigh-bells circling their ankles. All sorts of vices and sexual obscenities were performed in private rooms in the dive, and sometimes right out in the open. These actions were so visibly decadent, journalist Oliver Dyer wrote in *Packard's Monthly*, that John Allen was "The Wickedest Man in New York City."

Allen was so proud of his new moniker he made up business cards, saying:

John Allen's Dance Hall
304 Water Street
Wickedest Man in New York:
Proprietor

John Allen's Dance Hall was so prosperous, in just 10 years Allen banked more than $100,000, making him the richest pimp in New York City.

Soon, Allen came up with a new angle to make even more money. Falling back on his seminary background, Allen decided to turn his dance hall into a semi-religious experience. In spite of the sexual romps that were going on nightly inside his joint, Allen placed a Bible in every room, and on Saturday nights he gave away copies of the New Testament, as souvenirs to his guests. In time, Allen held religious sing-a-longs, in which his scantily-clad girls would croon spiritual songs, while Allen read passages of the Bible. Showing no shame, Allen placed on every bench and table in his joint the popular hymn book, *The Little Wanderer's Friend.*

Yet, Allen's intended monetary windfall never materialized. His usual guests fled his premises and headed for other joints like The Haymarket, McGuirk's Suicide Hall, and Paresis Hall. So Allen decided to go with another gimmick.

Allen turned his dance hall into a place for local clergymen to hold marathon prayer meetings. Religious men, like the Reverend A.C. Arnold, paid Allen $350 a month to hold such meetings in Allen's establishment. Allen even thickened the crowd by paying "newly reformed sinners" 25 cents a head to take part in the festivities. Allen was so certain he would hit the religious jackpot, he closed his dance hall and put a sign on the outside door saying, "This Dance Hall is Closed. No gentlemen admitted unless accompanied by their wives."

Unfortunately, Allen had overlooked the power of the press. In a shocking expose', the *New York Times* ran a series of stories exposing Allen in the worst possible light. Immediately, the duped reverends stopped holding their prayer meetings at Allen's joint, causing his cash flow to disintegrate. Allen tried opening his bawdy dance hall again, but his previous customers chose to stay away. After a few months of bleeding money, Allen closed down his dance hall for good.

Allen disappeared from the public eye for a while. Then he resurfaced in late 1868, when Allen and Little Suzie were arraigned in the Tombs Police Court, for stealing $15 from a sailor. The Allens were released on $500 bail, which they promptly jumped, then fled to places unknown.

"The Wickedest Man In New York City" died from causes unknown in West Perth, Fulton County, New York, in October 1870.

After Allen's death, a *New York Times* reporter revealed for the first time Allen's true intentions when he appeared to go all pious. Years earlier, Allen had confessed to the reporter, "I duped them religious fellers because I thought I could make more money out of silly church folk, than I could out of bad sailors."

Anti-Abolition Riots of 1834

It started as a peaceful service given by a black minister at the Chatham Street Chapel, but it transformed into four days of riots that turned the streets of New York City into a cauldron of hate.

In the early 1800's, there was a vibrant movement in the United States to end slavery. Yet, there was no other place in the country that displayed more animosity towards blacks than the mean streets of Manhattan's Lower East Side. The Abolitionist Movement (to abolish slavery) was spearheaded by men like William Lloyd Garrison, and bothers Arthur and Lewis Tappan. Yet, the hatred for black slaves permeated throughout New York City and was incited by the ruling Irish faction of Tammany Hall. This malevolence was punctuated by a multitude of atrocities, perpetrated against the slaves by the Irish Five Points street gangs, which Tammany Hall overtly protected from prosecution for their heinous crimes.

In 1833, aided by the fiery speeches of William Lloyd Garrison, slavery was abolished throughout the British Empire. Many of the Brits living in America also spoke out vociferously against slavery. This did not go over too well with the powers that be at Tammany Hall, which had convinced the Irish street gangs that the Abolitionists were looking to transform America back into a British colony.

Anti-Abolitionist James Watson Webb provoked the Irish gangs even further, when he printed in his *Courier and Enquirer* that, "Abolitionists had told their daughters to marry blacks, black dandies in search of white wives were promenading Broadway on horseback, and Arthur Tappan had divorced his wife and married a negress."

All Webb's statements were lies, but they were believed by the rabble nevertheless.

On July 7, 1834, a group of black slaves gathered in the Chatham Street Chapel to hear a sermon by a black minister. In the audience, lending his support, was Arthur Tappan. The sermon had just begun, when members of the New York Sacred Music Society broke in, claiming they had rented the chapel for the evening. The slaves, who had already paid for the use of the chapel, refused to leave. The street gangs, with members of the Plug Uglies, Forty Thieves, and Roach Guards, banded together and attacked the slaves with leaded canes, seriously injuring several slaves.

An angry mob had formed outside the chapel, and as the police arrived to try to quell the disturbance, Tappan hurried from the scene to his house on Rose Street, which is now the site of the New York City Municipal Building. Knowing he was an avowed abolitionist, a crowd followed Tappan, and as he rushed inside, they pelted his home with rocks.

Webb's paper predictably lied again, when he described the event as a "Negro riot," owing to "Arthur Tappan's mad impertinence." *The Commercial Advertiser*, another pro-slavery rag, said, "Gangs of blacks were preparing to set the city ablaze."

This was just the beginning of a string of atrocities. The next night, a mob of gang members broke down the door of the Chatham Street Chapel. And while they held an impromptu meeting inside, W.W. Wilder yelled, "To the Bowery Theater!"

The reason for their attack on the Bowery Theater was because its manager, and British actor, George P. Farren, another avowed abolitionist, had recently said of the pro-slavery crowd, "Damn the Yankees; they are a damn set of jackasses, and fit to be gulled."

Farren had also just fired an American actor, and as a result, anti-abolitionists posted handbills, detailing Farren's actions, throughout New York City.

An estimated 4000 rioters broke down the doors of the Bowery Theater, interrupting the performance of beloved American actor Edwin Forrest, who was a favorite of the Five Point gangs. Forrest tried to quiet the angry mob, but they insisted on knowing the whereabouts of Farren, who was hiding somewhere on the premises. Before the mob could take the place apart looking for Farren, with the intention of hanging him, a large contingent of police officers arrived and drove the mob from the theater with billy clubs.

Still, the mob was not through. They yelled, "To Arthur Tappan's house!"

Tappan and his family had already escaped before the mob showed up. Yet, when the mob did arrive, they tore down Tappan's house, board by board. They also piled Tappan's furniture into the street, and set it on fire until there was nothing left but a painting of George Washington.

As one rioter tried to throw the Washington painting into the fire, another one ripped it from his hands saying, "It's George Washington! For God's sake, don't burn Washington!"

The mob rampaged through the city, torturing and raping black slaves and even gouging out the eyes of an Englishman, after they had ripped off his ears. The worst rioting was in the Five Points area, where dozens of houses, including St. Phillip's Church, were burned to the ground. Several English sailors and black slaves were captured and mutilated. Word soon spread in the streets that every house in the Five Points area that did not have a candle burning in its window would be burned down. In minutes, candles appeared in every window; saving the neighborhood from destruction at the hands of the out-of-control racist lunatics.

On the afternoon of July 11, Mayor Cornelius Lawrence issued a proclamation asking all good citizens to band together to stop the rioting. He also ordered Major General Shadford to call in the 27th Regiment of the National Guard Infantry. At 9 p.m., around 300 Five Point Gang members assembled before the Laight Street Church, which was run by vocal abolitionist Reverend Samuel Hanson Cox. The church was guarded by several New York City policemen, but the mob charged anyway, forcing the outmanned policemen to run for their lives.

As the mob destroyed the church, Mayor Lawrence ordered the infantry into action. Armed with clubs, bayonets, muskets, and pistols, the infantry drove the rioters from several downtown churches, and the surrounding streets, back into the Five Points area.

The next day, armed soldiers and policemen scoured the Five Points, looking for known mob members. They rounded up and arrested 150 Five Pointers, but then, inexplicably, Tammany Hall stepped in and released almost all of them.

Only 20 gang members, out of the thousands who pillaged the streets of New York City in July of 1834, were ever tried, convicted, and sent to jail.

Astor Place Theater Riots of 1849

One of the worst riots in New York City history took place on May 10, 1849. It started over an impassioned disagreement over who had the better Shakespearian Actor: the United States, or hated Mother England.

British actor William Macready was considered to be the most accomplished actor on both sides of the pond. Yet Macready, who called himself an aristocrat, was a snob, who looked down on America in general and their inferior actors in particular. One of those actors who caused Macready to sniff in superiority was the Philadelphia-born Edwin Forrest, a self-taught thespian, who was the darling of the rough and tumble New York City crowd. To make matters worse for Forrest and his followers, the New York City aristocracy much preferred the foreigner Macready instead of the homegrown Forrest.

In 1848, Forrest, on a mission to prove to the world that he was the equal of any actor alive, traveled to London, England, to play Hamlet. Even though Forrest dined with Macready the night before Forrest's performance, when Forrest took the stage he was brutally hissed by the audience. Forrest's performance was panned viciously in the London newspapers and repeated in the American press. Forrest blamed this on Macready, and by the time Forrest arrived back in the United States, there was a global feud ready to explode.

Two New Yorkers were instrumental in fanning the flames of discontent concerning the rude treatment of their homeboy Forrest in England. One was Captain Isaiah Rynders, who owned the notorious Empire Club on Park Row. Rynders was also the mob boss, who controlled all the vicious gangs in the Five Points area. The other instigator was E. Z. C. Judson, who wrote under the pen name - Ned Buntline. Both men hated the English, and in the weekly newspaper, *Ned Buntline's Own*, Buntline turned a mere heated actors' dispute into an international incident.

The tension mounted, when it was announced in the New York City press that Macready would make a four-week "farewell" appearance in America, commencing on May 7, 1849. His first show was scheduled to be at the new Astor Place Theater, on Astor Place in Manhattan. As soon as Macready graced the stage with his presence, Rynders rose from his seat, and in concert with hundreds of his gang thugs in attendance, they peppered Macready with rotten eggs, ripe tomatoes, and old shoes. Macready, incredulous at the blatant disrespect for his great talents, thundered off the stage. He canceled the rest of his four-week engagement and vowed never to appear in the United States again.

This caused great consternation among the blue-bloods in New York City's society crowd. Quickly, they assembled a petition with 47 signatures, which included those of Washington Irving and Herman Melville, begging Macready to stay and continue his tour. Macready, against his better judgment, caved in and agreed to give it one more try.

The news hit the newspapers, that on May 10, just three days after he was rudely chased from the stage, Macready would appear as Macbeth in *Macbeth*; again at the Astor Place Theater. Coincidentally, Forrest also opened that same night, playing Spartacus in *The Gladiator*, in a playhouse a mile south of the Astor Place Theater. The newspapers played up the rivalry and the British crew of a docked Cunard liner said they would make their presence known at Macready's performance, lest an unruly American mob again tried to insult their countryman.

This incited Captain Rynders to plaster New York City with thousands of posters saying, *"Workingmen, shall Americans or English rule this city? The crew of the English steamer has threatened all Americans who shall dare to express their opinion this night at the English Aristocratic Opera House! We advocated no violence, but free expression of opinion is to all men!"*

New York City mayor Caleb C. Woodhull anticipated a riot, and he sent 350 policemen, under the command of Police Chief G.W. Matsell, to the Astor Place Theater to quell any possible disturbances. In addition, General Sanders, of the New York Militia, assembled eight companies of guardsmen and two troops of Calvary to patrol the area around the playhouse.

When the show started, all 1,800 seats had been sold, with the pro-Macready crowd vastly outnumbering the pro-Forrest crowd. It was estimated that more than 20,000 people stood outside the theater, making Astor Place, from Broadway to the Bowery, one large sea of discontent.

At 7:40 p.m., the play started, and the first two scenes played out without any interruption. However, when Macready majestically strode on stage for the third scene, all hell broke loose. Captain Rynders and his gangs hooted and hollered and hissed at Macready. Outside, the angry crowd, hearing the animosity inside, started to bum-rush the theater. They threw rocks and stones, breaking all the theater's windows. And just because they could, the mob smashed all the street lamps in the area too.

The police attacked the angry mob with clubs, but to no avail. The mob screamed "Burn the damned den of aristocracy."

The police were getting the worst of the riot, and at 9 p.m., the first of the militia arrived. They too were pelted by bricks and stones. Ned Buntline was at the head of the angry mob chanting, "Workingmen! Shall Americans or Englishmen rule? Shall the sons whose fathers drove the baseborn miscreants from these shores give up liberty?"

Chief Matsell, after being hit with a 20-pound rock in the chest, gave the order for the militia to shoot into the crowd. And they did just that, hitting men, women, and children, and even a lady who was sleeping in her bed 150 yards from the theater.

When the dust cleared hours later, 22 people were killed and 150 were injured. Five of those who were injured, died within five days. 86 rioters were arrested, including Ned Buntline, who received a year in jail and a $250 fine. Captain Rynders escaped without arrest, or injury, only to torment the city for many years to come.

The lawmen were not without their own injuries. More than a hundred policemen and militia were injured by rocks and stones, and another six were shot; but none died.

The next night, another mob tried to burn down the Astor Place Theater. But they were beaten back by a new battalion of militia, which had been brought into the city in case of further disturbances.

On the night of May 12, another crowd assembled at the New York Hotel, where Macready was staying, screaming for him to come out and be hanged like a man. However, Macready somehow slipped away. He boarded a train to New Rochelle, and then to Boston. From Boston, he sailed to England, never again to set foot in America.

Bow Kum -- The Vicious Killing of Bow Kum

In 1899, the Tong Wars began in New York City's Chinatown, when the smaller Hip Sing and Four Brothers Tongs joined forces against the powerful On Leong Tong, in a battle for the immense illegal profits generated in Chinatown from gambling and drug dealing. There were sporadic killings throughout the first decade of the 20th Century, but the blood started flowing more rapidly in 1909. It was sparked by the vicious murder of a Chinese slave girl named Bow Kum, known as "The Little Flower."

In the Canton Region of China, Kum was sold by her father for a few paltry yen. She was then brought to the United States where she was sold at the slave-trade market in San Francisco, for the huge sum (at the time) of three thousand dollars. The buyer was Low Hee Tong, a high-ranking member of the Hip Sing and Four Brothers Tongs.

Kum lived with Tong for four years, but then the San Francisco police discovered the illegal servitude. When Tong could not produce a marriage license, Kum was taken away from Tong and placed in a Christian mission run by Donaldina Cameron, a Scotswoman famous for helping young Chinese slave girls escape from the terrible tongs. Soon, gardener Tchin Lee, a member of the On Leong Tong, married Kum and took her to New York City.

Tong was furious he had lost the services of his female slave, but more furious over the loss of his three thousand dollars. As a result, Tong demanded that Lee give him back the money he spent on purchasing Kum.

Lee refused.

Tong then listed his grievances in a letter to the Hip Sing and Four Brother Tongs in New York City. Tong's Tongs agreed with him, and they demanded that the On Leong Tong force Lee to return Tong's money. Their request was denied, and immediately the Hip Sing and Four Brothers Tongs flew the red flag from their building on Pell Street, indicating they were declaring war against the On Leong Tong.

On August 15, 1909, a Hip Sing assassin broke into Lee's apartment at 17 Mott Street. The assassin stabbed Kum three times in the chest, cut off several of her fingers, and then mutilated her torso. This started a bloody war that resulted in over fifty killings in just a few short months.

In late 1909, Captain William Hodgins, the Commander of the 5th Precinct on Elizabeth Street, interceded, and he tried to make peace between the factions. He approached the On Leong Tong first, and they agreed to end the war, but only if the other two tongs gave them, as reparations, a Chinese flag, a roasted pig, and ten thousand packs of fireworks. The two smaller tongs considered this a huge insult, and the killings intensified for another year.

In late 1910, the United States government became involved. The Chinese Minister, in Washington D.C., appointed a committee of 40 Chinese merchants, teachers, and students to mediate the Tong Wars. An agreement was forged between the On Leong Tong, and the Hip Sing Tongs. However, the Four Brothers Tong refused to participate in the peace. As a result, the killings continued but not at the same pace as before.

Kerosene was thrown on the fire in 1912, when a new Tong, the Kim Lan Wui Saw Tong, suddenly appeared in New York City. In a battle for the illegal buck, these upstarts inexplicably declared war on the other three established tongs. This was a dumb move, since the three older Tongs, instead of fighting among themselves, turned all their venom on the outmanned Kim Lan Wui Saw Tong.

The bodies continued to pile up in Chinatown, bringing outside business into the area to a halt. Finally, the Chinese government on mainland China, in conjunction with the New York City Police Department, compelled the warring factions to formally agree to halt the hostilities. The treaty was signed on May 22, 1913, by the Chinese Merchant's Association.

Since tourists were no longer afraid to enter Chinatown (and get caught in the cross hairs of the daily gunfire), peace and prosperity returned to the area.

That is, until 1924, when the bloody Tong Wars resumed.

Bowery Boys Street Gang

The Bowery Boys street gang ruled the Bowery area, just north of the Five Points, from 1840 through 1860.

The Bowery Boys were an anti-Catholic, anti-Irish gang, who fought tooth and nail with the other Lower Manhattan gangs, most notably the Dead Rabbits from the Five Points area. Unlike the other gangs of its era, who were predominantly thugs, robbers, and murderers, the Bowery Boys were mostly butchers, mechanics, bar bouncers, or small businessmen. They wore a uniform of sorts, consisting of red shirts, and black trousers; the pants of which were shoved inside their calfskin boots. Most of the men had oil-slicked hair, covered by black stovepipe hats.

The Bowery Boys were ardent volunteer firemen, who aligned themselves with the Know-Nothing, or American Political Party (which lasted from 1849 to 1856) and later the Democratic Party. All of the big politicians of the time, including William "Boss" Tweed and future first United States President George Washington, were at one time volunteer firemen in Lower Manhattan. The Bowery Boys were attached to various firehouses, with names like the White Ghost, Black Joke, Dry Bones, and Red Rover. Each of the other downtown gangs, like the Dead Rabbits, Roach Guards, and the Plug Uglies, were also affiliated with various firehouses too, and the competition over who would arrive first at a fire was fierce and often bloody.

The Bowery Boys were said to love their fire engines almost as much as the loved their women. The worse thing that could happen was to arrive at a fire and find that all the fire hydrants had already been taken by other firehouses. The Bowery Boys often used a scheme to prevent this embarrassment.

As soon as a fire alarm sounded, the biggest Bowery Boy available would grab an empty barrel from a grocery store, and run to the fire plug closest to the burning building. He would turn the barrel over, cover the fire hydrant with the barrel, sit on it, and defend his position, battling men from other firehouses, who were trying to remove him, and the barrel, from the fire hydrant. It was said that the fights for the fire hydrants were so ferocious, the battling volunteer firemen sometimes didn't have enough time to actually extinguish the fires, which caused many buildings to burn to the ground.

The most famous Bowery Boy of his time was "Butcher" Bill Poole, a butcher by trade, and a volunteer at Red Rover Fire Engine Company No. 34, at Hudson and Christopher Streets. Poole was a bare-knuckle fighter of much renown. His arch enemy was John Morrissey, an Irish immigrant and strong-arm-man for Tammany Hall. Morrissey was a prodigious fighter too (he later became World Heavyweight Champion), and he challenged Poole to a bare-knuckles fight. Poole hated the Irish and Catholics with a passion (Morrissey was both), and he gladly accepted the challenge.

On July 26, 1854, the men squared off at the Amos Street Dock, near Christopher Street. After Morrissey extended his hand, in a symbolic gesture to start the fight, Poole feinted, and instead of fighting, he grabbed Morrissey is a frontal bear hug. Poole lifted Morrissey up into the air and squeezed the breath out of him for a full five minutes. Before Poole could crush Morrissey to death, wiser heads prevailed, and they separated the men. Morrissey was hurt so badly he couldn't walk the streets of New York City for six months. When he finally did, it was curtains for Poole.

On February 25, 1855, Lew Baker, a friend of Morrissey's, shot Poole at Stanwix Hall, a bar on Broadway, near Prince Street. Poole lingered for a little more than a week, but he finally died on March 8, 1855.

The downfall of the Bowery Boys started during the savage three-day New York City Draft Riots. On July 13, 1863, incensed at the imminent possibility of being drafted into the war down south they wanted nothing to do with, thousands of gang members took to the streets of New York City. These out-of-control maniacs looted and burned down stores, factories, and houses. Then they violently mutilated and killed Negroes, whom they blamed as the cause of their predicament.

The Bowery Boys, in actions normally adverse to their nature, were an integral part of these deadly riots, in which more than a thousand people were killed and thousands injured. The New York State Militia was called in to quell the riots, and when the dust settled three days later, the drafting of New York City men into the armed forces continued, but only for a short time.

Many Bowery Boys were drafted into the war. Some died, some

returned badly injured, or missing arms and legs; others joined rival gangs. By the end of the 1860's, the Bowery Boys ceased to exist, but other gangs rose from their ashes, to take their place of ignominy in downtown Manhattan.

Bristol Bill The Burglar

He was a hardened criminal, who escaped from a British prison in Australia and made his way to New York City. In the 1840's, the New York City Police Gazette wrote that Bristol Bill the Burglar was, "the most celebrated bank robber and burglar of our time."

The London police knew his real name, but they never revealed it. However, we do know the following about Bristol Bill:

He was born in the early 1800's, to an aristocratic family, the son of a Bristol MP. When Bristol Bill was in his second year at Eton College, his family adopted a 16-year old orphaned daughter of a poor cleric. Bristol Bill was the handsomest of men; almost 6-feet tall, with piercing brown eyes and a broad forehead. In no time, he had seduced the young girl and got her pregnant. Bristol Bill's father was so outraged when he found out about the young girl's delicate condition, he beat Bristol Bill to a pulp, then banished the girl from his home. His father sent Bristol Bill back to Eton, but Bristol Bill soon located his love, and they both absconded to London.

A child was born, and to pay the bills, Bristol Bill got a job at a local locksmith. Soon, Bristol Bill was so adept at key, lock, and tool making, he started selling his wares to a London Gang called the Blue Boys. The Blue Boys were so successful at burglarizing and bank robbing, they soon made Bristol Bill their leader.

This went on for half a dozen years, until Bristol Bill had accumulated approximately $200,000 in American money. With his newfound riches, and with the police nipping at his heels, Bristol Bill abandoned his wife and child and headed to Liverpool, where he planned to board a ship to America. However, a certain London policeman was on his trail, and this policeman arrested Bristol Bill in Liverpool. This same policeman would eventually play a big part in Bristol Bill's life on the other side of the pond.

After his arrest, Bristol Bill's money was confiscated, and he was sentenced to 14 years in prison at a penal colony in Botany Bay, Australia. After serving 10 years, Bristol Bill escaped by swimming four miles to an American whaler. He first landed in Bedford, Mass., but soon Bristol Bill made his way to New York City, where, at the time, almost all the professional thieves were of British extraction.

Bristol Bill's mission was to hook up with a robbery gang, which was called "the most extensive association of burglars, counterfeiters, and swindlers the Western world has ever seen." The London contingent consisted of such noted "crossmen" (a London term for thieves) as Billy Fish, Billy Hoppy, "Cupid" Downer, Bill Parkinson, Bob Whelan, Jim Honeyman, and Dick Collard. They were joined by two New Yorkers: Joe Ashley, and "One-eye" Thompson.

The brains of the operation was a shady character named Samuel Drury, who was known as a banker and a financier, but was, in fact, a counterfeiter of great renown and a prodigious fence of stolen goods. Whatever his gang robbed, Drury would buy and sell, and keep the majority of the money for himself.

Bristol Bill met a girl named Catherine Davenport, who was an expert sneak-thief and pickpocket. Davenport also worked for Drury as a "koneyacker," or a passer of counterfeit cash. Davenport informed Drury that the famous Bristol Bill was in New York City, and that he wanted to join their operation. When Bristol Bill first met Drury, he thought he looked familiar.

"Were you ever a policeman in London?" Bristol Bill asked Drury.

Drury admitted he had been.

"I knew it!" Bristol Bill said. "You're the same hound that tracked me to Liverpool and had me pinched for 14 years."

Drury told Bristol Bill that he was caught stealing himself, and he had to leave London for New York City. Drury told Bristol Bill, "If you have any grudge against me, you must forget it. I can make you a fortune in this country."

Bristol Bill worked with Drury and his crew for a full four years, robbing banks, valuables, and jewelry, from various places as far away as New Orleans. He even traveled to Montreal, to steal a large quantity of silver plate from the home of the Governor-General of Canada.

Bristol Bill's specialty was making his own burglary tools, and he was the best lock-picker in the entire United States. He once escaped from jail with a key he had made from silver oak. Another time, Bristol Bill opened his cell door with a key he had fashioned from a piece of stove pipe.

Bristol Bill's biggest heist was the robbery of the barge "The

Clinton." After opening the ship's safe with a key he had made from a wax impression, Bristol Bill walked away with $32,000 in cash. He kept $10,000 for himself and sold the rest of the money to Drury for $7,000, which Drury disposed of, little by little, from a bank he owned in upstate New York.

By 1849, Bristol Bill had earned over $400,000 in America, which he spent mostly on his three "wives": one living in Manhattan, one in Brooklyn, and one in New Jersey. The three women were fast friends, and they usually accompanied Bristol Bill on his out-of-town robberies; one posing as his wife and the other two as his sisters.

Living the lush life, Bristol Bill thought it was finally time to exact his revenge on Drury. Bristol Bill knew that Drury had bombed the home of a lawyer with whom Drury had quarreled. Not needing Drury as a fence anymore, Bristol Bill, at the request of the *New York Police Gazette*, provided information to the police about Drury's involvement with the bombing. While Drury and his son, along with One-Eyed Thompson, were in jail awaiting arraignment, the police raided Drury's mansion in Astoria. They found counterfeit plates and thousands of dollars in counterfeit cash.

For his help in nailing Drury, the New York City police gave Bristol Bill a pass. Knowing New York City was not safe for him any longer, Bristol Bill traveled to Vermont with his current squeeze, a former opera singer known only as "Gookin' Peg." Bristol Bill was also accompanied by a counterfeiter named Christian Meadows and a London crook, English Jim.

They leased a cottage in Groton, near the Canadian border, and got ready to engage in what they did best: robbing banks. In the spring of 1850, acting on information supplied by the *New York Herald* and the *New York Police Gazette*, the Vermont police raided the cottage. They found Bristol Bill's home-made burglary tools, a counterfeit machine, and freshly made bills. In addition, there were several diagrams of the banks Bristol Bill had planned to rob.

Faced with insurmountable evidence, Bristol Bill and Meadows were arrested. English Jim was not at the cottage when the police arrived, and for some reason, "Gookin' Peg" was never charged. Bristol Bill and Meadows were sentenced to ten years at the Windsor State Prison. When Bristol Bill was released, he was almost 60 years old, and he disappeared from the American crime scene. Some said

Bristol Bill went back to London. Others said, he died broke in America.

While he was in prison, Bristol Bill confided to fellow inmates that the biggest mistake he had ever made was inventing an unpickable lock in his early locksmith days in London. This lock was subsequently sold widely in the United States.

Bristol Bill said there were many times when he encountered his own invention on bank vaults and on the front doors of homes, which made his mission of breaking, entering, and stealing almost impossible.

Capone - Al "Scarface"

Most people associate Al Capone with Chicago, but in fact, Al Capone was born and bred, and got his start in the mob in the borough of Brooklyn, New York.

Alphonse Gabriel Capone was born the fourth of nine children, on January 17, 1899, on Navy Street, in the section of Brooklyn now known as DUMBO (Down Under the Manhattan Bridge Overpass). Capone stayed in school until the 6th grade, when in a fit of rage, he beat up one of his teachers. A resulting trip to the principal's office caused Capone to get beat up himself, and after licking his wounds, Capone left school for good.

Capone hooked up with a street mob called "The James Street Gang," which was an offshoot of the powerful Five Points Gang in Lower Manhattan. "The James Street Gang" was run by the rough and ruthless Johnny Torrio, who became the teenaged Capone's mentor for many years to come.

Torrio, along with his partner Frankie Yale, hired Capone to be their chief bouncer at their bar/brothel in Brooklyn. It was there that Capone got his nickname "Scarface," after his cheek was slashed by a hoodlum named Frank Galluccio, in a bar fight over a girl, whom Capone had insulted (apparently, the girl was Galluccio's sister, and Capone had made a tasteless remark about her shapely figure). Capone later told the press he had gotten his scar fighting for the "Lost Battalion" in France, during World War I. However, the truth was, Capone never served a day of military service in his entire life.

In 1919, Torrio moved to Chicago to run the rackets of his uncle-through-marriage: Big Jim Colosimo. Capone was suspected of a few murders in Brooklyn, so in order to avoid the heat, Capone headed west to Chicago to aid Torrio in his takeover of the town. Their first order of business was to take out Colosimo, who was a hindrance to Torrio and Capone getting into the illegal booze business. Brooklyn pal Frankie Yale traveled to Chicago, and he took care of Colosimo, personally and permanently, with bullets.

With Colosimo out of the way, the Torrio/Capone duo attempted to organize Chicago into separate but equal fiefdoms, each with protection and exclusivity in their own territories. Irish mobster Dion O'Banion, the head of Chicago's "North Side Gang," told Torrio he wanted nothing to do with Torrio's proposal, signing his death warrant in the process. Again, Frankie Yale was called into action, and O'Banion was shot to death by Yale and two associates in O'Banion's florist shop, in November of 1924.

After Torrio was seriously wounded in an assassination attempt by O'Banion's successor, Hymie Weiss, Torrio went into retirement at the age of 43, willing all his rackets to the 26-year-old Al Capone.

Capone took Chicago by the throat, and he had over 1,000 experienced gunmen under his control. Even the Chicago police turned a blank eye to Capone's murderous activities.

Capone once boasted, "I own Chicago, and I own the police."

Add aldermen, mayors, legislators, governors, newspapermen, and congressmen to the list of people on Capone's payroll. To deflect any possible heat from people not on his payroll, Capone widely limited his business endeavors to things that were popular with the people: booze, gambling, and prostitution.

Capone once boasted to his adoring press, "I'm just an honest businessman who's giving the public what they want."

Capone was so popular with the common man he was wildly cheered at Chicago Major League baseball games.

Capone's downfall started on February 14, 1929, when he orchestrated the "Valentine's Day Massacre." While Capone was sunbathing in Miami, his shooters lined up seven men against a garage wall in Chicago. The killers machine-gunned the seven men to death, but they missed Capone's main intended target and owner of the garage: George "Bugs" Moran.

All of a sudden, Capone was no longer the people's choice. Even the jaded citizens of Chicago were aghast at the savagery of the vicious murders. Despite the fact the government had no proof of Capone's involvement in the "Valentine's Day Massacre," they plotted to put him in jail, any way they could.

As a result, Capone was hit with 11 counts of income tax evasion, and in 1931, he was tried, convicted, and sentenced to 11 years in prison.

In 1934, Capone was transferred to Alcatraz, a maximum security prison called "The Rock." There, the effects of syphilis Capone had acquired in his brothel days in Brooklyn took control of his mind. Capone was diagnosed with dementia, and when he was released in November 1939, Al Capone was a broken man, given to outbursts of rage, over anything: from the government, to the Communists, to his old foe "Bugs" Moran.

Capone spent his last years flowing in and out of lucidity, and on January, 21, 1947, he died of a heart attack at his home in Miami Beach, Fla.

Civil War Draft Riots of 1863

Never in the history of New York has there been a more brutal mass insurrection than the New York City Civil War Draft Riots of 1863.

In March of 1863, the seeds were planted for these riots when President Abraham Lincoln issued a proclamation, called The Conscription Act (or Enrollment Act), stating he needed 300,000 more men to be drafted into the Northern Army, to beat back the Southern Rebels in the Civil War. This act required every male citizen, between the ages of 20 and 40, to be drafted into the war. Each man who joined the army was given a bounty of up to $500, as an enlistment bonus. The gravest inequity, however, was that for the sum of $300 a man could buy himself out of being drafted. The rich could afford the $300, but the poor could not, which led to the Civil War being called "A rich man's war and a poor man's fight."

New York City (only Manhattan at the time) had more than 800,000 citizens, of which more than half were foreign. Of that half, half again were poor Irish, who had no desire to fight in a war to end the slavery of Negroes, whom they despised. These poor, low-class Irish people had settled in the Five Points and in the Mulberry Bend areas in downtown Manhattan (the 6th Ward), and also in the 4th Ward near the East River. In these slums, gangs like the Plug Uglies, the Bowery Boys, the Roach Guards, and the Dead Rabbits, committed atrocious crimes. And this downtown area is where the draft rioters began their bloodthirsty march.

President Lincoln had announced that Draft Day in New York City would commence on Saturday, July 11. On that day, with only minor disturbances throughout the city, 1,236 men were drafted into the war. When the draft ended that day, it was announced that the draft would bypass Sunday and continue again on Monday morning.

However, the seeds of discontent grew during the rest of the weekend, spurred by an article in Saturday evening's *Leslie's Illustrated*, which stated, "It came like a thunderclap on the people, as men read their names in the fatal list, the feeling of indignation and resistance soon found vent in words, and a spirit of resistance spread fast and far. The number of poor men exceeded that of the rich, their number to draw from being that much greater, but this was viewed as proof of the dishonesty in the whole proceeding."

As Monday morning drew near, the poor slum-living Irish began planning how to voice their displeasure, and it wouldn't be pleasant. At 6 a.m. Monday, men and women started spilling out of the downtown slums, and they began their resolute march to the north. At every street corner, more discontents joined their forces, and the group became so huge it split into two groups. It was estimated that eventually 50,000 to 70,000 people took part in the four-day Draft Riots, and the New York City Metropolitan Police had only 3,000 men to combat the rioters.

As the rioters moved north along Fifth and Sixth Avenues, they turned east and made a beeline toward the main draft office, at 46th Street and Third Avenue. Police Superintendent John A. Kennedy, realizing trouble was brewing, dispatched 60 police officers to guard the Third Avenue Draft Office, and another 69 to guard the draft office at Broadway and 29th Street.

The rioters on Third Avenue were led by the volunteer firemen attached to Engine Company 33, known as The Black Joke. They consisted of members of the Plug Uglies street gang, who by now had stopped traffic completely and were pulling people out of their carts. Signs in the crowd were held saying "NO DRAFT!!", when suddenly someone in the crowd shot a pistol up into the air, and the riots commenced.

The mob threw bricks and stones at the draft office, breaking all the windows in the building. Then they surged forward, thousands of them, while 60 cops tried in vain to hold them back. The rioters stepped over the now-battered and unconscious policemen, and as draft officials jumped out the rear windows of the building, the mob set fire to the Third Avenue Draft Office.

Meanwhile, Superintendent Kennedy had left Police Headquarters at 300 Mulberry Street, wearing civilian clothes as a disguise. He took a horse carriage to 46th Street and Lexington Avenue, but when he saw the smoke, he jumped out of the carriage and proceeded on foot.

Kennedy was immediately recognized, and beaten to a bloody pulp, until he was unconscious. A Good Samaritan named John Egan saved Kennedy, when he announced to the mob that Kennedy was dead. Kennedy was covered with a gunny sack and put into a wagon, which drove him to Police Headquarters. When he was examined by doctors, Kennedy was found to have 72 bruises on his body and over two dozen cuts.

The rioters then attacked the Colored Orphans Asylum, on Fifth Avenue and 46th Street. As the rioters stormed the building, 50 matrons and attendants snuck 200 Negro children out a secret back exit. The mob rushed in, stole blankets, toys, and bedding, and then set fire to the building. One young Negro girl, who was accidentally left behind, was found hiding under a bed. She was dragged out and savagely beaten to death.

All throughout the streets of New York City, angry Irish mobs chased Negroes, whom they blamed for the drafts in the first place. The Negroes who were caught, were beaten to death and sometimes hanged. As their bodies hung from trees and rafters, mad Irish woman, glee in their eyes, stabbed the dead Negroes' bodies, while they danced under lit torches, and sang obscene songs.

Finally, Mayor George Updyke wired the War Department in Washington D.C. for help. During the next three days of unspeakable mayhem, hundreds of buildings were burned down, innumerable business looted, and Negroes were killed for no other reason than for the color of their skin. When the order was given, the United States Militia, armed, trained, and 10,000 strong, stormed New York City to quell the riots.

On Tuesday, July 14, New York Governor Horatio Seymour stood on the steps of City Hall, and said to the assembled crowd "I have received a dispatch from Washington that the draft is now suspended."

Governor Seymour was booed and jeered, and the riots continued for two more days.

It is impossible to estimate how many people were killed in the four-day riots. The New York Post reported that, under the blanket of darkness, the bodies of dead rioters were shipped across the East River, and quietly buried in Brooklyn. Police Superintendent Kennedy put the total dead at 1,155, but that did not include those buried secretly at night. Of the tens of thousands of rioters involved, and despite the brutal murders of scores of Negroes, only 19 people were tried and convicted of any crimes. The average prison sentence was a mere five years.

Diarist George Templeton Strong summed up the disgrace of the

1863 New York City Civil War Draft Riots, when he wrote "This is a nice town to call itself a center of civilization."

Cole - Vincent "Mad Dog"

He was known throughout the underworld as the "Mad Mick," but when he gunned down five children in Harlem, Vincent Cole forever became known as "Mad Dog" Cole.

Vincent Cole was born on July 20, 1908, in Gweedore, a small town in County Donegal, Ireland. When he was an infant, Cole's parents relocated to America; settling in a cold-water flat in the Bronx. After five of his siblings died, from either accidents or disease, his father left the family, never to be seen again.

Cole's mother died from pneumonia when he was seven, and Cole and his older brother Peter were taken by the state of New York and put in the Mount Loretto Orphanage, in Staten Island. The Cole brothers stood at the orphanage for three years, both being beaten repeatedly for insubordination. Finally, the Cole Brothers escaped, and insinuated themselves into New York's Hell's Kitchen, where they became members of the notorious street gang called The Gophers.

Soon, the Cole Brothers were working as go-fers for the infamous bootlegger Dutch Schultz. They were paid a hundred bucks a week to do Schultz's dirty work, which included a few killings when requested. Finally, fed up with Schultz's known cheapness as far as paying his crew, Cole approached Schultz, and demanded he become a full partner.

"I ain't your nigger shoeshine boy," Cole told Schultz. "I'll show you a thing or two."

Cole started up a small gang, which included his brother Peter, and his girlfriend and future wife, Lottie Kreisberger, who did little more than keep Cole company. Cole's first move on Schultz was a brazen daytime robbery of Schultz's Sheffield Dairy in the Bronx. Schultz was so angry at Cole's treachery, he thundered into the 42nd Precinct, and announced to a room full of cops, "I'll buy a house in Westchester for anyone in here who can kill that Mick (Cole)."

Cole then tried to lure Schultz's gang members into Cole's gang. Through an old school acquaintance named Mary Smith, the Cole brothers set up a meeting with one of Schultz's top boys, Vincent Barelli. At that meeting in a Bronx apartment, when Barelli rebuffed their advances, the Cole Brothers calmly shot him to death. Mary Smith, horrified at what she had just seen and unwittingly set up, tried to escape from the apartment. Cole chased her down, and shot her in the head, killing her in the middle of the street.

A few days later, members of Schultz's gang machine-gunned Peter Cole as he was driving in Harlem. The death of Peter Cole precipitated a large-scale war between Vincent Cole and Schultz, which resulted in at least 20 more killings.

Needing fast cash, Cole accepted an assignment from Italian Mob boss Salvatore Maranzano, to kill Lucky Luciano in Maranzano's midtown office. Maranzano paid Cole $25,000 up front, with another $25,000 due upon completion of his task.

Cole was in the lobby of Maranzano's office building, with a machine gun hidden under his coat and waiting for the elevator, when three men rushed out of the stairwell and plowed right into Cole. Knowing who Cole was, the men told Cole they had just killed Maranzano and for Cole to beat it before the cops arrived. Cole smiled, did an about-face, and he exited the building, whistling a happy tune, knowing he had just pocketed twenty-five grand for doing absolutely nothing.

To further inflate his bank account, Cole started kidnapping top aides of big-time gang leaders like Owney "The Killer" Madden, an Irishman himself. Madden paid Cole $35,000 for the return of his partner Big Frenchy DeMange, who was co-owner with Madden, in the Cotton Club in Harlem. Cole then kidnapped Madden's front man at the Stork Club, the very popular Sherman Billingsley. Again Madden paid the ransom, and Billingsley was soon back at the Stork Club, still in fine health.

Next on Cole's hit list was Joey Rao, Schultz's top numbers man in Harlem. Rao and a bunch of his boys were standing in front of their Helmar Social Club on East 107th Street, divvying out pennies to neighborhood kids, when Cole and his gang came barreling around the corner in a touring car. Cole let go with several blasts from a machine gun, missing Rao and his men completely, but instead striking five children. Little five-year old Michael Vengali took several bullets in the stomach, and he died before he could be rushed to the hospital.

Incensed at the killing of a child, the New York City newspapers ran frightening headlines about the "Baby Killer." They dubbed Cole -- Vincent "Mad Dog" Cole. And like any "mad dog," the public, and the underworld, demanded that Cole be put down. New York City Mayor James Walker offered a $10,000 reward for anyone who provided information that led to Cole's arrest. Madden and Schultz upped the ante, each offering $25,000 to any mug who could put the "Mad Dog" down with bullets.

Cole hid out in various parts of the Northeast, before finally returning to New York City with Lottie. They were holed up in the Cornish Arms Hotel on West 23rd Street, when the cops, acting on a tip, barged in and arrested Cole. Cole's trial was expected to be a slam-dunk for the prosecution, but the brilliant legal tactics of Cole's lawyer, Samuel Liebowitz, got Cole off the hook.

After his trial, Cole held court with the press outside the Criminal Courts Building.

He told the reporters, "I've been charged with all kinds of crimes, but baby-killing was the limit. I'd like nothing better than to lay my hands on the man who did this."

Cole was back on the streets, but still a marked man by the mob. He married Lottie at City Hall, but they were constantly on the run, moving quickly from hideout to hideout.

On February 1, 1932, four men busted into a home in the north Bronx, guns blazing. They shot a table full of people playing cards. Two Cole gang members were killed (Fiorio Basile and Patsy Del Greco), and another one wounded. Also killed was Mrs. Emily Torrizello, who just happened to be in the wrong place at the wrong time. Another unidentified woman was wounded. Miraculously, two babies lying in their cribs were found unharmed. Luckily for Cole, he showed up at the house a half hour later, just as the police arrived.

As a result, Cole went on the run again. After hiding separately for a while, Cole wound up back with Lottie at the Cornish Arms Hotel. Cole decided this was a good time to start kidnapping again, but this time with a twist. Cole phoned Madden, and told him he wanted $100,000, *not* to kidnap Madden.

"Imagine how the Dagos and Kikes is gonna feel when they have to shell out a hundred grand to save your sorry ass," Cole told Madden. "Pay me now, up front, and I'll save you the trouble."

Madden said he needed some time to think it over.

On March 8, 1932, Madden phoned Cole, and told Cole to call him from the phone booth at the drug store across the street from his hotel. At 12:30 am, Cole strode into the New London Pharmacy on West 23rd Street, and he headed for the phone booth in the back. While he was talking to Madden on the phone, a man with a machine gun hidden under his coat, calmly walked to the back of the drug store and opened fire. The gunman riddled Cole's body with 15 bullets.

Hearing the commotion, Lottie arrived a few minutes later, to see her husband's dead tattered body. Lottie Cole refused to speak with the police, but she cried to someone standing nearby, that their life savings, at the time, was a measly hundred dollar bill, she had stuffed inside her bra.

This proved, without a shadow of a doubt, that Vincent "Mad Dog" Cole, despite his dreadful bite, had died doggone broke.

Crowley - Francis "Two Gun"

They called him a "Half-Pint Moron," and "The Puny Killer." Yet for a short three-month span in 1931, Francis "Two Gun" Crowley was the most dangerous man in New York City.

Crowley was born in New York City, on October 13, 1912. His German mother was not married, and as soon as little Francis saw his first light of day his mother gave him up for adoption. It was rumored Crowley's father was a cop, which explained his hatred for anyone in a blue uniform. Crowley was brought up by a woman named Anna Crowley, and he took her name, calling her his only mother.

By the time Crowley was 18, despite the fact that he stood only 5-foot-3 inches and weighed 130 pounds, he was already a full-blown criminal and a murderer. Crowley teamed up with the hulking Rudolph "Fats" Duringer (who was said to be the largest man ever to sit in Sing Sing's electric chair). Soon, the Mutt and Jeff crime team soon started terrorizing New York City.

On February 21, 1931, Crowley, Fats, and another unidentified male, burst into an America Legion Dance Hall in the Bronx. They were uninvited, and when a slew of Legionnaires tried to toss them out, Crowley began firing with two guns, which gave him his nickname "Two Gun" Crowley. No one was killed, but two men were injured, and Crowley was now hunted by the police for attempted murder. Crowley was cornered in an office building on Lexington Avenue, but he shot his way out of the arrest, plugging Detective Ferdinand Schaedel in the process.

Crowley continued his crazed crime spree in rapid fashion. First, Crowley and his crew robbed a bank in New Rochelle. Then they staged a home invasion of the West 90th Street apartment of rich real estate investor Rudolph Adler. Crowley shot the feisty Adler five times, and just as he was ready to fire the final bullet into Adler's skull, Adler's dog Trixie went into attack mode and chased Crowley and his crew from the apartment.

Some tough guys.

In Crowley's first involvement in a murder, he wasn't even the shooter.

On April 27, 1931, Crowley was driving a stolen car, with his pal Fats in the back seat. Fats was busy trying to make the moves on a dance hall girl, Virginia Brannen, who had just come along for the ride. Brannen told Fats, in no uncertain terms, to keep his chubby hands to himself. This did not please the hulking gangster too much, so Fats shot Brannen dead. Crowley and Fats discarded Brannen's body outside the St. Joseph Cemetery in Yonkers.

After finding Brannen, the New York City and the Yonkers police departments, put out an all-points bulletin for the fat and skinny psychopaths. On April 29, a passing police car spotted Crowley as was driving a green Chrysler on 138th Street in the Bronx. The cops sped in hot pursuit after Crowley, firing shot after shot at the speeding Chrysler. Crowley returned fire, and somehow he managed to escape. The next day, the police found Crowley's abandoned car, riddled with bullets and smeared with blood.

The manhunt for Crowley continued.

On May 6, Crowley was smooching in a car with his 16-year old girlfriend Helen Walsh, in a secluded spot on Morris Lane in North Merrick, Long Island. Patrolmen Frederick Hirsch and Peter Yodice approached the car, and they asked for Crowley's identification. Instead of drawing his wallet, Crowley pulled out a pistol, firing. He shot Hirsch to death and wounded Yodice, before he fled the scene.

Now branded a cop-killer, the daily newspapers brought Crowley instant fame. The *New York Daily News* wrote: "Francis Crowley, who glories in the nickname 'Two Gun Frank,' and is described by the police as the most dangerous criminal at-large, was hunted throughout the city last night."

On May 7th, the police traced Crowley to a top-floor apartment on West 90th Street. Crowley was holed up there with Fats and Helen Walsh, and what transpired next will forever be known as "The Siege on West 90th Street": the most fierce gun battle in New York City's history.

First, two detectives tried to enter the apartment to arrest Crowley and his crew peacefully. But Crowley would have none of that. Crowley screamed through the door, firing lead, "Come and get me coppers!"

The detectives retreated down to the street, where they were joined by an estimated 100 police officers rushed in from all parts of the city. Crowley yelled down at the assembled cops, "I'm up here!

Come and get me!"

Over the course of the next several hours, and while an estimated 15,000 onlookers gawked from the streets and open tenement windows, more than 700 bullets were fired into Crowley's apartment. Crowley had an arsenal himself, and he brazenly returned fire. Safely under the bed, Helen Walsh and Fats reloaded Crowley's guns for him.

At one point, the police cut a hole in the roof, and they dropped gas canisters into Crowley's apartment. Crowley calmly picked up the smoking canisters and threw them out the window, overcoming several police officers below. Finally, a dozen cops broke down Crowley's door, and with four slugs in Crowley's body, the police were finally able to subdue him. Fats and Helen gave up without a whimper.

The newspapers had a field day with this one. Crowley was described as "A Mad Irish Gunman" (even though he was actually German), with "the face of an altar boy." Crowley and Fats were convicted of the murder of Virginia Brannen and Crowley of the murder of patrolmen Frederick Hirsch. They were both sentenced to die in the Sing Sing electric chair.

In jail, Crowley kept up his tough-guy act. He made a club from a wrapped-up newspaper and some wire from under his bed. Then he tried to fight his way out of prison, by cracking a guard over the head with his handmade club. His escape attempt having failed, Crowley set fire to his cell. And when that didn't work, he took off all his clothes and stuffed them into his toilet, flooding his cell. For these disturbances, Warden Lewis E. Lawes forced Crowley to sit naked in his cell for several days until the young maniac quieted down.

During his last days on earth, Crowley mellowed a bit. A bird flew into his cell, and he nurtured it. Crowley also began drawing pictures, a skill for which he had more than a little talent.

On December 10, 1931, Fats got the juice first. After Fats and Crowley hugged a last goodbye, and Fats started his last lonely trek down the hall to the chair, Crowley told a guard, "There goes a great guy, a square-shooter, and my pal."

Crowley was not so charitable to Helen, whom he refused to see, even though she visited the prison almost every day.

"She's out!" he told the newspapers, "She's going around with a cop! I won't even look at her!"

On January 21, 1932, Crowley followed the same path to the electric chair which his old pal Fats had traveled. After the black leather mask was pulled over his face, Crowley's last words were, "Send my love to my mother."

The lever was thrown, and Francis "Two Gun" Crowley was executed at the tender age of 19.

Daybreak Boys

When the Daybreak Boys formed their treacherous little gang in the late 1840's, there were said to be three dozen members, none of whom was over the age of 20. Some of the Daybreak Boys were as young as 10 years old. However, lack of age never meant a paucity of violence.

The Daybreak Boys' first leaders were Nicholas Saul and William Howlett, who were 16 and 15 years-old, respectively, when they took control of the gang. Other noted members were murderers like Slobbery Jim, Sow Madden, Cow-legged Sam McCarthy, and Patsy the Barber.

It was rumored that every member of the gang had committed at least one murder and scores of robberies before they reached the age of 16. The police said The Daybreak Boys not only murdered in the course of a robbery, but also for the sheer ecstasy of doing so, even if there was no hope of cashing in on a score. The police estimated in the three years that Saul and Howlett were their leaders, the Daybreak Boys robbed over $100,000, and killed as many as 40 people.

The Daybreak Boys' base of operations was the Slaughter House Point, owned by Pete Williams, located at the intersection of James and Water Streets. On August 25, 1852, a passing policeman looked in at the Slaughter House Point, and he saw Saul and Howlett huddled in a corner with low-level gang member Bill Johnson, who was half-sloshed. The policeman suspected the three men were up to no good, and he decided to drop by later. When he did, the three men were gone.

In the darkness, Saul, Howlett, and Johnson had taken a row boat, and navigated the East River to a ship named the *William Watson*, intent on stealing valuables they had heard were on board. The three men were met by the night watchman, Charles Baxter, and they shot Baxter dead on the spot. Thinking the gunshot would attract attention, the three men jumped ship from the *William Watson*, empty-handed, and they rowed back to shore.

The policeman, who had spotted the three men earlier, saw the rowboat dock, and he watched as Saul and Howlett dragged Johnson, who was now totally drunk, from the boat and carry him into the Slaughter House Point. Soon after, the body of the night watchman on the *William Watson* was found, and a group of 20 policemen, armed to the hilt, bum-rushed the Slaughter House Point.

After a long and bloody battle, in which a score of Daybreak Boys tried to thwart the capture of their three cronies, Saul, Howlett, and Johnson were finally arrested. After a short trial, Johnson was sentenced to life imprisonment, but Saul and Howlett were smacked with the death sentence. On January 28, 1853, Saul and Howlett were hanged to death in the courtyard of the Tombs Prison. Saul was barely 20 years old and Howlett was one year younger.

After the deaths of Saul and Howlett, Slobbery Jim assumed the leadership of the Daybreak Boys. However, Jim soon had to take it on the lam, after he whacked his old pal Patsy the Barber.

In 1857, The Daybreak Boys continued their decline. The Slaughter House Point, which had been the base of their operations for a decade, closed its doors (with a little prompting from the New York City Police Department). In 1858, more than a dozen gang members were killed in shootouts with the police and with the newly created Harbor Patrol. Scores of other Daybreak Boys were arrested and sent to jail.

By 1859, the Daybreak Boys basically ceased to exist, when its remaining members took up with other gangs in the Bowery and in the other Five Points areas.

Dead Rabbits – Irish Street Gang

The Dead Rabbits Irish Street gang was as vicious as any gang in the history of New York City. In the mid 1800's, the Dead Rabbits prowled the squalid area of Lower Manhattan called the Five Points. If a member of any other gang dared to set foot in the Dead Rabbits' territory, bad things happened to them fast.

There is some dispute as to how the Dead Rabbits got their name. One version is that the word "Rabbit" sounds like Irish word "ráibéad," meaning a "man to be feared." "Dead" was an 1800's slang word that meant "very." So a "Dead Rabbit" was a "man to be very feared."

Another version is that the Dead Rabbits were an offshoot of an older gang called the "Roach Guards." Two factions within the Roach Guards constantly quarreled, and during a fistfight at an especially violent gang meeting, someone threw a dead rabbit into the room. When the fighting subsided, one group took the name "Dead Rabbits," while the other kept the name "Roach Guards." Predating the present street gangs, the Crips and the Bloods, by more than 125 years, to mark which gang a man belonged to, a Dead Rabbit wore a blue stripe on his pants, while a Roach Guard wore a red stripe on his pants.

Besides the Roach Guards, the Dead Rabbits' archenemy was the Bowery Boys. On July 4 1857, the Dead Rabbits and the Bowery Boys squared off at the corner of Bayard and the Bowery. The incident started when an embattled policeman, being chased out of the Five Points by a group of Dead Rabbits, ran for safety into a Bowery Boys' saloon. The Dead Rabbits followed the policeman into the dive, and they were beaten back by an angry group of Bowery Boys.

Taking offense at their turf being invaded, a large group of Bowery Boys marched into the Five Points area, looking for trouble. They were cut off by a battalion of the Dead Rabbits, and a two-day war started, with as many as a thousand combatants fighting with hatchets, knives, stones, and even guns. The police sent in reinforcements, but they were beaten back by both gangs, and told, in no uncertain terms, to mind their own business. The war swayed back and forth into both territories, with Canal Street being the boundary line.

By the end of the second day, the two gangs were near exhaustion, and the Seventh Regiment of the National Guard was called in by New York City Mayor Fernando Wood. The National Guard, joined by the New York City Police, busted into what was left of the skirmish, and they started cracking the heads of the weary warriors. When the dust settled, eight gang members were dead and hundreds more were injured.

This did not end the animosity between the Bowery Boys and Dead Rabbits. In August 1858, on the corner of Worth and Centre Street, a small group of Bowery Boys were pummeled by a larger group of Dead Rabbits. As the Bowery Boys ran off licking their wounds, two unsuspecting men exited a house at 66 Centre Street, and they walked right into the path of the angry Dead Rabbits. Thinking these two men were Bowery Boys coming back for more, the Dead Rabbits descended upon them with a vengeance. One man was able to escape, but Cornelius Rady was not so lucky. Rady was hit in the back of the head with a rock from a slingshot, and he died soon afterwards. Dead Rabbit Patrick Gilligan was arrested for Rady's murder, but it is not clear if he was ever convicted.

The Civil War started two years later, and many of the gang members were drafted, against their wills, into the war and sent to faraway places, mostly in the South. When the war ended, the Dead Rabbits were either dead themselves, or in no physical condition to continue tormenting the streets of Lower Manhattan.

However, in New York City, the creature that it was, and in some cases still is, other street gangs soon followed to take the ignominious place of the Dead Rabbits.

Diamond, Jack "Legs"

Jack "Legs" Diamond was shot and injured so many times he was dubbed "The Gangster Who Couldn't be Killed."

Diamond was born on July 10 1897, of parents from Kilrush, County Clare, in Ireland. Diamond spent the early years of his life in Philadelphia. When Diamond was 13, his mother died from a viral infection. Soon, Diamond, and his younger brother Eddie, fell in with a group of toughs called "The Boiler Gang."

Diamond was arrested more than a dozen times, for assorted robberies and mayhem, and after spending a few months in a juvenile reformatory, Diamond was drafted into the army. Army life did not suit Diamond too well. He served less than a year, then he decided to go AWOL. Diamond was soon captured and sentenced to three-to-five years in the Federal Penitentiary in Fort Leavenworth, Kansas.

Diamond was released from prison in 1921, and he decided that New York City was the place he could make his fortune. Diamond and his brother Eddie relocated to Manhattan's Lower East Side, where they fell in with an up-and-coming gangster named Lucky Luciano. Diamond did various odd jobs for Luciano, including a little bootlegging, in conjunction with Brooklyn thug Vannie Higgins. Diamond's marriage to Florence Williams lasted only a few months (he was never home). However, Diamond's luck changed when Luciano introduced Diamond to Arnold "The Brain" Rothstein, a notorious gambler and known financial wizard. This was the break Diamond was waiting for, and he made the most of it.

After starting out as a bodyguard for Rothstein, Rothstein brought Diamond in as a partner in his lucrative heroin business. When his pockets were full with enough cash and his need for Rothstein diminished, Diamond, in concert with his brother Eddie, decided to branch out on their own.

The Diamond Brothers figured they could make a bundle, hijacking the bootlegging trucks of other mobsters, including those of Owney Madden and Big Bill Dwyer. This was not a very good idea, since Madden and Dwyer were part of a bigger syndicate of criminals that included Luciano, Dutch Schultz, and Meyer Lansky.

In no time, Diamond was persona-non-grata in the gangster world and free pickings for anyone who wanted to get rid of him.

In October 1924, Diamond was driving a Dodge sedan up Fifth Avenue, when at 100th Street a black limo pulled up alongside him. A shotgun was fired at Diamond from the back window of the limo, but Diamond was too quick to be killed. He ducked down and hit the accelerator, without looking where he was going.

Miraculously, Diamond was able to escape his shooters and drive himself to the nearby Mount Sinai Hospital. The doctors removed pellets in his head, face, and feet, and when the cops arrived to question him, Diamond dummied up.

"I dunno a thing about it," Diamond told the fuzz. "Why would anyone want to shoot me? They must of got the wrong guy."

Soon, Diamond became friends with a gangster not looking to kill him. His name was "Little Augie" Orgen. Orgen installed Diamond as his chief bodyguard. In return, Orgen gave Diamond a nice share of his bootlegging and narcotics businesses. This friendship went just fine, until October 15, 1927, when Louis "Lepke" Buchalter and Gurrah Shapiro gunned down Orgen on the corner of Norfolk and Delancey Street, with Diamond supposedly standing guard over Orgen.

Diamond was shot in the arms and legs (probably by accident), necessitating another trip to the hospital. Upon his release, Diamond made nice with Lepke and Shapiro, and as a result, the two killers gave Diamond Orgen's bootlegging and narcotics businesses as a reward for being stupid enough to get in the way of bullets meant for Orgen.

Now, Diamond was on top of the world. He had plenty of cash to throw around, and he became a mainstay in all of New York City's top nightclubs, usually with showgirl Kiki Roberts on his arm (despite the fact he was still married to his second wife Alice Kenny). Diamond was seen regularly at the Cotton Club, El Fay, and the Stork Club, and his picture was frequently in the newspapers, which portrayed Diamond not as a gangster, but as a handsome man-about-town.

Soon, Diamond was part owner of the Hotsy Totsy Club, located on Broadway between 54th and 55th Street, with Hymie Cohen as his fronting partner. The Hotsy Totsy Club had a back room where Diamond frequently settled business disputes, usually by shooting his adversaries to death, then carrying them out as if they were drunk.

Diamond's downfall started on July 13, 1929, when three unruly dockworkers got loaded and started a ruckus at the Hotsy Totsy Club's bar. Diamond jumped in, with his gang member Charles Entratta, to stop Diamond's manager from being throttled.

"I'm Jack Diamond and I run this place," Diamond told the dock workers. "If you don't calm down, I'll blow your (expletive) heads off."

The talking didn't work and soon the shooting started. When the smoke cleared, two dockworkers were dead and the third one was injured. As a result, Diamond and Entratta took it on the lam.

While they were in hiding, Diamond decided that before he could go back to doing what he was doing before, the bartender and three witnesses had to be killed. And soon they were, Cohen turned up dead, too, and the hat check girl, the cashier, and one waiter disappeared from the face of the earth.

Diamond and Entratta, with everyone out of the way who could possibly harm them, calmly turned themselves into the police and said, "I heard we were wanted for questioning."

No charges were ever brought against Diamond and Entratta for the Hotsy Totsy Club murders, but Diamond realized New York City was no longer safe for him. As a result, Diamond closed the Hotsy Totsy Club, and he relocated to Greene County in upstate New York.

From upstate New York, Diamond ran a little bootlegging operation. However, after a few months of impatience, Diamond sent word back to gangsters in New York City, namely Dutch Schultz and Owney Madden (who had scooped up Diamond's rackets in his absence), that he was coming back to take back what was rightfully his. This put a target in the middle of Diamond's back, and he soon became known as the "clay pigeon of the underworld."

Diamond was sitting at the bar of the Aratoga Inn, near Arca, New York, when three men, dressed as duck hunters, barreled into the bar and filled Diamond with lead. The doctors gave him little chance for survival, but four weeks later, Diamond walked out of the hospital and told the press, "Well, I made it again. Nobody can kill Jack 'Legs' Diamond."

A few months later, as Diamond was leaving an upstate roadside inn, he was shot four times: in the back, leg, lung, and liver. Yet again, Diamond beat the odds the doctors gave him, and he survived.

In December 1931, Diamond was not so lucky, when after a night of heavy drinking at the Kenmore Hotel in Albany, Diamond staggered back drunk to his nearby boarding room and fell asleep. The landlady said afterwards, that she heard Diamond pleading for his life, then she heard three shots. Apparently two gunmen had burst into Diamond's room, and while one held him by his two ears, the other put three slugs into his brain.

The killers escaped in a red Packard, putting an end to the myth that Jack "Legs" Diamond was the "gangster who couldn't be killed."

Eastman, Monk

Monk Eastman was born Edward Osterman, in 1875, in the Williamsburg section of Brooklyn. Edward's father owned a restaurant, and to keep the young Osterman busy, his father bought him a pet shop. Osterman's business venture failed, reportedly because he kept fighting with customers who wanted to purchase pets he became especially fond of. Out of business, young Osterman relocated to lower Manhattan, and to make money, he dived headfirst into a life of crime. He operated under several aliases, before finally settling on the last name of Eastman.

The short and stocky Eastman was nicknamed "Monk," because he resembled a monkey stalking the streets. He had an unkempt appearance, and his pumpkin-sized head and frazzled hair were covered by a derby two sizes too small. Eastman became known as a feared brawler, and he was the bouncer at one of the roughest nightclubs on the Lower East Side, the New Irving Social Club on the Bowery.

While he patrolled the club keeping the peace, Eastman carried a four-foot stick, which he used to crack the heads of any patron who was not behaving properly. In just a few short months, Eastman had whacked the heads of 49 near-do-wells, and not liking crooked numbers, he conked the skull of an innocent man just to make it an even 50. Eastman sent so many people to Bellevue Hospital, the hospital staff jokingly called their emergency room, "The Eastman Pavilion."

Yet Eastman apparently had a soft spot for women. If anyone of the female persuasion needed to be reckoned with, he reportedly dropped his stick, took off his brass knuckles, and hit the woman just hard enough to give her a black eye. No hospital visit was necessary for the lucky young lady.

Eastman also was a willing killer; for hire, or for just plain fun, especially when he was drunk, which was often. Eastman believed in "Dead Man's Eyes," which is the concept that when a person dies, the last thing that person he sees is permanently imprinted on the retina of their eyes. When Eastman killed someone, he truly believed he was leaving proof on the victim's eyes that he was the killer. So

Eastman, being the cautious bloke that he was, after he shot someone dead, not to leave any incriminating evidence, he shot out his victim's eyes out, too.

Eastman assembled a rough and tumble gang that reportedly numbered close to 2,000, mostly Jewish men. Eastman curried favor with politicians by doing them "little favors," like patrolling polling places during elections, to make sure each voter cast their vote for the proper man. The politicians returned the favor by springing Eastman out of jail, whenever an ambitious policeman decided to do something foolish, like actually arresting Eastman for one of his many crimes. However, Eastman was so out-of-control with his thievery, thuggery, and killings, he soon ran out of political favors.

In 1904, Eastman was finally sent to prison for robbing and beating a man uptown. He was sentenced to 10 years at Sing Sing Prison, but he was released after serving only five.

When Eastman got back to his old hunting grounds, he discovered his gang had been dismantled, and his former men were now working for other scattered ringleaders. Eastman was reduced to performing petty crimes in the streets for a while, until he had the bright idea of joining the army. Eastman wound up serving in World War I, in France, with the 106th Infantry Regiment of the 27th Infantry Division. Eastman was honorably discharged in 1919, and he immediately went back to the streets of the Lower East Side, causing his usual mayhem.

Eastman soon became involved with a crooked Prohibition agent named Jerry Bohan. On the night of December 26, 1920, the two men got into a drunken argument, and Bohan, knowing full well about Eastman's reputation for killing easy, shot Eastman dead, in front of 62 East 14th Street.

Fein, Benjamin "Dopey"

Benjamin "Dopey" Fein was born on the Lower East Side of Manhattan in 1889. He was nicknamed "Dopey" because an eye condition made his eyelids droop, and he seemed either to be falling asleep, or under the influence of a narcotic: in the street vernacular, "dope."

Fein dropped out of school at an early age, and he became involved is various street crimes, like pickpocketing and petty robberies. Fein enlisted groups of youngsters, particularly from the school he dropped out of (PS 20 on Essex Street), and soon he had scores of preteen criminals terrorizing the streets of the Lower East Side.

In 1905, Fein's luck turned sour, when he was arrested for assault and robbery, and sent upstate to the Elmira State Penitentiary, where he cooled his heels for three years. Fein was released and arrested twice more, before he finally hit the streets in 1910 and joined "Big" Jack Zelig's notorious gang.

After Zelig was murdered in 1912, Fein embarked on an upwardly horizontal career move. Fein started working for the bosses of several labor unions, especially the Garment Workers Union (GWU). Fein and his men became "schlammers," which meant they broke the heads of any union members who did not toe the line the union bigwigs had laid out for them.

After the Triangle Shirtwaist Factory Fire in 1911 (which killed 146 people, 123 of them women), Fein became involved with the ILGWU: the International Ladies Garment Workers Union. Fein had a reputation of making sure the woman in his union got paid the exact same salary for their work as did the men in the GWU, which was contrary to the common practice at the time.

Being on the ladies' side was a Machiavellian maneuver, which allowed Fein to use these ILGWU women as "toters," or carriers of concealed weapons, to which Fein and his gang had ready access whenever needed. Fein's female accomplices hid guns, knives, and brass knuckles, in mufflers, or in their hair puffed up high on their heads, in a unique hairdo called the "Mikado Tuck-up."

Fein's main foe at the time was Jack Sirroco. Sirroco was also heavily involved in the labor movement; not with the unions, but rather with the manufacturers, which put him at cross purposes with Fein. Fein and Sirroco's gangs fought numerous battles, especially when both sides showed up representing opposing parties at a labor strike.

In January 1914, Fein and his gang ambushed Sirroco's gang at a party at Arlington Hall, on St. Mark's Place. Only one person was killed, and it turned out to be an innocent bystander named Fredrick Strauss, who just happened to be a County Clerk officer. This put another nail in Fein's quickly closing coffin.

The final nail was inserted in the fall of 1914, when Fein threatened to kill B. Zalamanowitz, an official from the butchers union, who refused to pay Fein $600 to protect his striking butchers. Zalamanowitz, knowing Fein's murderous reputation, ran frightened to the police. On Fein's next meeting with Zalamanowitz, hidden cops watched as Fein repeated his intentions to harm Zalamanowitz if he did not pay up right away. The police arrested Fein on the spot; on first-degree extortion charges.

After a few days in the slammer, Fein, realizing his union influence was on the wane, decided to become a canary for the cops. Unknown to his associates in the labor unions, Fein had kept meticulous records on all his "labor transactions." He had written down everything, including who was involved in what, when, where, and how. This led to the arrest and convictions of dozens of people, including high-ranking officials of the Garment Workers Union and the International Ladies Garment Workers Union.

Fein was set free, but because he was considered a rat, he lost all of his union partners-in-crime, and any political influence he may have had. Fein was reduced to committing petty crimes in the streets, until he was arrested in 1931 for throwing acid in the face of a competitor: Mortimer Kahn. That set Fein up in Sing Sing Prison for a few more years.

In 1941, Fein was arrested again for stealing over $250,000 worth of clothing and fabric from the Garment Center. Fein was tried, convicted, and sentenced to life imprisonment. However, Fein, for some unknown reason, had his sentence reduced to 10-20 years.

When Fein was released from prison for the last time, he went right back into the garment industry, but this time as a legitimate tailor, a skill he had learned from his father. Fein moved from the Lower East Side of Manhattan to Brooklyn, where he married and raised a family.

Fein, unlike most of his contemporaries, who were either killed in the streets or fried in the electric chair, died of cancer and emphysema in 1962.

Forty Thieves

Based on "Ali Baba and the Forty Thieves," the Forty Thieves were considered to be the first organized street gang in New York City.

In 1825, the Forty Thieves originated at a produce store located on Centre Street, just south of Anthony (now Worth Street), in an area called The Five Points. The proprietor of the store was Rosanna Peers, who sold rotted vegetables out front and ran an illegal speakeasy in the back, where she sold rotgut liquor at prices much cheaper than licensed establishments. Soon, the joint became a haven for pickpockets, murderers, robbers, and thieves, and a dour gentleman named Edward Coleman rose as their leader.

Coleman gave out strict assignments to his men, with quotas on which and how many crimes he expected each man to commit. If after a period of time, a man did not meet his quota, he would be banished from the gang and sometimes even killed, as a message to others about the importance of meeting quotas.

Coleman's downfall was precipitated by one of the gang's few legal ventures: the Hot Corn Girls.

Coleman would send out scores of pretty young girls onto the streets, carrying baskets filled with hot roasted ears of corn. The Hot Corn Girl, dressed in spotted calico and wearing a plaid shawl, would walk barefooted in the streets, singing; "Hot Corn! Hot Corn! Here's your lily white corn. All you that's got money. Poor me that's got none. Come buy my lily hot corn. And let me go home."

The Hot Corn Girls were not allowed off the streets by Coleman until every single ear of corn in their basket was sold.

All the Hot Corn Girls were fairly attractive and the pretty ones were fought over by the amorous young men mingling on the streets. The best looking one of the lot was called "The Pretty Hot Corn Girl" and Coleman fell for her hard. After fighting off several other suitors, Coleman married "The Pretty Hot Corn Girl," and then he put her back out on the streets selling corn.

However, after his wife consistently did not meet her quotas, Coleman felt, in order to save face and be consistent with his orders, he had no other choice but to kill her. And that he did. As a result,

Coleman was arrested and convicted of murder. On January 12, 1839, Coleman became the first man ever to be hanged at the newly constructed Tombs Prison.

After Coleman's death, the men in the Forty Thieves drifted into other street gangs: including the Plug Uglies, the Dead Rabbits, and the Bowery Boys.

In the early 1850's, a juvenile street gang sprung up in the Five Points called the Forty Little Thieves, which consisted of homeless children of both sexes, from the ages of 8 to 12, who emulated the escapades of the old Forty Thieves. The head of the gang was Wild Maggie Carson, only 12-years-old herself.

The Forty Little Thieves soon outgrew their gang, and their members became assimilated into the older and more famous gangs; all except for Wild Maggie Carson, who was taken off the streets by Reverend Lewis Morris Pease, founder of the Five Points House of Industry. Under Pease's guidance, Little Maggie got a legitimate job sewing buttons. According to Pease, when she was 15, Little Maggie met and married a well-to-do gentleman. And she lived happily ever after.

That is, according to Pease.

Flour Riots of 1837

The flour problem began with the 1835 Great New York City Fire, which destroyed almost 700 downtown buildings. Nearly the entire New York City financial center, including the city's lifeblood - the banks - was burned to the ground. Unable to obtain loans, owners of factories and other downtown businesses, were not able to rebuild, putting tens of thousands of New Yorkers out of work.

By 1837, New York City had sunk into the depths of a recession. With no jobs and no money, people's diets sometimes consisted of little more than simple buttered or jammed bread. The poor of the city began to panic, when they discovered that flour, needed to make their daily bread, would become so expensive they would not be able to afford to buy it.

Matters were made worse, when reports from Virginia and other wheat producing states said there was a scarcity of wheat, from which flour was made, and a rise in price was inevitable. At the beginning of January 1837, wheat started at $5.62 cents a barrel. Within days, it had risen to $7 a barrel; then to $12 a barrel. There were rumors that in a few weeks, wheat would go to an incredible $20 a barrel.

The hardest hit were the poor people, who lived in the slums of the Five Points, Bowery, and the Fourth Ward areas on the Lower East Side of Manhattan. Besides the increase in the price of wheat, meat prices had doubled and coal to heat their hovels rose to $10 a ton. People became desperate, and poor souls who were not normally crooks felt they had no choice but to commit petty crimes in order to put food on their family's table.

On February 1, 1837, news circulated that New York City had only four weeks supply of flour left and that the large flour and grain depot in Troy, New York, contained only 4,000 barrels of flour, rather than the usual 30,000 barrels. The newspapers began sensationalizing the issue, when they stated in their editorials that certain merchants were hoarding wheat and flour in anticipation of the rising prices.

The Tammany Hall politicians were adept at causing unrest between the poor Irish, who populated the slums of Lower

Manhattan, and anyone with either money or prestige. Never letting a crisis go to waste, Tammany Hall began spreading unfounded rumors that England was refusing to send flour to the United States. The message was compounded by the untruth that the Old Mother Country's intention was to starve the poor Irish in America, as a repayment for the rancor between Ireland and England which had existed for centuries.

On February 10, 1837, a crowd of nearly 6,000 slum-dwellers, from the Five Points, Fourth Ward, and Bowery areas, met at City Hall Park. Running the meeting from atop the steps of City Hall were Tammany Hall titans like Moses Johnson, Paul Hedle, Warden Hayward, and Alexander Ming Jr. There it was decided that two businesses in particular - Hart and Company on Washington Street, and SH. Herrick & Company on Coenties Slip - were packed with both flour and wheat, and were holding back distribution, hoping for future monetary gain when the prices rose.

One of the speakers said, "Fellow citizens, Mr. Eli Hart has 53,000 barrels of flour in his store. Let us go there and offer him $8 a barrel, and if he does not take it......"

The speaker stopped in mid-sentence, but his implication was clear.

When the talking was over, the crowd stampeded from City Hall Park, and they headed down Broadway, west on Cortland and onto Washington Street. When the watchmen protecting Hart's Store saw the surging mob, they quickly ran inside, and they locked the three huge iron doors. But they forgot to insert the inside bar on the center door.

Eli Hart was viewing the mob unrest from a safe distance, and he immediately ran to City Hall, asking for police protection. Twenty policemen rushed to the scene, but they were beaten back by the rioters and their clubs taken away from them. The newly elected mayor of New York City, Aaron Clark, hurried up the steps of the store, and he tried to quell the angry mob. However, after he was showered with stones and bricks, Clark was forced to run for this life.

The rioters then rushed into the building and wrenched one of the iron doors from its hinges. Using it as a battering ram, they bashed down the other two iron doors, then they busted inside. Once inside, the mob entered the storerooms, then rolled approximately

1,000 bushels of wheat and 500 barrels of flour into the street. They smashed the bushels and barrels, until thousands of rioters were knee deep in the flour and wheat.

People started to sing, "Here goes flour at eight dollars a barrel!"

Women filled their apron and skirts with flour, while men used their hats and pockets to pilfer the goods. Even young children got into the act, scooping up what they could carry on their frail bodies.

Suddenly, the 27th Regiment of the National Guard arrived, and they confronted the rioters. Using bayonets and clubs, the National Guard stabbed and clubbed as many rioters as they could lay their hands on. Eventually, they captured scores of the worst offenders, and they started marching them to the Tombs Prison. However, before they got very far, more rioters attacked the National Guard, and they rescued dozens of prisoners, and in the process, tore the police commissioner's coat right off his back. Forty rioters were finally hustled to the Tombs, where they were tried and convicted, and sent to Sing Sing Prison.

While the rioters carted off their dead and wounded from in front of Hart's store, another contingent headed to the store of S.H. Herrick & Company. There the mob smashed the doors and windows with stones and bats, and within ten minutes, they were able to destroy an additional 30 barrels of flour and 100 bushels of wheat.

Then, without any apparent reason, the mob suddenly disbursed and headed back to their slums, their thirst for destruction finally sated.

The very next day, the price of flour increased one dollar.

Gallus Mag

Dating back to the 1700's, the waterfront of the 4th Ward was a haven for robbers, killers, and pirates. Vicious gangs like the Daybreak Boys, Buckoos, Hookers, Swamp Angels, and Slaughter Houses, prowled the streets, robbing and murdering any poor fool with cash in their pockets who was stupid enough to wander into their sacred domain. Yet, the most feared denizen ever to set foot in the 4th Ward of the mid-19th Century was not a man, but an amazon woman named Gallus Mag.

Gallus Mag was an Englishwoman who stood over 6-feet-tall. She was the bouncer at a Dover Street dive called the Hole-In-The-Wall Bar. The Hole-In-The-Wall Bar was originally built in 1794, and is now the site of the famed Bridge Cafe. The Hole-In-The-Wall Bar was owned by one-armed Charlie Monell, and ruled by Mag, who got her nickname "Gallus" because she kept her skirt from falling down with suspenders, or galluses, as they were called at the time.

Mag stalked the bar looking for troublemakers, with a pistol stuck in her belt and a bludgeon strapped to her wrist. If anyone was dumb enough to challenge her mettle, Mag would hit them with her club, then clutch their ear in her teeth, drag them to the front door and throw them out into the gutter. If the patron put up a stink, Mag would bite off their ear and store it in a large bottle of alcohol that she kept in plain sight behind the bar (They called it "Gallus Mag's Trophy Case"). The New York City police of that time proclaimed Gallus Mag the "most savage female they had ever encountered."

Mag was challenged one day by another woman, Sadie the Goat, a member of the Charlton Street Gang. Sadie the Goat got her name because her preferred manner of robbery was slamming her head into the stomach of her victim, whereas her male companion would then nail the sucker in the head with a rock from a slingshot, then rob him of all his valuables. One day in the Hole-In-The-Wall Bar, Sadie, three sheets to the wind, foolishly challenged Mag to a fight and was beaten to a pulp. As was her wont, Mag severed one of Sadie the Goat's ears with her teeth, and she deposited it into a liquor jar behind the bar. Sadie was glad to escape with her life, and she fled the 4th Ward for the foreseeable future. She then prowled the West Side piers, looking for other suckers to rob.

Years later, after she had made considerable cash performing her specialty on the streets of the West Side, Sadie returned to the Hole-In-The-Wall Bar and made her peace with Mag. Mag was so touched by Sadie's gesture, she immediately went into a liquor jar, removed Sadie's severed ear and returned it to its rightful owner. The legend is that Sadie was so overjoyed by the return of her ear, she wore it in a locket around her neck until her final days.

In 1855, after a slew of seven murders were committed on the premises in the space of three months, the Hole-In-The Wall Bar was closed down for good by the authorities.

There is no record of the year of Mag's demise, but her ghost is said to haunt the Bridge Cafe to this very day.

Gophers

The Gophers street gang was formed in the 1890's from a conglomerate of other Irish street gangs that patrolled the west side of Manhattan. The Gophers were given their name, because after they performed one misdeed or another, to avoid arrest, they hid themselves in the cavernous cellars that snaked throughout the neighborhood. The Gophers originally ruled the area west from Seventh Avenue to 11th Avenue, and north from 14th Street to 42nd Street. However, later they moved as far north as 57th Street. The Gopher's numbers swelled and eventually reached over 500 men, all murderous hooligans of the worst kind.

The Gophers' first base of operations was a notorious saloon called Battle Row, also the name of the area on 39th Street, between 10th and 11th Avenue, where the Gophers committed most of their mayhem. Battle Row was owned by a thug named Mallet Murphy, who was given his nickname because he corrected drunks and other miscreants with a wooden mallet instead of a bludgeon, which was the weapon of choice of that day.

Due to the death or imprisonment of their bosses, the Gophers went through several leaders. The most famous Gopher boss was Owney "The Killer" Madden. Madden's reign ended in 1913, when he was sent to the slammer for 10 years for killing Little Patsy Doyle, his girlfriend's ex-boyfriend and an ambitious man intent on replacing Madden as the leader of the Gophers.

Another such boss was One Lung Curran, who originated a practice that determined the fashion wear of his gang. One day Curran, dismayed that his girlfriend did not have a proper winter coat, snuck up behind a passing policeman, clubbed him over the head and stole his winter police coat. Curran gave the coat to his girlfriend, and after a few alterations, she produced a swell model with a military cut.

Other Gophers followed this trend, and soon there was an epidemic of police officers staggering back to their station house on West 47th Street, blood dripping from their heads and dressed only in their shirts, shoes, and trousers. This prompted the police captain of that precinct to send groups of four and five cops into the Gophers' domain. They bludgeoned enough Gophers that their sartorial vogue soon ended.

Another Gophers leader was Happy Jack Mulraney, called Happy Jack because his face was set in a permanent smile. Mulraney's smile was not intended, but, in fact, caused by a quirky paralysis of Mulraney's face muscles. His cohorts enjoyed inciting the psychopathic-killer Mulraney into a rage, by telling him someone had made fun of his unintentional grin.

One day, Paddy the Priest, a bar owner on 10th Avenue and a close friend of Mulraney's, made the horrible mistake of asking Mulraney why he didn't smile out of the other side of his face. Mulraney immediately shot Paddy the Priest in the head, killing him instantly. Then adding insult to injury, Mulraney emptied Paddy the Priest's cash register. For his temporary lapse in judgment, Mulraney was sentenced to life in prison.

In August of 1908, several Gophers wandered out of their West Side domain, and smack into the middle of a shootout on the Lower East Side between Monk Eastman's gang and Paul Kelly's Five Pointers. Not wanting to miss out on the fun, the Gophers opened fire, shooting at members of both warring gangs.

One Gopher later said, "A lot of guys were poppin' at each other, so why shouldn't we do a little poppin' ourselves?"

For years, the Gopher's main source of income was plundering the freight cars and the train depot of the New York Central Railroad, which ran along 11th Avenue. The New York City police was unable, and sometimes unwilling, to stop these shenanigans. So, the railroad organized its own "police force," which was comprised mostly of ex-cops, who had been brutalized by the Gophers in the past and were looking for revenge. This "police force" went into Hell's Kitchen, beating the Gophers from one end of the neighborhood to the other, or as a member of the "police force" said, "From hell to breakfast." Sometimes they used clubs, and if needed, they fired guns. Being former policemen and well-trained in firearms, they were much better at gunplay than were the Gophers.

In 1917, after the arrest of One Lung Curran, and with Madden still in jail and Mulraney in prison for life, the Gophers gradually dissipated. By 1920, the Gophers street gang ceased to exist, only to be replaced in later years by another murderous group called "The Westies."

Great New York City Fire of 1835

It was the worst fire in New York City's history. But that didn't stop the poor Irish, living in the slums of the Five Points, from going on a dazzling display of looting, which led to one of the biggest free champagne parties in the history of America.

The city was in the throes of one of the coldest winters on record. On the days preceding "The Great Fire," the temperature had dropped as low as 17 degrees below zero. By the night of December 16, 1835, there was two feet of frozen snow on the ground and the temperature was exactly zero frigid degrees. It was so cold, both the Hudson River and East Rivers had completely frozen.

Around 9 p.m., a watchman (the precursor to a New York City policeman) named Warren Hayes was crossing the corner of Merchant (now Beaver Street) and Pearl Street, when he thought he smelled smoke. Hayes looked up at the last floor of a five-story building at 25 Merchant Street, rented by Comstock and Andrews, a famous dry-goods store, and he spotted smoke coming out of a window. Unbeknownst to Hayes, a gas pipe had ruptured and had ignited some coals left on a stove.

Hayes immediately ran through the streets yelling "Fire!!" In minutes, the great fire bell that stood above City Hall began peeling loudly, summoning what was left of the New York City Fire Department. The bell at the Tombs Prison, about a mile north, also started ringing, summoning the volunteer firemen in that area.

In 1832, New York City was stricken with the worst case of cholera in the city's history. Four thousand people died, and more than half of the city's quarter million population fled the city in fear. This decimated the New York City Fire Department, and by 1835, the Fire Department had less than half of its previous members.

The volunteer fire department that responded on December 16, 1835, had spent the previous night fighting a fire on Burlington Street, on the East River, and they were now near exhaustion. By the time the local fire department arrived 30 minutes later, due to 40 mile-a-hour winds, the fire had already spread to 50 structures. Buildings were going up in flames on Water Street, Exchange Place, Beaver, Front, and South Streets. By midnight, the fire had also consumed Broad and Wall Street, which was the heart of the business and financial center of New York City, if not the entire country. Most of the city's newspaper plants, retail and wholesale stores, and warehouses, were also engulfed by the conflagration.

The call went out to every fire department in the city, but it was of no use. 75 hook and ladder companies were at the scene less than two hours after the fire had started. Hundreds of citizens pitched in, carrying water in buckets, pails, and even tubs. Unfortunately, because of the cold weather, the fire hoses were mostly useless.

In addition, the entire city's cisterns, wells, and fire hydrants were frozen too. Whatever water did stream thinly from the hydrants through the hoses, only went 30 feet into the air, then quickly turned into ice. What made matters worse, due to the high winds, this ice/water mixture, feebly coming out of the hoses, was blown back onto the fireman themselves, and soon scores of firemen were living ice structures. Many firemen poured brandy into their boots to keep their feet from getting frostbite. Some drank the brandy, too, in order to keep the rest of their body warm.

Other firemen raced to the East River, and they started chopping the ice to reach the water below. Black Joke Engine No. 33 was dragged onto the deck of a ship, and it started pumping water through the holes in the ice. Engine No. 33 directed the water though three other engines, until it finally reached the fire on Water Street. However, in just a few hours, those four engines were frozen too and were no longer of any use.

Two buildings were saved in an extremely odd way. Barrels of vinegar were rolled out of the Oyster King Restaurant, in the Downing Building on Garden Street. This vinegar was poured into several fire engines and used to douse the fires in the Downing Building, and in the Journal of Commerce Building next door. However, the vinegar soon ran out and could not be used to save any more structures.

As the city was engulfed in mayhem, a man ran into a church on Garden Street, and he began playing a funeral dirge on an organ, which could be heard all throughout Lower Manhattan. Minutes later, that church caught fire too, and the organist was seen sprinting from the flaming church.

Soon, the fire spread to Hanover Square, Williams Street, Hanover Street, and Exchange Place. Burning cloths and twines from various buildings were blown into the air, and they flew across the East River, igniting the roofs of homes in Brooklyn. The city's blaze was so intense, smoke could be seen as far south as Philadelphia and as far north as New Haven. New York City was so desperate, Philadelphia firemen were summoned from 90 miles away to help fight the blaze.

After consulting with experts, New York City Mayor Cornelius W. Lawrence agreed that the fire could be stopped, if they blew up certain buildings in strategic places, so that the flames could not travel from building to building. The only problem was, the sale of gunpowder was forbidden in New York City. The nearest ample supply was in the Brooklyn Navy Yard, in Red Hook, Brooklyn, as well as on Governors Island.

Mayor Strong sent word that the gunpowder was needed immediately, but it did not arrive until noon on December 17, accompanied by 80 marines and a dozen sailors. The military, with the help of James Hamilton, the son of former Secretary of the Treasury Alexander Hamilton, began blowing up buildings. In a few hours, the blaze was contained at Coenties Slip.

As downtown Manhattan continued smoldering, hundreds of Irish men, women, and children, from the slums of the Five Points area, rushed into the devastated area, eyes sparkling, and hands a-grabbing. For a full 24 hours, the hoodlums looted whatever they could get their hands on: stealing cloaks, frock coats, plug hats, and silk and satin of the finest quality.

Cases and kegs of booze, beer, and wine were smashed open, and the mob drank heartily in the smoky frigid streets. Fights broke out between the drunk and delirious rioters, over who had the right to steal what. Ten thousand bottles of the finest champagne were stolen, too, and what the mob could not guzzle on site, they lugged back to their slums for later consumption.

Noted diarist and future Mayor of New York City, Philip Hone, later wrote, "The miserable wretches, who prowled around the ruins, and became beastly drunk on the champagne and other wines and liquors, with which the streets and roads were lined, seemed to exult in the misfortune of others."

Finally, the area was placed under martial law, and patrolled by the marines from the Navy Yard, and from the Third and Ninth Military Regiments. However, this did not completely stop the looters from continuing their felonious frenzy. Dozens rushed to unaffected areas outside the burn zone, and they torched buildings, so they could loot those buildings too. Five arsonists were arrested by the Marines. But a sixth one, who was caught torching a building on the corner of Stone and Broad, was captured by angry citizens and immediately hung from a tree. His frozen body stood dangling there and was not cut down by the police until three days later.

From the start of the fire, three days had passed until the last spark was extinguished. By then, 17 blocks of lower Manhattan, covering 52 acres and consisting of 693 buildings, had burned to the ground. Two people were killed, and the damages were assessed at $20 million, almost a billion dollars by today's standards.

There was 10 million dollars in insurance money owed for the damages, but only a scant amount of that money was ever paid, since the insurance companies, and the banks, had also burned to the ground, forcing them out of business. Not being able to collect on their insurance, and not being able to get loans from banks that no longer existed, hundreds of businesses that burned to the ground during "The Great New York Fire of 1835" never re-opened.

In 1836, the downtown area was rebuilt, with structures made of stone and concrete, which were less susceptible to spreading fires. Some of those buildings are standing to this day.

Hicks, Albert E.

Albert E. Hicks, called "Hicksey" by his pals (if he had any) and "Pirate Hicks" by the police, was the last man to be executed for piracy in the United States of America.

Hicks was a freelance gangster, who lived with his wife and son at 129 Cedar Street in downtown Manhattan, only two blocks from the East River. Hicks felt his criminal enterprises were better served if he worked alone, and as a result, Hicks never joined any of the other gangs that prowled the waterfront in the treacherous 4th Ward. Working solo, the police suspected Hicks committed scores of robberies and over a dozen murders.

However, Hicks scoffed at that notion. "Suspecting it and proving it are two different things," he said.

In March 1860, Hicks tied on a big one at a Water Street dive, and he became so drunk, he could not walk the two blocks home. Instead, he staggered into a Cherry Street lodging house, figuring he'd sleep until he was sober enough to walk the rest of the way home. The owner of the establishment was a known crimp, or a man who specialized in shanghaiing, which was the practice of "kidnapping men into duty as sailors on ships, against their will, by devious techniques such as trickery, intimidation, or violence." Hicks asked the crimp for a nightcap, and that he got, as the crimp, not aware of Hicks' reputation, laced Hicks' rum with laudanum, which is an alcohol solution containing opium.

The nightcap knocked Hicks out cold and when he awoke the next morning, he found himself at sea, on the ship the *E. A. Johnson*," which was bound for Deep Creek, Virginia, to pick up a load of oysters. Five days later, the *E. A. Johnson* was found abandoned at sea, a few miles off the coast of Staten Island. The ship seemed to have collided with another vessel, and when it was finally secured, Coroner Schirmer and Captain Weed of the Second Precinct Police Station, boarded the boat to examine the cause of its condition. No one was on board, but in the ship's cabin they found the room ransacked, and the floor, ceiling, and bunks filled with blood. On the deck, they found four human fingers and a thumb lying under the rail.

The next day, two residents of the Cedar Street house, where Hicks lived with this family, told the police that Hicks had returned home with a considerable sum of money, and was now gone, with no trace of him, or his family. In fact, Hicks had packed his belongings and escaped with his family to a boarding house in Providence, Rhode Island.

New York City Patrolman Nevins traced Hicks, and with the help of the Providence police, he arrested Hicks's entire family. When Patrolman Nevins searched Hicks's belongings, he found a watch and a daguerreotype (an early version of a camera), which belonged to Captain Burr, the captain of the *E. A. Johnson*. The two other missing seamen were brothers, Smith and Oliver Watts, but nothing could be found belonging to them and their fate remained a mystery.

As a result, Hicks was arrested and locked up in the Tombs Prison. At his trial in May, it took the jury only seven minutes to convict Hicks of piracy and murder on the high seas. He was sentenced to be hanged at Bedloe's Island on Friday the 13th, which was certainly a double-bad-luck day for Hicks.

A week after his trial, Hicks decided to become downright chatty. Hicks summoned the warden and several newspapermen to his cell, and he began spilling the beans about the whole sordid affair.

"I was brooding about being shanghaied," Hicks said "And I decided to avenge myself by murdering all hands on the ship."

Hicks told the assembled crowd that he was steering the ship, while Captain Burr and one of the Watts brothers was sleeping in the cabin below. The other Watts brother was on lookout at the bow. Hicks lashed the steering wheel to keep the ship on course, then he picked up an iron bar, sneaked to the bow of the ship, and hit the lookout over the head with the bar, knocking him out cold.

The other Watts brother heard the noise, and he rushed topside. By this time, Hicks had found an ax, and when the boy climbed onto the deck, Hicks decapitated him with one mighty blow. Hicks then rushed down to the cabin and confronted Captain Burr, who had just awakened from a deep sleep. The Captain put up a brave battle, but in the end, he too was decapitated.

Hicks said he then heard rumblings from up top. Hicks rushed up to the deck, and he found the first Watts boy staggering around in obvious pain. Hicks knocked him down with a heavy blow. Then he picked him up, carried him to the rail and tried to throw the boy overboard. The boy clutched at the railing, and Hicks used the ax to chop off the boy's five fingers, after which the lad toppled into the murky waters below.

Hicks threw the other two bodies overboard. Then he rushed below and ransacked the cabin, looking for money and valuables. When he saw the coast of Staten Island, Hicks lowered a small boat, and he rowed the rest of the way to land.

Hicks's confession made him an instant celebrity. Hundreds of gawkers paid the prison guards small fees to see Hicks shackled in his cell. And for a few pennies more, they were allowed to speak with the condemned man himself.

Among Hicks's many visitors was circus owner P.T. Barnum, who offered Hicks $25, a new suit of clothes, and two boxes of cigars, in exchange for a plaster cast of Hicks's head, which Barnum, the enterprising chap that he was, had planned to display in his circus, after Hicks's execution. Hicks agreed, but later on his way to the gallows, he complained to the warden that the suit was cheap and it did not fit properly. The warden told Hicks it was too late for alterations.

On the morning of July 13, Hicks, led my Marshall Rynders and a crowd estimated at 1500 people, started a procession to the docks. Rynders and Hicks boarded the boat accompanied by several policemen, and they sailed for Bedloe's Island, where a gallows had been erected 30 feet from the water. Hundreds of boats followed the doomed man, and it was estimated that 10,000 people came to witness Hicks's execution.

After the noose was slung around Hicks's neck and the ground removed from beneath his feet, Hicks struggled for a full three minutes before he stopped moving. Hicks was then cut down and pronounced dead.

Hicks was buried at Calvary Cemetery. However, a few days later, Hicks's body was stolen and sold to medical students, intent on studying the brain of a man who could commit such vile atrocities without much remorse.

Holstein, Caspar – The Harlem Policy King

He was considered a genius; a compassionate man who gave freely to the poor. However, Caspar Holstein made his fortune in the Harlem numbers policy racket, a game of chance he helped invent.

Casper Holstein was born on December 7, 1876, in St. Croix, Danish West Indies. His parents were of mixed African and Danish descent, and his father's father was a Danish officer in the Danish West Indies Colonial militia. In 1894, the Holstein family moved to New York City. Holstein, an extremely bright teenager, graduated from high school in Brooklyn, which was no mean accomplishment for a black man before the turn of the century. After graduation, Holstein enlisted in the Navy, and during World War I he visited his homeland, which, by then, was known as the West Virgin Islands.

When Holstein was discharged from the Navy, he worked at various odd jobs, including being a doorman in an Upper East Side building. He also became a personal assistant to a wealthy white couple, and years later, after he had made his fortune and they had lost theirs, Holstein supported this couple, then paid for their funeral.

Looking to better himself, Holstein wandered down to Wall Street, where he got a job, first as a messenger, and then as head messenger for a commodities brokerage firm. Holstein became enamored of gambling, especially the horses. But he also dabbled in the stock market, perusing the daily figures from the Boston and the New York City Clearing Houses.

One day, an idea came to Holstein that would improve his lot dramatically. Holstein knew that people in black neighborhoods, such as Harlem, loved to gamble, but most didn't have enough spare cash to do so. When he had saved enough money to start his new endeavor, Holstein devised a scheme where people could bet as little as a dime on a random set of three digit numbers which would appear daily in the New York City newspapers.

Using the Boston and New York City Clearing House figures, Holstein took the two middle digits of the New York number and the one middle digit from the Boston number. So if the two clearing house totals were $9,456,131 and $7,456,253 respectively, the winning number would be 566: the "56" being the two digits before the last comma of the first figure, and the "6" being the last digit before the last comma of the second figure.

This system was so random, it could not be manipulated; like it would be later by gangster Dutch Schultz, after he muscled in on the Harlem numbers rackets and began using race track figures which he manipulated to decrease his losses. By the early 1920's, Holstein's system was the rage in Harlem. Holstein became known as the "Bolita King," earning an estimated $5000 a day.

Using his newfound wealth, Holstein contributed generously to worthwhile causes. He gave huge amounts of money to the St. Vincent Sanitarium and to the nationalist Garvey Movement. Holstein also funded prizes for *Opportunity Magazine's* literary awards, which discovered much of Harlem's young artistic talent. Holstein built dormitories at black colleges, and he financed many of Harlem's artists, writers, and poets. Holstein also helped start a Baptist school in Liberia, and he established a hurricane relief fund for his native Virgin Islands. The *New York Times* said that Holstein was, "Harlem's favorite hero, because of his wealth, his sporting proclivities, and his philanthropies among the people of his race."

Seeing how Holstein and Stephanie St. Clair had turned Harlem into a financial bonanza due to their numbers rackets, gangster Dutch Schultz barged in and took over their games. Just like that. Schultz had big politicians, including the disgraced Jimmy Hines, in his back pocket. Schultz also bought off the cops, and he killed, or had killed, black numbers runners who did not work for him. Schultz eventually forced St. Clair to work under him, but Holstein refused Schultz's offers to consolidate their numbers rackets.

In 1928, Holstein was kidnapped for $50,000 ransom, by five white gangsters, whom were presumed by the Harlem public to be goons sent by Schultz. The news of Holstein's kidnapping made national headlines. The *New York Times* reported that Holstein had been seen at Belmont Racetrack just days before his abduction, betting more than $30,000 on the ponies.

Holstein was released by his captors after three days in custody, insisting he had paid no ransom. Holstein's explanation was that his captors had felt sorry for him and had freed him with $3 cab fare in his pocket.

However, Holstein's tale carried very little weight, since he soon mysteriously cut down on his policy activities. A few years later, Holstein completely stopped his street operations, and he operated only as a lay-off better.

In 1935, despite the fact that he was barely in the game, Holstein was arrested for illegal gambling. Holstein was tried and convicted, and he spent one year in prison. Holstein claimed he was framed, possibly by Schultz, but he did his time in jail uneventfully. When he was released from prison, Holstein got involved in the real estate business, and he provided mortgages for people in Harlem whom the regular banks shunned.

Casper Holstein died on April 5, 1944, at the age of 68. More than 2,000 people attended Holstein's funeral at Harlem's Memorial Baptist Church. A scholarship at the University of the Virgin Islands and a housing development in St. Croix are named in Holstein's memory.

Hudson Dusters

The Hudson Dusters were an unruly street gang, which, starting in the late 1890's, ruled the Greenwich Village area of New York City. They were formed by the trio of Kid Yorke, Circular Jack, and Goo Goo Knox, who was a former gang member of the Gophers, a homicidal group that ran Hell's Kitchen a few blocks to the north.

Knox had tried to take control of the Gophers, failed, and then moved south to terrorize a different neighborhood, which was open to whichever gang could take control. The Hudson Dusters crushed local gangs like the Potashes, and the Boodles, and then they took command of the rackets in Greenwich Village. The Hudson Dusters also made big scores, plundering the docks along the Hudson River, a few blocks to the west.

After the Hudson Dusters committed one of their varied crimes, the snakelike streets of Greenwich Village were perfect for their getaways. Their most accomplished thief was Ding Dong, who would roam the streets with a dozen or so youths. When the opportunity arose, Ding Dong would direct the kids to jump on passing wagons, and to toss to him any valuables they could get their hands on. Before the police could respond, Ding Dong was long gone, having disappeared through the maze of streets that comprised Greenwich Village.

The Hudson Dusters became street legends, but they were not particularly famous for their fighting prowess, as were other brutal New York City gangs. The Hudson Dusters hung out in the taverns and gin mills of the Village, mingling with the famous writers and artists of their time. The print journalists also favored the Hudson Dusters, whom they portrayed in the newspapers as nothing more than a fun-loving bunch, who drank more than they committed crimes. One of Hudson Dusters' party pals was playwright Eugene O'Neil, who frequented the gang's hangout - the Hell Hole on Sixth Avenue and 4th Street. It was there that O'Neil garnered most of his characters for his most famous play: *The Iceman Cometh*; the Iceman meaning "death."

At their inception, the Hudson Dusters moved their base of operations frequently, finally settling on a house on Hudson Street, just below Horatio Street, later the site of the Open Door Mission. More interested in partying than pillaging, the Hudson Dusters installed a piano, and they danced the nights away, in a cocaine-induced stupor, with the prostitutes who prowled the West Side piers a few short blocks away. This annoyed the neighboring homeowners and business owners to no end, but they all were afraid to make a complaint to the police, because the Hudson Dusters had the reputation of seeking revenge in a hot moment against anyone who dared rat them out. After a night of carousing, the Hudson Dusters were known to parade in the streets, boozed out and hopped-up on coke, looking to cause mayhem on anyone or anything in their path.

One night, the Hudson Dusters asked a local saloon keeper to provide them with a few kegs of beer for a party, on the arm, meaning they did not expect to pay the man for his stock. The saloon keeper refused, and the Hudson Dusters descended up his establishment. They wrecked the joint and carried away every ounce of booze on the premises. The saloon keeper ran to his friend, Patrolman Dennis Sullivan. Patrolman Sullivan opted to declare war on the Hudson Dusters. He rounded up ten Hudson Dusters, including their then-leader Red Farrell, and arrested them for vagrancy.

The Hudson Dusters decided to retaliate, and with the blessing of a Greenwich Village politician who used the Hudson Dusters for intimidation on Election Day, they ambushed Patrolmen Sullivan, as he was about to arrest one of the Hudson Dusters on a robbery charge. The Hudson Dusters attacked Patrolman Sullivan from behind and stole his jacket, gun and shield, while beating him with stones and blackjacks. As many as 20 Hudson Dusters took turns kicking and punching the distressed policeman after he was down. When Patrolman Sullivan was finally unconscious, four Hudson Dusters rolled him onto his back, and then they ground the heels of their boots into his face, causing permanent scars. Patrolman Sullivan was finally taken to the hospital, where he stayed, recuperating for over a month.

The Gophers Street Gang congratulated the Hudson Dusters on their cop-beating accomplishment. Gopher leader, "One Lung" Curran, felt moved enough to write a poem praising their actions. The poem reads:

Says Dinny "Here's me only chance
To gain meself a name;
I'll clean up the Hudson Dusters,
and reach the Hall of Fame."
He lost his stick and cannon,
and his shield they took away.
It was then he remembered,
Every dog had his day.

The Hudson Dusters loved this poem so much, they printed up hundreds of copies, and distributed them on the streets of Greenwich Village, even dropping one off at the Charles Street Station House where Patrolman Sullivan was assigned.

By 1916, the Hudson Dusters had dissipated, as most of their gang members were either coke addicts, dead, or locked up in jail. Another Greenwich Village gang, the Marginals, led by Tanner Smith, took over the Hudson Dusters' rackets. The Marginals controlled the Village, until Tanner was killed by Chicky Lewis, inside the Marginal Club on Eighth Avenue, on July 29, 1919.

For all practical purposes, that was the end of a street gang presence on the Lower West Side of Manhattan.

Ida "The Goose"

Ida "The Goose" Burger was a strikingly beautiful dance hall girl, and sometimes prostitute, who was the favorite of several members of the five-hundred-strong Gophers gang, which controlled New York City's Hell's Kitchen. The Gophers passed Ida the Goose around from boss to boss, and even down to the low-level members of their gang. Make no mistake, Ida belonged to the treacherous Gophers, and anyone who thought otherwise would be dealt with severely.

Jack Tricker was a saloon keeper/gangster, whom, after Monk Eastman was sent to prison for armed robbery, headed up one faction of the Eastman gang on the Lower East Side. Tricker owned a bar on Park Row in downtown Manhattan. But after it was closed by authorities (for basically being a den of iniquity), Tricker decided to branch out of the Lower East Side and into Hell's Kitchen, which was enemy territory. Tricker decided, that maybe, because of the Gophers' internal battles, they were not so tough anymore. In an act of defiance, Tricker bought the Old Stag Bar on West 28th Street, smack in the middle of Gopher territory, and he renamed it the Maryland Cafe.

One of Tricker's men, Irish Tom Riley, somehow won the affections of the glorious Ida the Goose. Riley spit in the Gophers' face, when he took Ida away from the Gophers and brought her to the Maryland Cafe, where they immediately installed Ida as the main attraction - the "Belle of The Ball," so to speak.

The Gophers sent an emissary to Tricker, demanding the return of Ida the Goose. Tricker told the emissary that he would not get involved, one way or another, and that it was their problem, not his. Immediately, threats spewed from the Gophers to Tricker's gang, who armed themselves heavily in anticipation of a street war. However, after weeks had passed and nothing happened, Tricker's gang relaxed a bit, thinking the Gophers were all talk and no action.

In October of 1910, four Gophers, one of whom was Ida's former boyfriend, swaggered into the Maryland Cafe. They approached the bar and ordered four beers, which they were quickly served. Six Tricker gangsters, who were sitting at a large round table nearby, were so surprised by the bold move, they sat transfixed and said not a word, let alone try to evict the invaders.

Outraged, it was Ida the Goose who spoke first. She screamed at the Gophers, "Say!! Youse guys have some nerve!"

The Gophers calmly finished their beer, then one turned around slowly, and said, "Well, let's get at it."

The four Gophers each drew two guns, and they began spraying the bar's walls, mirrors, and tables with bullets. The two bartenders, who were not part of Tricker's gang, dived behind the bar for cover. Five of Tricker men's were shot and disabled. The sixth, who was Ida's newfound lover, Riley, was so far untouched and un-bloodied. Seeking refuge, Riley dived under Ida's flowing skirt.

Nonplussed, Ida stared down at Riley in disdain.

Then she shrugged her shoulders and said, "Say, youse! Come on out and take it."

Ida stepped back, and she shoved Riley into the center of the floor. Smiling broadly, the four Gophers pumped four bullets into Riley's torso. Then Ida's former boyfriend stepped forward, and he put one final bullet into Riley's brain.

Proud of their accomplishments, the four Gophers strode out of the Maryland Cafe, followed closely by Ida the Goose, glowing with pride that such a battle had been fought over her affections.

As a result, Ida the Goose was again the exclusive property of the Gophers, never to stray from their embrace.

Johnson, Ellsworth (Bumpy)

Ellsworth "Bumpy" Johnson was known as a murderous policy numbers baron in Harlem during the 1930's, but he was, in addition, the conduit between the Italian Mob and the Harlem rackets for almost three decades.

Ellsworth Johnson was born in Charleston, South Carolina, on October 31, 1905. He got the nickname "Bumpy" because as a child he had received a huge dump on the back of his head. Johnson was a brilliant youth, and by the time he was eight years old, he had already skipped two grades.

When Johnson was 10, his brother Willie was accused of killing a white man. Knowing a lynch mob was looking for Willie, Johnson's parents sent Willie to live up north.

Growing toward adulthood, Bumpy Johnson was a proud black man, defiant of the segregation and the violence perpetrated against blacks in the deep south. Johnson's parents were worried Johnson, who had a violent temper, would follow in his brother Willie's footsteps. So, in 1919, they sent Johnson to Harlem to stay with his Aunt Mabel.

After graduating from Boys High in Brooklyn and attending City College for a few semesters, Johnson got involved with a wild element in Harlem. As a result, he made several trips to prison, for such crimes as armed robbery and burglary. In a 10-year stretch of prison life, Johnson, because of his penchant for violence, spent a full three years in solitary confinement. When he was released in 1932, Johnson had spent more than half of his life behind bars.

Back on the streets causing mayhem, Johnson caught the eye of Stephanie St. Clair, called "Madame Queen" in Harlem. Johnson became chief lieutenant to St. Clair. But it was rumored they were also lovers, even though St. Clair was 20 years Johnson's elder.

St. Clair was a numbers baron, who was being squeezed out of the rackets by crazed gangster Dutch Schultz. Schultz used every trick in the book to drive St. Clair out of Harlem, including killing her numbers runners and paying off the cops to arrest St. Clair's numbers runners on sight.

Johnson, knowing Schultz was not a reasonable man, went to

Italian mob boss Lucky Luciano, and he asked Luciano to intercede on St. Clair's behalf. Luciano was impressed with Johnson's gumption and intelligence. But he told Johnson there was not much he could do as far as Schultz was concerned, since he and Schultz were partners in several other illegal activities. Johnson decided to take the war to Schultz, and for the next three years, the two gangs shot each other on sight, resulting in numerous casualties on both sides.

In 1935, Johnson and St. Clair caught a break, when Luciano, tired of the murderous Schultz's unpredictable violence, had Schultz gunned down in a New Jersey steakhouse. Luciano gave Schultz's numbers rackets to "Trigger" Mike Coppola, a captain in what was later to be called the "Genovese Crime Family."

However, Luciano, remembering Johnson's capabilities, cut a deal with Johnson, allowing Johnson and St. Clair to keep their independent Harlem numbers business intact. This made Johnson an instant hero to the black people in Harlem, and it also gave Johnson respect and credibility with the Italian mob. Soon, St. Clair opted for retirement, and she turned over her number business to Johnson.

With the backing of the Italian mob, Johnson became "The Man" in Harlem. Johnson rubbed elbows with many Harlem celebrities, including Bill "Bojangles" Robinson, Lena Horne, Billie Holiday, and World Middleweight Champion Sugar Ray Robinson. Johnson was also the uncrowned "Crime Boss of Harlem," and no one could run an illegal operation in Harlem without clearing it with Johnson first and cutting him in for a piece of the pie.

From 1940 until 1968, Johnson acted as a "middleman," between the Genovese Crime Family, who operated out of Italian Harlem (the area surrounding East 116th Street), and the black gangsters operating out of the main section of Harlem. Johnson brokered numerous drug deals between black drug dealers and the Italian suppliers, who were importing the drugs from overseas. Johnson was also known as a "persuader," or a high-level gangster, who could settle mob disputes before they erupted into violence. It is estimated that during the time he was in power in Harlem, Johnson brokered deals, mostly drug affairs, involving tens of millions of dollars with the Genovese Crime Family.

In 1952, Johnson was indicted for conspiracy to sell heroin. He was convicted and sentenced to 15 years in prison. While he was at

Alcatraz, it was rumored Johnson helped three fellow inmates escape. Although he stood put himself, Johnson was said to have arranged to have a boat to pick up the three escapees, once they slipped out of prison and made it to San Francisco Bay.

Johnson was released from prison in 1963, and when he returned to Harlem, the local folk threw him a ticker tape parade. In December 1965, Johnson led a sit-down strike in a police station, refusing to leave, as a protest against the cops conducting unreasonable surveillances on his crew. Johnson was charged with "refusal to leave a police station," but at trial he was found not guilty.

On July 7, 1968, Johnson, under indictment by the feds for drug conspiracy, was at Wells Restaurant in Harlem at 2 a.m., munching on a meal of chicken legs and hominy grits, washed down by coffee. Suddenly, Johnson grabbed his chest, and he toppled to the floor.

With two lifelong friends at his side, Ellsworth "Bumpy" Johnson died of a heart attack at the age of 63, forever to be known as the "Harlem Godfather."

Kaplan, Nathan (Kid Dropper)

Nathan Kaplan was born on the Lower East Side of Manhattan in 1891. Kaplan took to the streets as a youth, and soon he became engaged in petty swindles, such as the "dropper" scheme.

When no one was watching, Kaplan would conveniently "drop" a wallet full of counterfeit money on the sidewalk. Then he would immediately "find" the wallet, and look for a sucker, whom he told, "Lookit, I don't have time to locate the owner. You take the wallet and find the owner. Give me half of what you think the reward money will be."

Dupes constantly fell for this scheme, hence Kaplan was given the nickname "Kid Dropper."

Because of his expertise in making an illegal buck, Dropper joined Paul Kelly's (Paolo Vaccarelli) Five Points Gang, which was quite unusual for the Jewish Dropper, since the vast majority of Kelly's gang members were of Italian descent.

Yet, Dropper did not last too long with the Five Pointers. In 1911, he was arrested for armed robbery and sentenced to seven years in Sing Sing Prison. By the time Dropper was released in 1917, Kelly's gang had been disbanded. Dropper, considered a minor criminal before he went to jail, fancied himself as successor to Kelly, and he grabbed Kelly's labor rackets business.

In his past life, Dropper was a habitual wearer of slovenly attire, in other words, he dressed like a bum. Now as a boss, Dropper started to dress accordingly. He threw away his normal rags, and started prancing around the streets in loud checkered suits, pointed shoes, shirts and ties with loud colors and outlandish designs, and a straw hat or a derby tilted rakishly over one eye.

Dropper soon compiled a motley crew of low-level gangsters. He called his gang, "The Rough Riders of Jack Dropper." However, Dropper soon found himself in a war for control of Kelly's old rackets with an old foe who had just been released from prison himself.

Before his incarceration, Dropper had made a very bad enemy in fellow Five Pointer Johnny Spanish, a Spanish Jew; real name Joseph Weyler. The two men had been pals, until 1911, when

Spanish had to take it on the lam for a shooting which resulted in the death of an innocent eight-year-old girl. Spanish split town for a few months, and when he came back he found Dropper had stolen his girlfriend. Spanish, who carried four guns with him at all times, proceeded to pepper his former lover with multiple gunshots. Somehow the woman survived, but Spanish got seven years in prison for his actions.

When he was released in 1917, Spanish took dead aim at Dropper and every illegal activity Dropper controlled. Each man had approximately three dozen shooters under their wings, and these shooters went to work, resulting in the deaths of several men on both sides. The war ended, when Dropper got the drop on Spanish, so to speak, after he and two of his men ambushed Spanish as Spanish exited a restaurant at 19 Second Avenue. When the dust settled, Spanish was dead, and Dropper was now in charge of all the strong-arm tactics used by several unions to control their men.

Between 1920 and 1923, Dropper and his gang were responsible for more than 20 murders. However, in these rackets, when you kill one competitor, another one usually emerges from the shadows intent on doing to you what you did to the other guy, to gain control of whatever illegal activities you dominated. This person emerged in the name of Jacob "Little Augie" Orgen.

Little Augie had in his stable a crew of every capable killers, which included Jack "Legs" Diamond, Louis "Lepke" Buchalter, and Gurrah Shapiro. In 1922 and 1923, Dropper's gang and Little Augie's gang turned Manhattan into one big shooting gallery. The result was 23 murders, including the death of one innocent man who just happened to be in the wrong place at the wrong time.

In 1923, Dropper was arrested on a concealed weapons charge. He was soon released outside the Essex Market Court, on Second Avenue and Second Street. There were rumors that a death squad was awaiting his release, so as he stepped into a waiting taxi, Dropper was surrounded by a phalanx of cops.

Dropper was sitting in the back seat of the taxi next to Detective Jesse Joseph, when a minor thug working for Little Augie, named Louis Kushner, rushed from behind the cab and shot Dropper through the closed window, twice in the head.

Dropper's wife rushed to her mortally wounded husband, and said, "Nate! Nate! Tell me you were not what they say you were."

Dropper gasped, and with his last breath he said, "They got me."

Then he keeled sideways, dead, his head nestled on Detective Joseph's shoulder.

Kushner, restrained by several burly cops, was obviously proud of his handiwork. He smiled at the coppers, and snapped, "I got him! Now give me a cigarette!"

Kelly, Paul (Paulo Vaccarelli)

In the early 1900's, Paul Kelly was the most high-profile gangster in New York City. Real name Paulo Vaccarelli, Kelly was born in Sicily in 1879. He immigrated to America in the early 1890's, and soon became a bantamweight boxer of some repute. He changed his name from the Italian Vaccarelli to the Irish-sounding Kelly, in order to get more fights, at a time when being Italian in America was considered being a low-class citizen of ill repute.

Unlike most gangsters of his day, Kelly was an intelligent, erudite man, who could speak three languages. Kelly was a dapper dresser and an easy person to like, which is why he was able to recruit so many quality gangsters to work for him.

After Kelly retired from boxing, he formed the notorious Five Points Gang in Lower Manhattan. The 1,500-member Five Points Gang was the breeding ground for some of the most famous gangsters ever to set foot in America. Their members included Johnny Torrio and Al Capone (both of whom later emigrated to control Chicago), Meyer Lansky, Bugsy Siegel, Lucky Luciano, and Frankie Yale.

While Kelly's gang was almost entirely comprised of Italians, his main nemesis was Monk Eastman, who headed a 2000-strong, mostly Jewish gang. Kelly and Eastman's crew fought often and violently. The dividing line between their territories was the Bowery. Kelly's domain was west of the Bowery, and Eastman ruled to the east of the Bowery. Everything else was neutral territory, and that's where the trouble began, resulting in disputes over who controlled what and where.

Both Kelly and Eastman worked for Tammany Hall as head-busters on Election Day, when either one group, or the other, would stand guard at all the polling places, making sure that the Tammany Hall-backed candidate won the election. Finally, the two gangs became so out-of-control dangerous to the community, the Tammany Hall bosses ordered Eastman and Kelly to duke it out, mano a mano, with the winner getting control of the prized neutral territories.

The two men went at it for a full two hours, and even though the ex-boxer Kelly was 50 pounds lighter than the hulking Eastman, neither man was able to knock the other man out. The fight was ruled a draw, and Kelly and Eastman went back to their usual violent territorial disputes.

Kelly's base of operations was his fancy New Brighton Athletic Club on Great Jones Street, just north of Houston Street. In April 1905, police raided the club, and they arrested several members, including Kelly. Even though four policemen testified they had witnessed illegal activities in the club, due to the false testimony of a police captain named Burke and a Tammany Hall-appointed judge named Barlow, Kelly's case was summarily dismissed, to the roar of a cheering crowd of hundreds of Kelly's supporters assembled in the courtroom.

In November 1908, Kelly's luck ran out, when two of his former henchmen, Biff Ellison and Razor Riley, barged into the New Brighton Athletic Club, with guns blazing. Kelly was sitting at a table with his two bodyguards, Bill Harrington and Rough House Hogan. Kelly dove under the table, but not before he was shot three times. Harrington took a bullet in the head, and he died instantly. Kelly fired back from under the table, and he injured both Ellison and Riley.

Even though he recovered from his injuries, Kelly's clout was never the same after the shooting incident. Within days, since Kelly's new-found notoriety had cost him the favor of Tammany Hall, police shut down the New Brighton Athletic Club. Kelly relocated to Italian Harlem, and he toned down his criminal activities, to a point. Kelly became intimately involved in union activities, some legal and some not-so-legal. Through intimidation and strong-arm tactics, Kelly was eventually elected vice president of the International Longshoremen Association.

Unlike his arch enemy Eastman, who was shot to death on the streets in 1920, Kelly died in 1936 of natural causes.

Lansky, Meyer

Born Majer Suchowlinki on July 4 1902, in Grodno, Poland, Meyer Lansky was considered one of the great masterminds of the modern day mob.

In 1911, Lansky's family immigrated to New York City, and

they took up residence at 6 Columbia Street on the Lower East Side of Manhattan. As a boy, Lansky learned the trade of tool and die making. He also dabbled as an auto mechanic, and for a short time he worked in a factory. Tired of the 9-5 drag, Lansky hooked up with fellow Lower East Sider, Benjamin "Bugsy" Siegel (no one called him Bugsy to his face), and they started an auto-theft racket. Siegel would steal the cars. Lansky would get them in good working order, and then sell them.

They soon formed the violent "Bugs and Meyer Mob," which delved heavily in the illegal booze business. When Lansky and Siegel weren't hired as muscle to protect other bootlegger's shipments, they were hijacking liquor trucks themselves, sometimes even the trucks of the bootleggers whom they were supposed to be protecting.

The "Bugs and Meyer Mob" was also intimately involved in violent "schlammings" (beating up people for a fee) and a few murders, as long as the price was right. The murder business was so lucrative, several of the "Bugs and Meyer Mob" alumni eventually became key members of "Murder Incorporated," which terrorized the streets of New York City in the 1930's. These killers included Joe "Doc" Stacher, Joe Adonis, Abner "Longie" Zwillmen, and Arthur "Dutch Schultz" Flegenheimer.

As a young man, Lansky became fast friends with Italian mobster Lucky Luciano. Lansky and Luciano joined forces with men like Arnold "The Brain" Rothstein, and they began to run their crime enterprises like a business, with violence used only as a last resort.

In 1931, after the deaths of Mafia bosses Salvatore Maranzano and Joe "The Boss" Masseria (both were ordered killed by Luciano), Lansky and Luciano transformed the mob into one National Crime Syndicate, with men of assorted nationalities on their "Board of Directors." Not only did this Crime Syndicate engage in illegal activities, such as gambling, hijackings, shakedowns, and loansharking, but they also controlled the labor unions, which oversaw the shipping and trucking industries, as well as public works projects. Lansky also partnered with mob boss Frank Costello, to corner the illegal slot-machine markets throughout the country.

Even though most of his mob boss associates were in the Italian Mafia, Lansky had as much say as the Italians. In fact, most people considered Lansky "the brains of the operation," while the Italians mostly provided the muscle. Because he was short in stature, Lansky was dubbed "The Little Man," However, this was not a derogatory term. Lansky's vote on any crime issue usually took precedence over anyone else's vote.

After Luciano went to jail on a trumped-up prostitution charge, Siegel convinced Lansky that there was money to be made in the desert of Las Vegas, Nevada, which was then little more than a "comfort station" for weary travelers. Lansky formed the Nevada Projects Corporation, and Las Vegas was born.

Unfortunately, Siegel did not live long enough to reap the mob's Las Vegas profits. Siegel was suspected of skimming the mob's construction cash, and in 1947, Siegel was shot through the eye, as he sat in the living room of his girlfriend Virginia Hill's mansion in Beverly Hills. Rumors arose that Lansky voted against killing his longtime pal Siegel, but in fact, Lansky agreed, saying, "I had no choice."

Lansky invested heavily in the casino gambling operations in Cuba. However in 1959, Lansky lost everything, when Fidel Castro took over the rule of Cuba from Fulgencio Batista in a military coup.

With the United States government cracking down on the mob in Las Vegas, Lansky fled to Israel to avoid arrest. He tried to claim Israeli citizenship under "The Law of Return," a rule that gave citizenship to anyone born of a Jewish mother. After lengthy court battles, Lansky's pleas for citizenship in Israel were turned down, and he was sent back to America. In 1973, law enforcement officials tried to jail Lansky on tax evasion charges, like they had done with Al Capone four decades earlier. However, Lansky was acquitted at trial, which gave the government a big black eye.

After undergoing open heart surgery in 1973, Lansky spent the rest of his life as a sickly man. Stricken with lung cancer, Meyer Lansky died at his home in Miami Beach, Florida, in January 1983, at the age of 80.

Leslie, George Leonidas

George Leonidas Leslie started out in life as one of the privileged class. However, Leslie soon became a criminal, known by the New York City Police as "King of the Bank Robbers."

Leslie was born in Cincinnati in 1840. His father owned a brewery, and Leslie started out as an academic, graduating from the University of Cincinnati with honors and a degree in architecture.

After both his parents had died, Leslie sold his father's brewery. He gave up his architectural career, and he moved to New York City. There Leslie fell in with a bad crowd, and he decided he could make a darn good living by robbing banks. It is estimated, that in the 10-year period spanning 1874-1884, Leslie was responsible for 80 percent of all bank robberies committed in the United States; swiping cash estimated to be between 7-12 million dollars.

In New York City, Leslie posed as a man-about-town of considerable means. He belonged to the most exclusive clubs, and he was a regular theatergoer and a patron of the arts. Leslie used this false pretense to gain access to valuable bits of information, that made his bank-robbing life most profitable.

Leslie would often spend as much as three years planning a bank job. When he found a bank to his liking, Leslie would try to get the blueprints of the interior of the bank. If that were not possible, Leslie would visit the bank posing as a depositor. With his experience in architecture, Leslie would then draw up rough plans, detailing the intricacies of the inside of the bank. Sometimes, Leslie would have one of his gang members get a job at the bank, either as a night watchman, or a porter. These "inside men" would provide Leslie with the exact specifications of the inside of the bank, and the make and model of the bank vault.

After obtaining all this valuable information, Leslie would then buy a duplicate of the bank's safe. Leslie spent days, and sometimes weeks, perfecting the art of opening that safe. Leslie shied away from using dynamite to crack the safe, having decided that an explosion would cause too much noise and lead to them being detected.

Leslie method of opening safes included boring a hole

underneath the dial, then using a thin piece of steel to manipulate the tumblers into place. To cover almost any contingency in robbing a bank, Leslie had a set of burglar tools specially created for him, which cost the staggering sum of $3,000 - more than most people, at that time, earned in several years.

To perfect the job he was planning, Leslie sometimes set up a room in a loft he had rented downtown to resemble the inside of the bank he was planning to rob. There Leslie, and the men whom he had selected for that particular bank job, would spend considerable amounts of time practicing exactly how the bank robbery should develop. Leslie would darken the lights, and watch his men go through their maneuvers in the dark. He would then critique their work.

Leslie's cohorts consisted of various known criminals, such as Jimmy Hope, Jimmy Brady, Abe Coakley, Shang Draper, Red Leary, Johnny Dobbs, Worcester Sam Perris, Bill Kelly, and Banjo Pete Emerson.

In May of 1875, Leslie decided to rob the Manhattan Savings Institution at 644 Broadway. Leslie, through his "inside man" at the bank, Patrick Shelvin, found out the make and model of the lock on the bank's vault. Leslie procured an exact model from the manufacturers: Valentine & Bulter. Then, Leslie spent six months perfecting the opening of the lock.

On October 27, 1875, Shelvin let Leslie and Leslie's crew into the bank at night. When their work was done, they had stolen $3.5 million in cash and securities, almost $50 million in today's money. No one was arrested until May 1879, and as a result, Jimmy Hope and Bill Kelly were convicted and sent to prison. Abe Coakley and Banjo Pete Emerson were also arrested, but they were acquitted at trial. Leslie was never arrested, and his involvement in the bank robbery was not discovered until after his death.

Leslie's reputation grew to such gigantic proportions, he was often called in as a "consultant" by other bank-robbing gangs. It is believed, Leslie received more than $20,000, just to travel to San Francisco to look over plans for a local bank heist.

Yet, if Leslie had one weakness, it was for the affections of a woman. Leslie began an affair with the girlfriend of one of his cohorts: Shang Draper, a murderous thug of the worst sort.

On June 4, 1884, Leslie's decomposed body was found lying at the base of Tramps Rock, near the borderline between Westchester and the Bronx. He was shot twice in the head. Police speculated that Leslie was killed by the jealous Draper in a house at 101 Lynch Street in Brooklyn. Then Leslie's body was carted to Tramps Rock, by three of Draper's associates, who had been seen near Yonkers at the time Leslie's body was discovered.

However, there was little evidence of the crime, and no one was ever arrested for Leslie's murder.

Luciano, Lucky

Lucky Luciano was born Salvatore Luciana on November 24, 1896, in Lercara Friddi, a tiny town near Palermo, Sicily. Luciano immigrated with his family to America in 1907, and they settled in an apartment building at 265 East 10th Street. The rumor was that as a 10-year-old Luciano was a terror in Sicily, and he convinced a customs officer at Ellis Island to change his name from Luciana to Luciano, in order to avoid detection by several enemies he had made in the old country.

Luciano was not a model student. As a result, Luciano decided to work a racket in which he would confront skinny Jewish kids on their way to the public school he attended, and offer them, for a penny or two, protection from him not beating them up. Some kids paid, and some kids Luciano beat up badly. However, one skinny Jewish kid fought Luciano tooth and nail in an all-out street fight. The Jewish kid's name was Meyer Lansky, and they started a lifelong friendship that would be extremely profitable to both.

Luciano dropped out of school at the age of 15, and he worked in a hat factory for a while. Unfortunately, that was not the life for him. Looking for a different kind of work, Luciano started hanging out on Mulberry Street, and soon he became a charter member of the Five Points Gang, under the tutelage of their leader, Paul Kelly, with top-notch hoods Johnny Torrio and Frankie Yale as his mentors. Luciano became a "leg-breaker" for the Five Points Gang, and he was suspected of many beatings and maybe even a few murders. However, the Five Points Gang had their hooks into crooked cops and politicians, so Luciano was never brought up on any criminal charges.

By 1920, the Five Points Gang had splintered into several smaller gangs. Luciano saw potential in the rackets of Joe "The Boss" Masseria, who himself saw potential in the rough-and-tumble Luciano. Masseria treated Luciano like a son, and he made Luciano his top gun and second in command in all Masseria's operations.

However, Masseria didn't like the fact that Luciano did business with Jews like Lansky and Lansky's partner Bugsy Siegel; or even with Italians like Frank Costello, who was from Calabria, and didn't have Masseria's required Sicilian bloodlines.

Finally, Luciano decided Masseria had to go, and because Masseria was now involved in the Castellammarese War with rival Salvatore Maranzano, Luciano threw in with Maranzano with the intention of killing Masseria. To finalize his double-cross, Luciano lured Masseria to a Coney Island restaurant, and while Luciano was taking a bathroom break, Siegel and three other men barged in and shot Masseria to death.

After a few months under the strict rule of Maranzano, Luciano decided Maranzano, and his old-world ways, had to go, too. Furthermore, Maranzano felt the same way about the ambitious Luciano. As a result, Maranzano invited Luciano to a meeting in Maranzano's midtown office, where he planned to have Vincent "Mad Dog" Cole shoot Luciano into Swiss cheese.

Luckily for Luciano, he was one step ahead of Maranzano. Luciano sent four men, led by Samuel "Red" Levine, to Maranzano's office, where they shot and stabbed Maranzano to death. As they left the scene of the crime, the four men passed Cole in the ground floor hallway. They told Cole that Maranzano was already dead and not to bother going up to Maranzano's office. Cole shrugged, did an about-face and quickly exited the building, quite content in the fact that he had been paid in advance for doing absolutely nothing.

Luciano's next move was to unite all the disjointed mobs into separate, but equal groups; Italians and otherwise. With the assistance of Lansky, Luciano formed a National Crime Syndicate. However, Luciano's reign was short-lived.

In 1936, ambitious special prosecutor, Thomas E. Dewey, arrested, tried, and convicted Luciano on a trumped-up charge of prostitution. The key evidence against Luciano was provided by several pimps and prostitutes, who were more interested in staying out of prison than they were about giving truthful testimony. As a result, Luciano was sentenced to 30-50 years in prison.

However, after the end of World War II, Dewey, now Governor of New York, offered Luciano parole, for his "wartime services to his country." These services included Luciano's men providing protection on the New York City docks, most likely from themselves. The catch was, Luciano could never return to the United States and would instead be exiled forever to Italy. From Italy, Luciano still kept his fingers in mob affairs, even sneaking into Cuba to help Lansky run his lucrative casino businesses.

By the early 1960's, Luciano, due to several heart attacks, was an extremely ill man. Knowing his days were numbered, Luciano was contemplating providing details for a movie concerning his longtime connections to organized crime. Lansky and his pals were not too happy about these new turn of events. But before they could stop him, on January 26, 1962, Charles "Lucky" Luciano died of a heart attack at a Naples airport. He was on his way to meet an arriving scriptwriter to discuss the details of that never-made biographical flick.

Madden, Owney

Owney "The Killer" Madden was an anomaly in the world of the 1920 New York City gangsters, mainly because Madden was not Italian or even Jewish. Madden was British, the son of a relocated Irish dockworker, born and bred and dedicated for life to his homeland: merry old England. In fact, even though Madden was an American criminal for six decades, he didn't give up his English passport until 1950, after he was threatened with deportation.

Owen "Owney" Madden was born at 25 Somerset Street, in Leeds, England, on December 18, 1891. In need of work, his father moved the Madden family to Liverpool. In 1903, when young Madden was only 12, his father died, and his mother re-located her family to America, settling on the West Side of Manhattan in a treacherous neighborhood called "Hell's Kitchen."

Madden fell in with a rough-and-tumble gang known as the Gophers, and he became proficient in the favored crimes of the era: robberies, muggings, and labor racket beatings. Madden was adept at using a myriad of weapons, including a slingshot and brass knuckles. However, Madden's favorite weapon was a lead pipe, wrapped in newspaper.

Madden's main source of income was the "insurance business," where Madden sold "bomb insurance" to scores of local merchants who were worried about having their businesses bombed, of course, by none other than Madden himself. As a member of the Gophers, Madden was arrested 44 times, but managed to stay out of prison every time.

When he was 17, Madden earned his nickname "The Killer," after he shot to death an unarmed Italian in the street, for no reason, other than the fact that he could do so. After the killing, Madden stood over the dead body, and he announced to the assembled crowd, "I'm Owney Madden!"

By the time he was 23, Madden had at least five other murders to his credit.

One time, Madden's braggadocio almost cost him his life. On November, 6, 1912, at the Arbor Dance Hall, which was in the heart of the territory controlled by the Gopher's rivals, the Hudson

Dusters, Madden strolled into the hall by himself during a dance given by the Dave Hyson Association. Madden was watching the proceedings from the balcony, when 11 Hudson Dusters surrounded him and filled his body with six pieces of lead. Madden was rushed to the hospital where a detective asked Madden who had shot him.

"Nothin' doin,'" Madden said. "It's no business but mine who put these slugs into me. My boys will get them."

By the time Madden was released from the hospital, six of his 11 assailants had already been shot dead.

While Madden was recuperating, one of his fellow Gophers, Little Patsy Doyle, thought he could use Madden's weakened condition as a reason to take control of the gang. However, the main cause of Doyle's ire was that Madden had stolen Doyle's girlfriend, Freda Horner, away from him.

When word got back to Madden about Doyle's intentions, Madden used Miss Horner to lure Doyle to a saloon on Eighth Avenue and 41st Street, where Madden and two of his gunmen shot Doyle dead. Madden was arrested three days later, and at his trial, Miss Horner turned the tables and testified against Madden. Madden was sentenced to 10-20 years in Sing Sing Prison, but he did only eight, being released in 1923.

When he hit the streets again, Madden found his Gophers gang had dissipated, so he threw himself headfirst into the bootlegging business. As a result of his great bootlegging success, Madden moved up in class and was considered the equal of mobsters like Lucky Luciano, Frank Costello, Louis Lepke, Bugsy Siegel, and Meyer Lansky. Madden also dabbled in the night club business, opening the legendary Cotton Club in Harlem, which he bought from former heavyweight champion Jack Johnson.

His relationship with Johnson segued Madden into the boxing business, where he nurtured the career of Italian carnival freak, the 6-foot-6-inch, 285-pound Primo Canera. Madden fed Canera so many stiffs and setups, the no-talent Canera was able to win the heavyweight championship of the world. Canera did so by landing an invisible punch against champion Jack Sharkey in the 6th round at the Madison Square Garden Bowl, in Long Island City. Sharkey obviously took a dive and was reportedly paid handsomely to do so.

The first time Madden put Canera in tough, against Jewish heavyweight sensation Max Baer, Canera was knocked down 10 times, before the referee mercifully stopped the fight in the 11th round. Of course, Madden made big money betting on Baer, who, because of Canera's feared reputation, went into the fight as a slight underdog.

In 1932, Madden was arrested on a parole violation, and when he was released a few months later, he decided he had accumulated enough cash in a lifetime of crime to relocate to Hot Springs, Arkansas. There, Madden opened several casino/hotels, which were used as hideouts for New York City mobsters on the lam. To perpetuate his guise of respectability, Madden even married the Postmaster's daughter. In 1943, Madden was granted United States citizenship.

In 1965, after being stricken with emphysema, Madden died in his own bed, at the ripe old age of 74. He was said to have amassed a fortune of $3 million, but not surprisingly, none of that money was ever found after his death.

Mandelbaum, Fredericka "Marm"

Fredericka "Marm" Mandelbaum was born in 1818 in the country of Prussia. In 1848, she immigrated to the United States with her husband, Wolfe Mandelbaum. A big woman, tipping the scales at over 250 pounds, Mandelbaum opened a dry-goods store at 79 Clinton Street on the corner of Rivington. The dry-goods store was located on the ground floor of a three-story building, which Mandelbaum later purchased with her ill-gotten gains.

By 1854, the dry-goods store was a front for the biggest fencing operation in the history of New York City. Mandelbaum lived on the top two floors of the building with her husband, son, and two daughters. Their apartments were as lavishly furnished as any in New York City; furnished, of course, with stolen goods. Among the famous crooks Mandelbaum dealt with on a regular basis, were Shang Draper, George Leonidas Leslie, Banjo Pete Emerson, Mark Shinburn, Bill Mosher, and Joe Douglas.

Mandelbaum was known for throwing lavish parties in her apartment, attended by every known criminal, of both sexes, in New York City, including judges and politicians, whom she had in her back pocket. Knowing women were as good, or even better crooks than men, Mandelbaum became fast friends with female criminals like Black Lena Kleinschmidt, Big Mary, Ellen Clegg, Queen Liz, Little Annie, Old Mother Hubbard, and the notorious pickpocket and shoplifter Sophie Lyons. Lyons, along with her bank-robber husband Ned, moved right over the Hudson River to New Jersey, and she later became known as the "Queen of Hackensack."

In 1862, Mandelbaum first caught the eye of the police, and it is estimated that from 1862 to 1884, she handled between 5-10 million dollars of stolen property. Her business was so good, Mandelbaum decided to put some of her best crooks on salaries. However, Mandelbaum abandoned that idea quickly, when she caught a few of them peddling their stolen goods to other fences (What did she expect, honest crooks?).

As her business grew, Mandelbaum, imitating the Dickens character Fagin, decided to start a school for children on Grand Street, where little tykes could learn the noble profession from the ground up, starting as pickpockets and sneak thieves. For the older children, Mandelbaum offered courses in burglary, safe-breaking, blackmailing, and confidence games. Mandelbaum's school became so well-known, the son of a prominent police official applied for admittance, compelling Mandelbaum to shut down her school immediately and permanently.

Whenever Mandelbaum did get herself into trouble, she could always count on Little Abe Hummel and Big Bill Howe, from the law firm of Hummel and Howe (not to be confused with the law firm of Dewey, Screwem, and Howe), to find whatever loophole they could find, legal and illegal, to keep Mandelbaum out of jail. Hummel and Howe were of such good service to Mandelbaum, she placed them on an annual retainer of $5,000.

In 1884, the New York District Attorney, Peter B. Olney, hired the Pinkerton Detective Agency to infiltrate Mandelbaum's criminal organization. One of the detectives sold her a stolen shipment of silk, and when her house was raided the next day, Mandelbaum was arrested, along with her son Julius and clerk Herman Stroude. Mandelbaum was charged with grand larceny and receiving stolen goods (pieces of silk and satin worth $633). However, the wily Hummel and Howe arranged for Mandelbaum's release on bail. Resorting to form, Mandelbaum jumped bail, and she moved to Toronto, Canada, where she lived the rest of her life in comfort.

To add insult to injury, the state of New York got hoodwinked by Hummel and Howe, and a crooked bondsman, who was supposed to have held the property Mandelbaum had pledged for bail. Using backdated checks, these three gyp-artists transferred the property to Mandelbaum's daughter, along with other properties the state was in the process of putting liens on.

Jabbing her finger in the eye of the New York City police, Mandelbaum, still wanted for her numerous crimes, traveled several times to New York City, in disguise, to take up with her old criminal pals, helping them plan several heists.

In 1894, after having screwed the American government as much as any woman in American history, Marm Mandelbaum died of natural causes in Canada at the age of 76.

Big Bill Howe died peacefully in his own bed in 1903. However, in 1905, Little Abe Hummel was sent to prison after being convicted of several counts of legal malpractice.

To paraphrase Meat Loaf, one out of three ain't bad.

Maranzano, Salvatore

Salvatore Maranzano was the Mafia leader who organized the first Cosa Nostra in America.

Maranzano was born in Castellammare del Golfo, Sicily, in 1886. As a young man, the college-educated Maranzano studied to become a priest, but then he did a 180-degree turn and became a Mafioso instead. Maranzano came under the influence of Sicilian Mafia Boss, Don Vito Cascio Ferro, who groomed Maranzano to be his second-in-command.

In 1925, Ferro sent Maranzano to America to organize the Sicilian crime families into one powerful group. Ferro eventually planned to come to America himself and assume the title of "Capi de Tutti Capi" (Boss of All Bosses). Unfortunately, Ferro was arrested in 1926 by Sicilian prefect Cesare Mori, on a trumped-up charge and sentenced to life in prison. This opened the door for Maranzano to take Ferro's place at the top of the Mafia heap in America.

When Maranzano arrived in America, he worked ostensibly in the real estate business, when in fact, he was a major bootlegger, who specialized in "homebrew." Maranzano employed hundreds of people to produce illegal booze in their homes, which Maranzano's men distributed throughout New York and New Jersey, and even as far as Pittsburgh.

Maranzano's long-range plan was to unseat New York's top Mafia chief, Joe "The Boss" Masseria, then reorganize the fractured crime families, including non-Italians, into one large organization with several "Bosses" leading their individual families. Of course, Maranzano envisioned himself as the "Boss of All Bosses." Masseria did not exactly agree with Maranzano's vision, and the result was the Castellammarese War, where the casualty count, in both Masseria and Maranzano's ranks, totaled over 50 dead bodies.

In 1928, in order to achieve his goal, Maranzano tried to recruit Masseria's top lieutenant, Charles "Lucky" Luciano, to take out Masseria. Luciano balked at first, but in 1931, Luciano, tired of Masseria's greed, and also tired of Masseria's ban on Luciano working with non-Sicilians, switched sides and agreed to take out Masseria. Luciano lured Masseria to an Italian Restaurant in Coney

Island, and with Luciano conveniently in the men's room, four men, led by deranged killer Bugsy Siegel, filled Masseria's belly with lead, to go with the Chicken Parmesan he had eaten earlier.

With Masseria out of the way, Maranzano was now on top of the American Mafia world. Or so he thought.

Maranzano summoned more than 500 Mafioso to a meeting in the Bronx. At this meeting, Maranzano outlined a Roman Empire-style organization, with the entire New York Mafia divided into five families, each with a boss, an underboss, lieutenants, and soldiers. Maranzano dubbed his new organization the "Cosa Nostra," or "Our Thing." Of course, Maranzano officially anointed himself "Boss of All Bosses," which did not sit well with Luciano and his Italian pals, which included Frank Costello, Vito Genovese, and Joe Adonis; nor with Jewish gangsters Meyer Lansky, Louie "Lepke" Buchalter, and Bugsy Siegel.

Maranzano, ever the wily fox, knew Luciano had the adulation of many of the top New York City mobsters and would eventually try to wrest control of the organization from Maranzano. As a result, Maranzano compiled a "death list" of guys who had to go. Luciano's name stood right at the top of the list.

Maranzano struck a deal with kill-crazy, Vincent "Mad Dog" Cole, to murder both Luciano and Genovese, while they were present at a meeting in Maranzano's midtown office. Maranzano gave Cole $25,000 down, with $25,000 more, due upon the completion of his task. However, Luciano caught wind of the plot, and on the same day Luciano and Genovese were supposed to be killed, Luciano sent his own execution squad to Maranzano's office, which consisted of four Jewish gangsters led by capable killer, Red Levine.

On September 10, 1931, while Maranzano was awaiting the arrival of Luciano and Genovese, four men barged into Maranzano's outer office, flashing badges. They threw Maranzano's bodyguards against the wall, frisked them, and relieved them of their weapons. Then the four killers strode into Maranzano's inner office, where they stabbed and shot him to death.

The killers rushed from Maranzano's office, bypassed the elevator, and hurried down the emergency stairwell. They were followed by the two Maranzano bodyguards, who were now out of work, and seeking employment. The killers crossed paths with "Mad

Dog" Cole, who was ready to enter the stairwell to do in Luciano and Genovese, who were nowhere near the premises.

When Levine informed Cole about Maranzano's demise, Cole did an immediate about-face, and then rushed out of the building, whistling a happy tune. Due to the unexpected turn of events, Mad Dog Cole was $25,000 richer, without having to kill anyone.

Masseria, Joe (The Boss)

Joe "The Boss" Masseria was an uncouth mobster who enjoyed killing as much as he enjoyed eating, and he enjoyed eating a lot.

In 1903, the 5-foot-2-inch Masseria fled Sicily, because he had murdered someone and was not cool about cooling his heels in a Sicilian prison for the rest of his life. Masseria landed in New York City, and he immediately became part of the vicious Morello Gang, America's first Italian organized crime family.

The Morello gang was headed by Joe Morello and his brother Nick; killers so proficient, they were reportedly responsible for scores of murders themselves. The Morello Brothers also employed two other vicious henchmen: Lupo "The Wolf" (real name Ignazio Saietta, of the Black Hand fame), and half-brother Ciro Terranova, who later became the "Artichoke King" in New York City.

However, the greedy, ambitious, and treacherous Masseria did not like taking a back seat to anyone. As a result, after Lupo the Wolf, Joe Morello, and Terranova were sent to prison for various crimes, including a counterfeiting charge, Masseria planned to snatch the reins of the organized crime family from the Morello brothers. Masseria joyfully pulled the trigger himself, killing several Morello loyalists. After Nick Morello was killed by men from the Neapolitan Camorra (Naples' version of the Mafia) in Brooklyn, it left Masseria in charge of all the local Manhattan rackets.

For the next few years, there were several hit attempts on Masseria's life, but Masseria always emerged unscathed. In 1922, Masseria left his apartment at 82 Second Avenue, protected by two bodyguards. He was met by a hail of bullets, fired at close range by two men, one of whom Masseria recognized as Rocco Valenti. Masseria's two bodyguards were shot dead, but Masseria fled into a millinery shop next door. Amazingly, even though the two gunmen had emptied their guns at Masseria, Masseria was able to bob and weave, and avoid any contact with the lead.

Soon after, Masseria set up a meeting with Valenti at a restaurant on East 12th Street, ostensibly to make peace. Valenti arrived with two bodyguards, but three of Masseria's men were waiting in ambush. Seeing imminent danger, Valenti made a mad dash across the street, looking for cover. After Masseria's men wounded Valenti's bodyguards, Valenti jumped on the running board of a passing taxi. Valenti was firing back at his assailants, when he was shot dead, reportedly by a young Lucky Luciano, a hood who would later play an important part in Masseria's demise.

To keep his empire running smoothly, Masseria hired young gangsters like Luciano, Vito Genovese, Joe Bonanno, and Thomas Lucchese to do his dirty work for him. Masseria was so fond of Luciano, he eventually made him his second-in-command.

The relationship between Masseria and Luciano became strained, when Luciano started doing business with two Jewish gangsters, Meyer Lansky and Bugsy Siegel, and also with Frank Costello, an Italian from the mainland of Italy. Masseria had one strict rule. He and his men could only do business with fellow Sicilians. Period. This did not go over too well Luciano, and he waited for the right time to take out Masseria, and gain control of Masseria's rackets.

In 1927, Masseria encountered a new threat to his supremacy in the name of Salvatore Maranzano, who came over from Sicily, as the underboss to Don Vito Cascio Ferro, the most powerful Mafia leader in Sicily. What happened next, was the Castellammarese War: a two-year bloody confrontation between Masseria's and Maranzano's men. During this time, Luciano, and his pals, ostensibly stood loyal to Masseria. However, reading the writing on the wall, they finally decided to throw their lot in with Maranzano.

On April 15, 1931, Luciano lured Masseria to the Nuova Villa Tammaro Restaurant, in Coney Island. After Masseria had stuffed his belly with an enormous amount of Italian food (Masseria was said to have the eating habits of a "drooling mastiff"), Masseria and Luciano sat down to play cards.

At 3:30 p.m., Luciano excused himself to go to the bathroom. While he was taking care of business, four gunmen busted through the front door: Vito Genovese, Bugsy Siegel, Albert Anastasia, and Joe Adonis. The four men fired repeatedly at Masseria, hitting him six times, before he dropped dead to the floor holding the Ace of Spades in his right hand.

Minutes later, when the police arrived, Luciano told them, since he had been busy in the bathroom, he had not seen who had killed Masseria; nor did he have the slightest idea who would do such a terrible thing.

The police doubted the sincerity of Luciano's statement, but since Masseria was held in such high contempt by the law, no one was ever arrested for Masseria's murder.

Mock Duck

No, Mock Duck is not an item on the menu of a Chinese restaurant, but rather the name of one of the most notorious Chinese gangsters ever to set foot in America.

Real name, Sai Wing Mock, Mock Duck was born in China in 1879. In the late 1890's, Mock Duck traveled to the United States. He immediately took residence in New York City's Chinatown, where he joined the Hip Sing Tong, a small group of Chinese gangsters led by Lem Tong Sing.

At the time, Chinatown was controlled by the powerful On Leong Tong, whose boss was the murderous Tom Lee. Soon, Mock Duck pushed aside Lem Tong Sing as leader of the Hip Sing Tong, and he took control of the tong himself. Mock Duck's first act as boss of the Hip Sing Tong was to demand fifty percent of the profits from Tom Lee's On Leong Tong. This did not sit well with Lee, and as a result, the Tong Wars of the early 1900's started in full force.

Mock Duck, knowing his Hip Sing Tong couldn't compete in total gang members against the On Leong Tong, joined forces with the Four Brother's Society to even up the numbers a bit. Still, the Tong Wars became a bloody mess for three decades, with many casualties on all sides.

On January 24, 1906, as a group of On Leong Tong members exited a building at 32 Pell Street, a dozen Hip Sing Tong members jumped from an alley on Doyers Street, and the fired as many as hundred rounds of ammunition at their rivals. Two On Leong Tong members were killed, and two were badly injured. This rampage was reportedly planned by Mock Duck, who ordered murders to be done, but very rarely got his hands dirty doing the actual killings himself.

The one exception was in 1900, when Mock Duck allegedly murdered a New Jersey tailor named Ah See, in front of 23 Mott Street. Mock Duck was tried three times for See's murder, but was never convicted.

Mock Duck lived in a top floor apartment with his family at 21 Pell Street, in the heart of Chinatown. The rest of the apartments in this building also housed Hip Sing Tong members. There had been several attempts on Mock Duck's life, so he was forced to wear a "chain mail" vest, in addition to always carrying two guns and a small hatchet for protection, just in case.

On January 12, 1912, Mock Duck narrowly escaped death, when two On Leong Tong members casually entered an apartment at 21 Pell Street. They opened fire at a group of Hip Sing Tong members, as the Hip Sings played a game of fan-tan, killing Lung You, one of Mock Duck's top henchmen. Luckily for Mock Duck, he was out of the building at the time and was not a victim of the shooting, which was obviously intended for him.

Mock Duck was finally arrested by the police in 1912 for the minor crime of running a "policy game," more commonly known as the "numbers racket." Mock Duck was convicted and sentenced to two years in Sing Sing Prison. When Mock Duck was released in 1914, he returned to Chinatown, and he assumed a very low profile in the Hip Sing Tong.

In 1932, Mock Duck briefly resurfaced in the news, when he, in conjunction with the American and Chinese governments, arranged a truce, officially ending the Chinatown Tong Wars.

Unlike most of his fellow Chinese Tong members, who were killed in the streets of Chinatown, Mock Duck died of natural causes, at the age of 72, in his Brooklyn home in 1941.

Morrissey, John (Old Smoke)

John Morrissey started out as a feared bare-knuckle boxer, but later became a street-gang member and a leg-breaker for the Tammany Hall politicians.

Morrissey was born in Templemore, County Tipperary, Ireland in 1831. The famed potato famine was in its infancy, but Morrissey's parents saw the writing on the wall. They immigrated to America in 1833 and settled in Troy, New York. Not being educated, but good with his fists, Morrissey was relegated to working as a collection agent for the local Irish crime bosses. While working as a bouncer in a Troy brothel, Morrissey taught himself how to read and write. Realizing his future was limited in Troy, Morrissey made the short trek to New York City. There, Morrissey made a name for himself as a rough hooligan, fighting often in bars and on the piers, just for sport.

One day, Morrissey engaged in an impromptu fight with Tom McCann, at the indoor pistol gallery under the St. Charles Hotel. McCann was getting the best of Morrissey, when a powerful McCann punch drove Morrissey over burning coals from a hot stove, which had been overturned during the fight. Morrissey's clothes and flesh were on fire, and with smoke comes from his backside, Morrissey leaped forward, and he immediately battered McCann senseless. Hence, Morrissey was awarded the nickname "Old Smoke."

After winning a few more battles, inside and outside the ring, Morrissey challenged world heavyweight champion Yankee Sullivan to a fight for the World's Heavyweight Title. The fight took place on October 12, 1853, at Boston Corners, on the border of Massachusetts and New York. Morrissey was battered throughout the fight, but he won by disqualification in the 37th round, when Sullivan hit Morrissey while he was down.

Buoyed by his newfound fistic fame, and now a member of the Dead Rabbits, a feared street gang, Morrissey was hired by the Democrats from Tammany Hall to protect the polling places from the Bowery Boy's gang, led by Butcher Bill Poole. Poole and his pals terrorized the polling places on election days, in favor of the

Native American, or Know-Nothing political party.

On Election Day 1854, Poole announced that he and 30 of his Bowery Boys were headed to a certain local election site to destroy the ballot boxes. Tammany Hall called on Morrissey to protect their interests, and with John A. Kennedy, who later became New York City's Superintendent of Police, they assembled a gang of over 50 Dead Rabbits. Itching for a fight, they stood in wait inside the polling place for Poole and his gang's arrival.

A man of his word, Poole arrived at the polling place looking to do as much damage as possible. However, as Poole scanned the inside of the polling place, he immediately realized his group was vastly outnumbered by Morrissey and the Dead Rabbits.

Not a good thing for Poole.

Poole met Morrissey in the center of the room, and after staring menacingly at each other for a few moments, without saying a word, Poole abruptly turned and left, taking his gang with him. Tammany Hall was so overjoyed by Morrissey's heroics, they gave him a free gambling house (under the protection of the New York City police, of course).

In 1855, Morrissey challenged Poole to a bare-knuckles fight, on a pier near Christopher Street. Poole accepted, but once the two men squared off, instead of fighting with his fists, Poole tried to crush Morrissey to death by squeezing Morrissey in a mighty bear hug. When Morrissey was nearly unconscious, a group of men barged into the ring, and they stopped the murder attempt.

A few months later, Poole was shot and killed by Morrissey's close friend Lew Baker at Stanwix Hall, a bar on Broadway near Prince Street. Both Baker and Morrissey were arrested for Poole's murder, but after three mistrials (rumor had it that Tammany Hall influenced some jurors in Morrissey and Baker's favor), the charges were finally dropped.

In 1857, Morrissey retired from boxing, and he went full-throttle into the gambling business. Morrissey eventually opened 16 gambling houses throughout the state of New York, including an exceptionally profitable one in Sarasota Springs.

From 1867-71, and with the backing of Tammany Hall, Morrissey was elected United States Congressman from New York. In 1873, tired of Tammany Hall's illegal tactics, which were only surpassed by the illegal tactics Morrissey employed himself,

Morrissey testified against Tammany Hall chief and thief, William "Boss" Tweed. Based on Morrissey's testimony and the overwhelming evidence of Tweed's treachery, the jury convicted Tweed on several counts of misappropriating government funds. As a result, Boss Tweed was sent to prison, where he subsequently died.

In 1875, as a reward for his service to his country, Morrissey was elected to the New York State Senate. Morrissey was still a Senator, when he died of pneumonia in 1878 at the age of 47.

In 1999, John Morrissey, A.K.A., "Old Smoke," was elected to the International Boxing Hall of Fame.

Orgen, Jacob (Little Augie)

Jacob "Little Augie" Orgen was born on the streets of the Lower East Side of Manhattan in 1896. He quickly ditched school and became known as a "schlammer," for the Benjamin "Dopey" Fein mob. "Schlammers," or "Sluggers" were basically head-breakers, who kept the union workers in line, by "schlammin'" them on the side of the head, with a club, or with a baseball bat, if they went against what their union leaders decreed. Orgen formed a little side gang call the "Little Augies," but he was strictly a small-time player under Fein.

After Fein was arrested for improprieties concerning the Amalgamated Clothing Workers of America, rather than go to jail for a long period of time, Fein, not as dopey as his name, cut a deal with the cops. As a result of being a rat, Fein lost his job and his influence with the labor unions.

Enter rival gangsters Johnny Spanish and Kid Dropper, who while Orgen was cooling his heel in prison on a robbery charge, spent the next several years fighting over control of the labor unions. In 1919, Dropper eliminated Spanish with a few bullets, and Little Augie, fresh out of prison, put his eyes on Dropper's domain.

Orgen's gang of mostly Jewish criminals joined forces with the gang of Solomon Schipiro, whose men, strangely enough, consisted mostly of Italians. Orgen and Schipiro were fighting a losing battle against Dropper's forces, so they decided to cut off the head: Dropper himself.

As Dropper was being released from prison on a gun charge at the Essex Market Court on Second Avenue and Second Street, Little Augie and his gang stood anxiously in the street outside the court, mayhem on their minds. A dozen cops surrounded Dropper, with their eyes on Orgen, who was rumored to be there to kill Dropper. The police pushed Dropper into a waiting cab, when out nowhere, a nobody named Louis Kushner rushed the cab from the back and shot Dropper twice in the head. Kushner denied all involvement with Orgen (but the cops knew better), and he was sentenced to 20 years-to-life in prison for the murder of Dropper.

Orgen immediately took over Dropper's rackets, and he enlisted a dangerous crew of killers, including "Jack Legs" Diamond, Louis "Lepke" Buchalter, and Jacob "Gurrah" Shapiro, to keep in line people who needed to be kept in line.

Pressure from the police (who were embarrassed Dropper was killed right under their noses), forced Orgen to abandon the labor rackets. Dropper segued right into the bootlegging business, supplying illegal hooch to various speakeasies around town. This did not sit too well with the bootleggers whom he had displaced in those joints.

Orgen was told, in no uncertain terms, by Arnold Rothstein and by Meyer Lansky, to get out of the bootlegging business, or bad things would happen to him real quick. Orgen ignored these warnings, so the offended bootleggers struck a deal with Louie "Lepke" Buchalter and Jacob Shapiro, offering them employment in their vast operations if they murdered Orgen.

On October 16, 1927, Orgen was walking in front of 103 Norfolk Street, with his new bodyguard Jack "Legs" Diamond, when a black touring car pulled up alongside him, guns a-blazing. Orgen was killed and Diamond severely wounded, but Diamond lived to die another day.

Orgen was buried by his estranged father, in a huge cherry-wood coffin, lined with white satin. On the top of the coffins was a silver plate that simply said: "Jacob Orgen – Aged 25 years."

Orgen was 33 at the time of his death, but his father, a legitimate, God-fearing man, considered his son dead eight years earlier when he could not convince Orgen to get out of the rackets.

Pioggi, Louis (Louie the Lump)

Louis Pioggi, affectionately called Louie the Lump, was a diminutive and dapper Italian-American Five Points Gang member. Pioggi thrust himself into the spotlight one starry night in Coney Island, when he snuffed out the life of Kid Twist, the boss of the former Monk Eastman Jewish Lower East Side gang.

Kid Twist's gang and the Five Pointers were in a constant battle for control of the Lower East Side rackets. Under Kid Twist's reign, Twist and his gang had made great inroads into the Five Pointer's territory. The ire was so great between the two gangs, they made the Hatfields and the McCoys look like choir boys singing in church.

Born in 1889 on the Lower East Side, Pioggi was basically a footnote in the history of the American gangster. Pioggi was a small-timer, who as fate would have it, fell in love with the same dancehall girl the more illustrious Kid Twist (Maxwell Zwerbach) was seeing on the side.

It was the custom at the start of the 20th Century, for gangsters who had more than a few bucks in their pockets, to break free from the dumps and dives on the Lower East Side and "go out on the town," to the wondrous expanses of Coney Island in Brooklyn. On May 14, 1908, Pioggi took a trip out to Coney Island to see Carroll Terry, a gorgeous Coney Island dancehall girl who was the regular squeeze of Kid Twist.

Unknown to Pioggi, Kid Twist was also in Coney Island to see Miss Terry, and he was accompanied by his bodyguard, Cyclone Louie, real name Vach Lewis. Cyclone Louie was a killer for Kid Twist, but he was better known as a Coney Island circus strongman who bent large pieces steel around his neck for a living.

Pioggi visited the dancehall Terry worked in, and he enticed her to have a few dances with him, which was her job anyway. Pioggi became hopelessly lovesick, and before he left he begged Terry to promise him, after her had shift ended, she'd come back to New York City with him. Saying anything to get rid of Pioggi, Terry said she would, but only if Pioggi left at once so she could do her job without his interference.

The real reason Terry gave Pioggi the bum's rush was because she expected to see Kid Twist shorty. And that she did, when just moments after Pioggi left, Kid Twist and Cyclone Louie made their grand entrance into the dancehall. Terry joined them at a table, and after a few drinks her lips loosened, and she told Twist about Pioggi's amorous advances.

Soon after, Pioggi returned to the dancehall, and he saw Kid Twist holding hands with Terry, with Cyclone Louie standing guard nearby. Knowing he had been had, Pioggi wandered into a dive on Surf Avenue, to drown his sorrows on the second floor of the saloon. Minutes later, Kid Twist and Cyclone Louie burst into the saloon and climbed the stairs. They confronted Pioggi.

"I just seen Carroll," Kid Twist told Pioggi. "And she said youse is the biggest bum she knows. So she says you are an active cuss, always jumpin' around. Let's see how active youse is." Kid Twist pointed to the open window. "Take a jump out of the window."

Pioggi was in no mood for the 25-foot jump, but when Kid Twist made a move for the revolver in his belt, Pioggi, as requested, quickly jumped out of the window. Pioggi landed on all fours, but he later found out he had fractured his ankle. Pioggi limped to a telephone and called Paul Kelly, the boss of the Five Points gang. Pioggi told Kelly what had transpired concerning Kid Twist.

"I've got to cook him," Pioggi told Kelly.

"Sure you got to cook him," Kelly said. "I'll send a fleet down. When my boys get there, you get these bums on the street and open up with your cannons."

Kelly's boys arrived an hour later, and when they did, they saw Kid Twist and Cyclone Louie having a grand old time in Terry's dancehall, laughing and talking loudly about Pioggi's daring jump. Terry had vacated the premises for a while and was nowhere to be seen. Pioggi sent a kid inside with a note, telling Kid Twist that Terry was waiting for him outside.

As soon as Kid Twist and Cyclone Louie made it to the sidewalk, Kid Twist heard a voice call him from the side.

"Over this way, Kid," Pioggi yelled.

Before Kid Twist could react, Pioggi put a bullet in his head, killing him instantly. Cyclone Louie stood with his mouth open for an instant, then he started to run for his life. Pioggi and the Five Pointers chased Cyclone Louie, pumping bullets at him at a dazzling rate. Finally, shot five times in the chest and back, Cyclone Louie fell dead as a rock to the pavement.

Pioggi, still outraged, refused to stop shooting. As luck would have it, Terry showed up seconds later, and just for the fun of it, Pioggi pumped a slug into her hip. Terry fell on top of the dead Kid Twist, but she lived to dance another day.

As Pioggi jumped into a getaway car, a cop showed up at the scene. Pioggi fired again. This bullet knocked the cop's helmet off his head, but otherwise did him no harm.

Pioggi finally made his getaway, and he went into hiding, while Kelly contacted Tammany Hall to see if he could negotiate Pioggi a favorable deal.

A few days later, Pioggi turned himself in and pleaded guilty to manslaughter. He also testified that he had acted completely alone, which was quite disingenuous of him, since scores of people had seen the Coney Island executions.

Pioggi was sentenced to 11 months in Elmira State Prison. He left the courthouse sneering. "What's 11 months?" Pioggi said. "I could do that standin' on me head."

Rodgers, Mary, "The Beautiful Cigar Girl"

She was known as "The Beautiful Cigar Girl," but the 1841 murder of 20-year-old Mary Rogers remains one of the most baffling unsolved murders in New York City's history.

Rogers was a clerk in the upscale John Anderson's Tobacco Shop in downtown Manhattan. She was an amazingly beautiful girl, and famous writers like Edgar Allen Poe, James Fennimore Cooper, and Washington Irving, became her regular customers. Poet Fitz Green-Halleck was so smitten by Rogers, he wrote a poem in Rogers's honor. Many of the top newspaper editors and beat writers were also frequent customers at Anderson's; some just to get a brief glimpse of Rogers's beauty.

On Sunday morning, July 25, 1841, at a Nassau Street boarding house owned by her mother, Rogers told one of the boarders, her fiancé Daniel Payne, that she was going out for the afternoon to visit her sister, a Mrs. Downing. That night, New York was hit by a severe thunderstorm, and Rogers did not return to the boarding house. Both her mother and Payne figured, that because of the storm, Rogers was spending the night at her sister's house.

Yet on the next day, Rogers's sister told them that Rogers had never shown up at all, nor had she expected Rogers to visit. Joined by Rogers's ex-fiancé, Alfred Crommelin, they searched the city, but could find no trace of Rogers.

Unfortunately, this was not the first time that Rogers had disappeared. In October 1838, Rogers's whereabouts were unknown for several days. When she returned, she said she had visited a friend in Brooklyn, even though she had not told her mother, or her employers, of her intentions to do so.

After Rogers's second disappearance, Rogers's mother placed an ad in the *New York Sun* daily newspaper, asking if anyone knew "the whereabouts of a young lady, aged 20, last seen on the morning of the 25th, who was wearing a white dress, black shawl, blue scarf, Leghorn hat, light colored shoes, and light-colored parasol."

No one responded to the ad.

On Wednesday, July 28, at Sybil's Cave in Hoboken, New

Jersey, three men spotted something floating and bobbing on the New Jersey side of the Hudson River. The men jumped in a rowboat, and they quickly rowed to the area where the object was located. When they got there, they found the dead body of a young woman. They tired pulling the body onto the rowboat, but after a few unsuccessful attempts, they tied a rope under the dead woman's chin and rowed toward shore.

When the coroner examined the body, in addition to severe discoloration all over her once- beautiful face, he found a red mark, the shape of a man's thumb, on the right side of her neck. There were also several marks on the left side of her neck, the size of a man's finger, indicating Rogers had been strangled and her body dumped in the river. Crommelin, after reading the accounts in the newspapers of the body found in the Hudson River, traveled to Hoboken, and he identified the body as that of Mary Rogers.

Because of her popularity with the press, Rogers's death became front-page news in all the New York City newspapers. Members of the press cast suspicion on her fiancé Daniel Payne, who had told the police, that on the day of Rogers' disappearance, he had visited his brother and had spent the day bouncing to and from several bars and restaurants in New York City. To prove his innocence, Payne produced sworn affidavits from witnesses, saying he was indeed where he said he was on the day Rogers had disappeared.

The mystery of Rogers's death soon disappeared from the daily newspapers. The New York City police then consisted of motley night-time Watchmen and day-time Roundsmen, who were untrained and lowly paid commoners, with little incentive to solve crimes. These pseudo-policemen decided not to investigate any further, since the body of Rogers was found in New Jersey. The New Jersey police felt Rogers had most likely been killed in New York City and that the murder investigation was not their problem.

Frederica Loss owned a tavern called Nick Moore's House, near Hoboken, New Jersey, not far from where Mary Rogers's body had been found. On August 25, 1841, two of Loss's young sons, who had been playing in the woods, found various articles of women's clothing, including a handkerchief with the initials "M.R." on it. Mrs. Loss immediately notified the police of her sons' findings

This new discovery ignited an investigation by the New Jersey police, since they now decided Rogers had indeed been killed in

New Jersey. However, nothing became of the investigation and it soon ended.

Throughout the years, several criminologists tried to explain who killed Mary Rogers, and why. Yet no credible evidence has ever materialized and no one was ever charged with the crime.

A year after Rogers's death, Edgar Allen Poe, obviously saddened by the tragedy of "The Beautiful Cigar Girl," wrote his famous novel, "The Mystery of Marie Roget." The novel was set in Paris, and it duplicated the events that had occurred surrounding Rogers's death. In the novel, Poe's famous detective, Austin Dupin, concluded that the murderer was a naval officer of dark complexion, who had previously attempted to elope with Marie (Rogers), which explained her first disappearance in 1838. This mysterious Naval officer then killed Rogers in 1841 after she refused to marry him a second time.

Poe's novel closely mirrored the most credible explanation of Mary Rogers's death, which was put forth by author Raymond Paul in the early 1970s. Paul's theory was that Daniel Payne had murdered Rogers, but not on the Sunday she disappeared (for which Payne had a solid alibi), but on the following Tuesday. Because Rogers's body was still in rigor mortis when she was found, she could not have been dead for more than 24 hours. Rigor mortis starts scant hours after a person dies, but then after 24 hours it gradually dissipates.

Paul concluded, from the evidence compiled more than 130 years earlier, that Payne had gotten Rogers pregnant, and on Sunday July 25, 1841, he ferried her off to Hoboken to have an abortion. While her mother and former fiancée were looking for Rogers, Rogers was recuperating from the abortion in a Hoboken inn.

Payne then returned to Hoboken on Tuesday, July 27, to pick up Rogers and bring her back to New York City. When Rogers told Payne she was breaking off their relationship, Paul concluded Payne strangled Rogers, then dropped her body into the Hudson River. Paul also deduced from the circumstances that Rogers's brief disappearance in 1838 was for the same reason: to have an abortion.

After Rogers's death, Payne started drinking heavily. On October 7, 1841, Payne, after making the rounds of several New York City bars, purchased the poison laudanum. He took the ferry to Hoboken, then went to Nick Moore's House, where he got properly drunk. Soused, Payne staggered, holding a bottle of brandy, to the very spot in the woods where Rogers's clothing had been found.

There, Payne wrote on a piece of paper, "To the world, here I am on the very spot. May God forgive me for my misspent life."

Payne put the note in his pocket, drank the laudanum, and washed it down with the brandy. Then he laid down and died.

The newspapers, and the New York City police, thinking Rogers had been killed on Sunday, for which Payne had an airtight alibi, figured Payne had committed suicide because the love of his life had been murdered. Yet, the police investigation had been so cursory, incomplete, and totally inefficient, they never considered the fact that it was impossible for Rogers to have been killed four days before she was found, because her body was still in the state of rigor mortis.

Although the murder of Mary Rogers has never officially been solved, her death was not in vain. The complete incompetency of the New York City police force, combined with pressure from an outraged New York City press and populace, compelled the city to totally revamp its policing procedures.

Starting in 1845, Watchmen and Roundsmen became obsolete, as New York City finally created a police force, comprised of men specifically trained to prevent and investigate crimes.

Rothstein, Arnold (The Brain)

Arnold Rothstein was the most notorious gambler of his time; a bootlegger of great proportions and a master-fixer of everything imaginable. Rothstein was so adept at what he did, he reportedly fixed the 1919 World Series.

Rothstein was born on January 18, 1882, on the Upper East Side of Manhattan. His father, Abraham Rothstein, owned a dry-goods store and a cotton processing plant. Rothstein's father, a devout Jew, was also a mover and shaker in New York City politics, and he was called by his friends, "Abe the Just." Abe Rothstein was so popular with the New York City politicians, in 1919 a dinner was staged in his honor, which was attended by New York Governor Al Smith and Judge Louis Brandeis.

Yet, young Arnold wanted no part of his father's life. At the age of 15, Arnold began sneaking away from his fancy Upper East Side home to mingle with the fast-moving crowd on the Lower East Side of Manhattan. Rothstein loved to gamble, and soon he was a fixture at downtown card and dice games.

Having limited funds at that age, Rothstein would "borrow" money from his father in outlandish ways. As the Sabbath approached, Abe Rothstein would stash his money and jewelry in a dresser drawer in his bedroom. Young Rothstein, knowing his father's habits, would take the money from his father's drawer, spend all day gambling, then replace the money before sundown. One time, he even stole his father's watch and pawned it. That day, Rothstein won big at poker. Then before sundown, Rothstein redeemed his father's watch from the pawnbroker and put it back into his father's drawer, without his father being any the wiser.

Rothstein later explained his passion for gambling. He said, "I always gambled. I can't remember when I didn't. Maybe I gambled just to show my father he couldn't tell me what to do. When I gambled, nothing else mattered. I could play for hours and not know how much time had passed."

Successful gamblers sometimes make enemies, and Rothstein was no exception. In 1911, several gamblers, he had regularly taken to the cleaners, decided to teach Rothstein a lesson. As good as he was with dice and cards, Rothstein was even better with a pool stick. So his "pals" imported pool shark Jack Conway from Philadelphia to show Rothstein he wasn't the pool player he thought he was.

After Conway challenged him to a match, Rothstein got to pick the pool parlor in which they would play. Rothstein picked John McGraw's Pool Room, owned by the legendary former manager of the New York Giants. Every known New York City gambler was in the pool room that night, mostly betting against the cocky Rothstein. After Rothstein lost the first match to 100 (probably on purpose), he and Conway engaged in a 40-hour marathon, in which Rothstein won every 2 out of 3 matches they played. During that two-day period, Rothstein won thousands of dollars, and he earned a reputation of being cool and collected under pressure.

Rothstein's prowess at gambling caught the eye of local politician and a mighty fine crook himself: Big Tim Sullivan. Sullivan hired Rothstein, now called "The Brian" by his associates, to manage his gambling concession at the Metropole Hotel on 43rd Street. That was the big break Rothstein had been waiting for.

Rothstein parlayed his stint at the Metropole into owning his own gambling joint on Broadway, in the glitzy Tenderloin section of Manhattan. Rothstein's reputation attracted such known gamblers as Charles Gates (son of John W. "Bet a Million" Gates), Julius Fleischmann (the Yeast King), Joseph Seagram (Canadian Whiskey baron), Henry Sinclair of Sinclair Oil, and Percival Hill, who owed the American Tobacco Company. Playing poker, Hill once lost $250,000 in one night to Rothstein.

In 1919, after Prohibition was enacted, Rothstein became a major bootlegger. He fell in with several young criminals, including Lucky Luciano and Meyer Lansky, both of whom looked up to the classy Rothstein as their mentor. Rothstein made sure all his young Turks made money, by cutting them into every whiskey deal he was involved with. It was during this period, that Rothstein received his second nickname: "The Fixer."

Rothstein had sucked up to Tammany boss Charley Murphy, and using Murphy's clout, Rothstein fixed thousands of bootlegging criminal cases. Out of 6,902 liquor-related cases that made it to court, with Rothstein's influence, 400 never made it to trial and an incredible 6,074 were dismissed completely.

In 1919, through former featherweight champion Abe Attell,

several Chicago White Sox baseball players approached Rothstein about fixing that year's baseball World Series against the Cincinnati Reds. It's not clear whether Rothstein actually bankrolled the fix or turned them down completely. However, what is clear, is that Rothstein bet $60,000 on the Reds, and he pocketed a cool $270,000.

In 1928, the wear and tear of all his dealings and double-dealings had a severe effect on Rothstein. He started to lose more often than he won at cards. Rothstein's downfall started when he got involved in a marathon poker game, that began at the Park Central Hotel on September 8, and ended on September 12. Among the gamblers involved were Nate Raymond and Titanic Thomson. When the dust settled, Rothstein had lost $320,000 to Raymond and Thomson, which he refused to pay because he claimed the game was fixed.

On November 4, 1928, Rothstein was eating at Lindy's Restaurant, when he received a phone call requesting his presence at the Park Central Hotel to discuss the payment of his gambling debt. Before he left Lindy's, Rothstein told the waitress, "I don't pay off on fixed poker."

Because guns are traditionally not allowed at such meetings, Rothstein gave his gun to an associate to hold until he got back.

A few hours later, the Park Central doorman found Rothstein slumped over a banister in the hotel.

"Please call a taxi," Rothstein told the doorman. "I've been shot."

Rothstein was taken to the Polyclinic Hospital with a bullet in his gut. When the police asked him who had shot him, Rothstein replied, "Don't worry. I'll take care of it myself."

Rothstein fell in and out of delirium for several days. One afternoon, his estranged wife came to the hospital to see him. Rothstein told her, "I want to go home. All I do is sleep here. I can sleep at home."

Rothstein died a few hours later at the age of 46. No one was ever arrested for Rothstein's murder.

Arnold "The Brain" Rothstein's funeral was attended by every card-shark and gangster in New York City. Lucky Luciano said later about Rothstein, "Arnold taught me how to dress. He taught me how not to wear loud things, how to have taste. If Arnold had lived longer, he could have made me real elegant."

Schultz, Dutch (Arthur Flegenheimer)

Mob bosses come in all shapes and sizes. Some are brilliant. Some are just plain dumb. Almost all are homicidal maniacs. However, only one was a certified lunatic, and his name was Dutch Schultz.

In 1902, Schultz was born Arthur Flegenheimer to German/Jewish parents in the Bronx. His father abandoned the family at an early age, and young Flegenheimer took assorted jobs, including one at the Schultz Trucking Company. Despite his legitimate work at the trucking company, young Flegenheimer took up with a gang of crooks, who during Prohibition, did a little illegal importing of hooch (from Canada to New York City) on the side.

When he was pinched for the first time by the cops, Flegenheimer gave his name as Dutch Schultz, which was the name of the son of the boss of the Schultz Trucking Company. Later, the headline-happy Schultz would tell the press that he changed his name to Dutch Schultz because it fit in the newspaper headlines better than Arthur Flegenheimer did.

"If I had kept the name of Flegenheimer," Schultz said. "Nobody would have ever heard of me."

Schultz quit the trucking business, and he decided he could make a mint off the Harlem numbers rackets, where it was reported that the locals bet a staggering $35,000 a day. Schultz set up a gang that included crazed killer Bo Weinberg, mathematical genius Otto "Abbadabba" Berman, and Lulu Rosenkrantz, who could kill with the best of them too. Schultz and his crew invited the black gangsters, who ran the numbers show in Harlem, to a meeting. When the black gangsters arrived, Schultz put a 45 caliber pistol on the table and told them, "I'm now your partner."

And that cemented the deal.

Yet Schultz was not satisfied with just making a ton of cash off the Harlem numbers racket. He wanted to make 100 tons of cash; maybe even more. So, he enlisted the genius mind of Abbadabba Berman to rig the Harlem numbers game so that he could achieve his goal.

The *Harlem Age* newspaper, instead of using the *New York Clearing House Reports* for its daily three-digit number, used Cincinnati's Coney Island Race track to determine the winning numbers. The only problem was that Schultz owned that particular race track. So all Berman had to do was go over the thousands of slips bet that particular day, and before the seventh race at the track, he knew which numbers Schultz did not want to win. Then one phone call to the race track, and like magic, the final numbers were altered for Schultz's monetary benefit.

Schultz had one simple rule that helped propel him to the top: if someone stole a dime of his cash, that person would soon die. His longtime lawyer, J. Richard "Dixie" Davis, Schultz's conduit to the crooked politicians who protected Schultz's flank, once said, "You can insult Arthur's girl. Spit in his face. Push him around. And he'll laugh. But don't steal a dollar from his accounts. If you do, you're dead."

Two such men, who were deposited into the hereafter by Schultz, were Vincent "Mad Dog" Cole and Jack "Legs" Diamond. After Schultz's men pumped several bullets into Diamond's head in an upstate hotel, Schultz said, "Just another punk caught with his hands in my pocket."

The killings of Diamond and Cole propelled Schultz into the big time, and soon he became an equal in a syndicate of gangsters, which included Lucky Luciano, Louie "Lepke" Buchalter, Meyer Lansky, Albert Anastasia, and Joe "Adonis" Doto. While the rest of the crew were immaculate dressers, Schultz dressed one step above a Bowery bum. Even though he was raking in millions, Schultz never spent more than $35 for a suit, or $2 for a shirt.

Lucky Luciano once said of Schultz, "Dutch was the cheapest guy I ever knew. The guy had a couple of million bucks, and he dressed like a pig."

As for his insistence on not dressing up to his mob stature, Schultz said, "I think only queers wear silk shirts."

As time passed, the rest of the syndicate grew weary of Schultz's erratic ways. One such example of his lunacy was when Schultz, in order to beat a tax-evasion case in upstate Malone, New York, converted to Catholicism in order to butter up the all-Catholic jury. His scheme worked, and Schultz was acquitted on all counts.

Another time, at a syndicate meeting, Schultz became upset over a wisecrack Joe Adonis made about Schultz's chintzy clothes. Schultz, who had a bad case of the flu, grabbed Adonis in a headlock, and he blew hard into his face.

"See you (expletive) star. Now you've got the flu too."

Adonis did indeed catch the flu from Schultz, which did not make him and the rest of the syndicate particularly happy.

Schultz's downfall was his insistence that the syndicate kill New York City Special Prosecutor Thomas E. Dewey, who was on a mission to crack down on all the mobs, especially Schultz's. Schultz called a meeting of the nine-member syndicate, and he demanded Dewey's head on a plate. The other members thought killing Dewey was a terrible idea, because they were convinced, if Dewey was offed, an avalanche of criminal investigations would surely fall down on their heads. Schultz's proposal was voted down 8-1.

Schultz stormed from the meeting, saying, "I still say he ought to be hit. And if nobody else is going to do it, I'm gonna hit him myself. Within 48 hours."

The other syndicate members, knowing Schultz was not one to bluff, immediately voted unanimously that Schultz was the one who had to go; and quickly, before Dewey was dead.

On October 23, 1935, the day following the fateful votes, Schultz, Berman, Lulu Rosenkrantz, and Abe Landau were in the Palace Chop House and Tavern in Newark, New Jersey, ostensibly to discuss how best to do away with Dewey. Schultz was in the bathroom, when Charlie "The Bug" Workman and Mendy Weiss slipped quietly through the front door.

With Weiss standing guard outside the bathroom door, Workman quietly entered the bathroom, looking for possible witnesses. Instead, he found a started Schultz just zipping up his pants. Workman plugged Schultz once, right in the middle of the chest. Satisfied Schultz was dead, Workman and Weiss rushed into the main dining room, and they shot numerous holes into Berman, Rosenkrantz, and Landau, killing all three men.

Schultz was rushed to the hospital, and he lay delirious for two days. While lying in his hospital deathbed, Schultz spouted such idiocies as: *Oh Duckie, see we skipped again.* And, *Please mother, crack down on the Chinaman's friends and Hitler's commander.* And, *Louie, didn't I give you my doorbell?*

Schultz's temperature rose to 106 degrees, and on October 25 he fell into a coma and died. His former pals in the syndicate, overjoyed and more than little relieved, divided Schultz's prosperous operations equally amongst themselves.

Siegel, Benjamin (Bugsy)

Benjamin "Bugsy" Siegel is the man most responsible for the birth of the city of Las Vegas, which became the gambling capital of the world.

Siegel was born Benjamin Siegelbaum on February 28, 1906, in the Williamsburg section of Brooklyn. As a teenager, Siegel crossed the bridge to Manhattan, and he started a gang on Lafayette Street, which skirted the border of Little Italy, with another thug named Moe Sedway. Their main racket was shaking down pushcart owners for protection money, and if they weren't paid quickly enough, they burnt down the poor owners' pushcarts.

Soon, Siegel teamed up with Meyer Lansky, the man who would shape his life, and eventually, his death. Together they formed the "Bugs and Meyer Gang," which started out in auto theft and ended up handling hit contracts for bootleggers, who were having their shipments hijacked. This tidy little killing business was the forerunner to the infamous "Murder Incorporated," which handled hundreds of contract killings during the 1930's.

In the late 1920's, Siegel and Lansky hooked up with ambitious Italian mobsters Lucky Luciano, Frank Costello, Joe Adonis, Vito Genovese, Joe Bonanno, Albert Anastasia, and Tommy Lucchese. Together they formed a National Crime Commission, which controlled all organized crime in America, for many years to come. Siegel was the main hitman for the group, and in 1931, he led the four-man hit-squad which riddled Joe "The Boss" Masseria's body with bullets in a Coney Island Restaurant. Siegel developed the reputation as a man who not only killed frequently, but enjoyed killing, with the glee of a schoolboy on his first date.

In the late 1930's, The Commission sent Siegel to California to take over their West Coast rackets, including the lucrative racing wire, which transmitted horse race results to thousands of bookie joints throughout the country. Siegel pushed aside West Coast mob boss Jack Dragna, who was told by Lansky and Luciano, if he didn't step down and hand the racing wire reins over to Siegel, bad things would happen to him quickly. Dragna did as he was told, and Dragna soon disappeared from the California organized crime scene.

While in Hollywood, Siegel, who was movie-star-good-looking, was a renowned ladies man, who sometimes bedded down three or four starlets at a time. He hung around with such movie hunks as Clark Cable, Gary Cooper, George Raft, and Cary Grant. The girls he bedded included Jean Harlow, Wendy Barry, Marie McDonald, Virginia Hill, and Italian Countess Dorothy DiFrasso.

Even though Siegel was busy with the broads, he always found time to do a little killing on the side. In 1939, on orders from New York City Jewish mob boss Louis "Lepke" Buchalter, Siegel whacked Harry "Big Greenie" Greenberg, who was singing like a canary to the feds. Siegel was arrested for Greenberg's murder, but after a witness conveniently disappeared, Siegel was acquitted of all charges.

The bad publicity from the Greenberg trial ruined Siegel's man-about-town reputation in Hollywood. As a result, the Commission sent Siegel to the deserts of Nevada, to scout sites for a hotel/casino they wanted to build. Siegel found the perfect location in Las Vegas, and he convinced the boys from New York City, including his pal Lansky, to invest millions of dollars in an opulent night club, Siegel dubbed "The Flamingo Hotel."

The building of the "The Flamingo Hotel" was a disaster from the start. Siegel's insistence on only the best of everything skyrocketed the costs to a staggering $6 million, which annoyed his partners in New York City more than just a little bit. Furthermore, there were concerns that maybe Siegel was skimming a little construction money off the top, to fund his actions with the ladies.

In December 1946, the opening night of "The Flamingo Hotel" was an unmitigated disaster. Siegel had moved up the opening date from March 1947, while the hotel was still in the late stages of being built. Since "The Flamingo Hotel" did not show well (the lobby was draped with ugly drop cloths), the Hollywood crowd they had depended upon to generate business stayed away.

In a few short months, "The Flamingo Hotel" was more than a quarter of a million dollars in the red. Losing money on gambling was unheard of in the mob, and as a result, Siegel's partners in New York City made a business decision that Siegel's days on earth must end as soon as possible.

Contrary to what has been written in the past, longtime pal Lansky had no problem signing off on Siegel's death warrant.

Lansky said that "business is business," and Siegel was bad for business.

On June 20, 1947, Siegel was sitting on the living room couch, in the Beverly Hills home of his girlfriend Virginia Hill, reading the *Los Angeles Times*. Suddenly, two rifle bullets, fired from an open window, struck Siegel in the face. One bullet hit his right cheek and settled in his brain. The second hit him in the nose, then pierced his right eye.

Siegel's unseeing right eye was found on the floor, 15 feet from his lifeless body.

St. Clair, Stephanie (Madame Queenie)

She was chased out of the Harlem numbers rackets by Dutch Schultz, but when Schultz lay dying in a hospital bed from a bullet wound, Stephanie St. Clair had the last laugh.

Stephanie St. Clair was born in 1886, in Marseilles, a seaport in southern France. At 26, she emigrated to New York City, and she settled in Harlem. Almost immediately, St. Clair hooked up with the Forty Thieves, a white gang which were in existence since the 1850's. There is no record of what St. Clair did for the next 10 years, but it's safe to say, considering her ties to the Forty Thieves, a notorious shake-down gang, what she did was anything but legal.

In 1922, St. Clair used $10,000 of her own money, and she started Harlem's first numbers rackets. St. Clair was known for having a violent temper, and she often cursed at her underlings, in several languages. When people questioned St. Clair about her heritage, she snapped that she was born in "European France," and that she spoke flawless French, unlike the French-speaking rabble from the Caribbean. In Harlem, they called her Madame St. Clair, but in the rest of the city she was known as just plain "Queenie."

In the mid-1920's, known bootlegger and stone killer Dutch Schultz, decided he wanted to take over all the policy rackets in Harlem. Schultz did not ask St. Clair to back away too nicely, resulting in the deaths of dozens of St. Clair's numbers runners.

St. Claire enlisted the help of Bumpy Johnson, an ex-con with a hair-trigger temper, to take care of the Schultz situation. Johnson went downtown, and he visited Italian mob boss Lucky Luciano. Johnson asked Luciano to talk some sense into Schultz, before things got downright nasty. However, there was not much Luciano could do, since at the time Luciano was one of Schultz's partners in several illegal endeavors. Luciano suggested that St. Clair and Johnson throw in with Schultz, making them, in effect, a sub-division of Schultz's numbers business. This did not sit too well with St. Clair, and even though Johnson tried to convince her this was the smart move, St. Clair turned down Luciano's offer.

As a result of her refusal to buckle under to Schultz's demands, St. Clair began having trouble with the police, whom she was paying off to look the other way. This was the work of Schultz, who through his connections with Tammany Hall, had several politicians in his back pocket, as well as half of the New York City police force. While Schultz's number runners worked the streets of Harlem with impunity, St. Clair's runners, when they were not being killed by Schultz's men, were being arrested for illegal gambling.

St. Clair decided to fight back with the power of the press. In December 1930, St. Clair took several ads in Harlem newspapers, accusing the police of graft, shakedowns, and corruption. That did not go over too well with the local fuzz, and they immediately arrested St. Clair for illegal gambling. St. Clair was tried, convicted, and sentenced to eight months of hard labor on Welfare Island.

Upon her release, St. Clair appeared before the Seabury Committee, which was investigating graft in the Bronx and in the Manhattan Magistrates Courts. St. Clair testified that from 1923-1926, to protect her runners from arrest, she had paid the police in Harlem $6,000. She added that after the police took her money, they arrested her number runners anyway. Schultz had a good laugh over that one, since $6,000 was less than he paid monthly to keep the cops in New York City happy.

Nothing came from St. Clair's testimony before the Seabury Committee, so St. Clair decided to plead her case directly to New York City Mayor Jimmy Walker, who was almost as crooked as Schultz. St. Clair told Walker that Schultz was pressuring her to join his gang, or else. Walker, who was being investigated by the Seabury Committee himself, answered St. Clair by quitting his job as Mayor and relocating to Europe for the next few years, until the heat died down.

At her wit's end, St. Claire pleaded with the other black policy number bankers in Harlem to join forces with her in a battle against Schultz. Knowing that Schultz had too much juice in the government and too many shooters in his gang, the other Harlem policy bankers turned St. Clair down flat.

Bumpy Johnson soon found out that Schultz had put the word out on the streets that St. Clair was to be shot on sight. St. Clair went into hiding, refusing to even go outside to see the light of day. On one occasion, Johnson had to hide St. Clair in a coal bin, under a mound of coal, to save her from Schultz's men. That was the final straw for St. Claire. She sent word to Schultz that she would agree to his demands. Schultz sent word back to St. Clair, that she could remain alive as long as she gave Schultz a majority share of her numbers rackets. St. Clair reluctantly agreed.

Schultz had his own run of bad luck, when he demanded that Luciano and Luciano's pals, agree to the killing of Special Prosecutor Thomas E. Dewey, who was breathing down Schultz's neck. Schultz's proposition was turned down flat, and when he said he would kill Dewey himself, Schultz was shot in the belly, in the bathroom of a New Jersey restaurant.

Schultz lingered in a delirious state in a hospital for a few days before he died. As Schultz was laying there mumbling inanities, a telegram arrived, saying *"As ye sow, so shall you reap."*

The telegram was sent by the Queen of Harlem: Stephanie St. Clair.

Wanting to get away from all the tensions, St. Clair eventually turned over her number business to Bumpy Johnson. Not being the boss "Madame Queenie" any longer, St. Clair faded into obscurity, and she died in her sleep in 1969.

In the 1997 movie "Hoodlum," Lawrence Fishburne played Bumpy Johnson, Tim Roth played Dutch Schultz, Andy Garcia played Lucky Luciano, and Cicely Tyson played Stephanie St. Clair.

Sullivan, Timothy (Big Tim)

"Big Tim" Sullivan was a Tammany Hall hack who gave true meaning to the term "crooked politician."

Sullivan was born in 1863 at 25 Baxter Street, one of the worse slum buildings in New York City. At 25 Baxter Street, the squalor was so intense, in 1866, a *New York Times* article called it, "one of the filthiest tenements in New York City."

Sullivan's parents had emigrated from County Kerry, Ireland, and with them being so poor, Sullivan was thrust into the streets at the age of eight, to shine shoes and sell newspapers. Being the enterprising lad that he was, Sullivan soon saved up enough cash to start his own newspaper delivery service, in which Sullivan employed dozens of poor kids from the neighborhood to do his deliveries. In a few short years, Sullivan had enough cash to purchase four local bars; the first of which he opened on Christie Street, just east of the Bowery.

One of Sullivan's bar customers was Thomas "Fatty" Walsh, a notorious ward leader in Tammany Hall. Sullivan fell under Walsh's political wing, and in 1894, Sullivan was elected to the Third District's State Assembly.

Running roughshod over the rules, Sullivan became a large cog in Tammany Hall's corrupt wheel. Soon, Sullivan was appointed the District Leader of the entire Lower East Side of Manhattan.

That was like giving a vampire the key to the blood bank.

Sullivan bridged the gap between public service and common street thuggery, by recruiting infamous gang leaders, like Paul Kelly and Monk Eastman, to do his dirty work. This work included "voter influence" at election sites, which basically meant their gangs beat up voters who didn't see things exactly Sullivan's way.

In return for using his influence to keep these gangsters out of jail, Sullivan got a piece of all their illegal activities in the Lower East Side, including prostitution, gambling, loan-sharking, and extortion. To keep things looking on the up-and-up, Sullivan also entrenched himself in many legal endeavors, including becoming partners in the MGM and Loews cinema operations.

In Congress, Sullivan did pioneer a couple of key pieces of

legislation. In 1896, Sullivan introduced a law that made boxing legal, only to see it made illegal again in 1900 after several boxers were killed in the ring.

In 1911, Sullivan also passed the dubious "Sullivan Act" which made it illegal to carry guns, unless you could afford to pay a hefty registration fee. Needless to say, Sullivan's cronies made so much illegal dough, they all were able to cough up the cash needed to carry guns legally, in order to enforce their illegal activities. Yet, the common schmo on the street was so poor, he had no choice but to walk the mean streets of New York City without a firearm to protect himself.

In late 1911, Sullivan's evil ways finally caught up with him. Sullivan contracted syphilis, probably in one of the many prostitution houses in which he was a partner. As a result of this disease, Sullivan became paranoid and delusional. Sullivan was judged mentally incompetent, and he was removed from his seat in the Senate. In 1912, Sullivan's family placed him in a mental institution, which made his condition worse. While in the sanitarium, Sullivan complained he was being watched and that his food was being poisoned.

In 1913, while the guards were playing cards, Sullivan escaped from the sanitarium. Two weeks later, Sullivan's body was found near the railroad tracks in Pelham Parkway. It appeared, he had been hit by a freight train.

For some unknown reason, Sullivan's body was not claimed until 13 days later. The city declared him a vagrant, to be shamefully interred in a potter's field at Hart Island. As Sullivan's body was being readied for transport to Hart Island, a police officer made a final inspection of the corpse. He was astounded to discover that the dead man was, indeed, the missing Big Tim Sullivan. As a result, Big Tim was finally given a proper send-off.

After a jam-packed funeral ceremony at Old St. Patrick's Cathedral on Mulberry Street, an estimated 25,000 people lined the streets, as Sullivan's funeral reception made its way along Lower Manhattan and over the Williamsburg Bridge.

Sullivan was finally laid to rest at Calvary Cemetery in Long Island.

Torrio, Johnny

Giovanni "Johnny" Torrio, nicknamed "The Brain," "The Fox," and "Terrible Johnny," was born in Italy in 1882. His father died when Johnny was 2-years-old, and his mother emigrated with Torrio to America. They settled on the Lower East Side of Manhattan, where Torrio's mother remarried a grocer.

After working as a porter at his stepfather's grocery store (which was really a front for illegal activities), Torrio embarked on a life of crime. He soon became the boss of the James Street Gang, and with the money he saved from his ill-gotten gains, Torrio opened his own pool hall, which was the base of operations for his assorted crimes, which included burglaries, robberies, gambling, and loan-sharking.

Torrio caught the eye of Paul Kelly, the leader of the 1,500-member Five Points Gang. Kelly inserted the diminutive, but tough-as-nails Torrio as the bouncer at Kelly's nightclub on Pell Street, considered one of the roughest dives in Manhattan. In a short time, Kelly was so impressed with Torrio's business acumen, he made Torrio his second-in-command.

However, Torrio figured he could make more money by branching outside Kelly's gang. As a result, in 1912 Torrio moved his operations to Brooklyn, where he opened a bar with a hidden brothel, near the Brooklyn Navy Yard. His partner was the murderous Frankie Yale and one of their bouncers was a 19-year-old Al Capone.

In 1915, Torrio was summoned to Chicago by his uncle-through-marriage, "Big Jim" Colosimo, to help Colosimo rid himself of treacherous Chicago Black Hand shake-down artists. In Chicago, Torrio had killed whoever needed to be killed, and soon Torrio was in charge of Big Jim's numerous brothels. In 1919, Torrio brought Capone to Chicago, to help with the muscle he needed to keep things running smoothly in the flesh-peddling business.

In 1920, when Prohibition came into effect, Torrio saw the prospect for tremendous profits by importing, selling, and serving illegal booze. Torrio tried to convince Colosimo to pare down his brothels and to get into the illegal liquor business. However,

Colosimo did not see the potential of Prohibition, and he turned Torrio down flat.

Frustrated, Torrio concluded Colosimo was in the way of Torrio making some big money. In late 1920, Torrio imported Yale from Brooklyn, to put Colosimo permanently out of commission. A few bullets did the trick, and Colosimo was erased from the Chicago rackets.

After taking over all of Colosimo's interests, Torrio decided to convince Chicago's several other gangs: Italians, Irish, and Poles, to join forces, each with their own exclusive territory. Most fell into line, with the exception of the North Side Gang headed by Irishman Dion O'Banion. Again, Torrio called on his pal Yale, and in November 1924, while toiling in his flower shop, O'Banion was cut down by a barrage of bullets.

"Homicidal" Hymie Weiss took over O'Banion's operations, and his first order of business was to eliminate Torrio. When his limousine was ambushed by Weiss's shooters, Torrio narrowly avoided death. His dog and chauffeur were killed, but Torrio escaped with just two bullet holes in his hat. Torrio was not so lucky a few months later, when he was cornered in front of his apartment building and shot four times. The shooters were Weiss and George "Bugs" Moran.

For 10 days, Torrio was near death's door, and he was under constant watch by Capone and 30 of his best men. While Torrio was recovering from his wounds, he decided he would live longer if he got out of the Chicago rackets completely. Torrio was 43, and he had accumulated enough cash he could not spend it in several lifetimes.

So Torrio handed over all his operations to Capone, saying "It's all yours, Al. I'm retiring."

Torrio absconded with his wife to live in Italy for a few years, but then he returned to America. Back on his home turf, Torrio became a mentor to such notables as Lucky Luciano and Meyer Lansky, both of whom came to Torrio many times for advice.

In 1973, while sitting in a barber's chair in Brooklyn, Johnny Torrio died of a heart attack at the age of 75. Torrio died facing the door, his eyes wide-open, ever cautious to the very end.

Triangle Shirtwaist Factory Fire

If it weren't for the greed of the sweatshop bosses, this tragedy may never have occurred. However, on March 25, 1911, the Triangle Shirtwaist Factory Fire took the lives of 141 people, most of them women.

At the turn of the 20th century, working conditions in the New York City sweatshops were abysmal. Men, woman, and children toiled in dirty factories, warehouses, and tenements, doing menial tasks, that made the garment industry one of the most profitable businesses in the nation. Labor laws were inadequate and hardly ever enforced. Factory inspections were rare, and if they were done at all, the factory owners knew whose palms to grease to get high inspection marks, when the condemnation of their factory was the proper course of action.

In 1899, a law banning night work for women was declared unconstitutional. The absurd reason given by the courts, whose members were often in the sweatshop bosses' back pockets, was that the law "deprived woman of the liberty to work in factories at night, or for as long as they wished to." In 1907, this ruling was upheld by the New York Court of Appeals. Even though the International Ladies Garment Workers Union was formed in 1900, the sweatshop bosses hired thugs as strikebreakers, to keep the ladies' union in line, by force if necessary.

Of all the greedy sweatshop owners, the worst offenders were Max Blanck and Isaac Harris, who owned the Triangle Shirtwaist Company, located on the 8th, 9th, and 10th floors of the 10-story Asch Building at 22 Washington Place, on the corner of Greene Street. The factory produced women's blouses, known at the time as "shirtwaists." The firm employed around 500-600 people, most of whom were young female Jewish and Italian immigrants, who worked under horrible conditions, for 9 hours a day on weekdays, and 7 hours on Saturdays. The bosses were such tyrants, they charged their employees for needles and for other supplies. They also charged them a fee for using their chairs, and if one of the employees damaged a piece of goods, they had to pay three times the value of the item to replace it.

In 1908, Blanck and Harris formed a sham company union that served their purposes much better than it served their hundreds of employees. Several employees, who tried to join a legitimate union, like the International Ladies Garment Workers Union or the United Hebrew Trades, were quickly fired. The reason management gave for these firings was that because of poor economic conditions, they had to cut staff. Yet strangely enough, new workers were hired almost immediately after the dismissal of the others.

Because Triangle Shirtwaist Company had locked out their dismissed workers, Local 25 of the International Ladies Garment Workers Union called for a strike against them. Blanck and Harris hired union strike breakers, or "schlammers," to beat up the male pickets. They also hired prostitutes to mingle with the female workers in the picket lines, in order to cause disruptions. The police and the judges, obviously working at the behest of the owners, sided with Blanck and Harris. One judge even said at the sentencing of one picketer, "You are on strike against God."

On March 25, 1911, it was a cold and windy day. As the 5p.m. closing time approached, it was estimated that 600 employees, packed in like sardines, were working at the sewing machine at the Triangle Shirtwaist Company. Most were women between the ages of 13 and 23. The 5p.m. bell rang, and the women scrambled to get their coats and hats, and then they rushed for the elevators.

Suddenly, a fire broke out on the southeast corner of the 8th floor. It was later determined that the fire was inadvertently caused by a cigarette butt that had been thrown into a litter basket, near a sewing machine. An updraft of air sent the flames and smoke shooting upwards towards the roof.

The building had no sprinkler system, and the fire quickly enveloped the entire 8th, 9th, and 10th floors. Girls on the 8th floor ran to a stairwell on the Washington Place side of the building, but the door was locked from the outside. The fire was so intense, all the windows on the top three floors of the building blew out from the heat.

Some workers were able to jam themselves into the elevators, while the elevators were still working. Others, including Blanck and Harris, were saved because they were able to make it to the safety of the roof.

A passerby named Joe Zito, and an elevator operator named

Gaspar Mortillalo, used the only working elevator to make five trips up to the 9th floor; taking down 25-30 terrified people at a time. However, that elevator soon became inoperable too.

Within five minutes, the fire trucks had arrived, but there was not much they could do. Their extension ladders only reached the 6th floor and the stream from their hoses only reached the 7th floor. Rather than burn to death, people began jumping out of the windows, sometimes in groups of two, three, and four.

A man and a woman appeared in a 9th floor window, their clothes ablaze. They kissed, then hugged, and jumped together, their bodies smashing on the cold pavement below.

The firemen brought out safety nets to catch the jumpers, but it was hopeless.

One fire chief later said, "Life nets? What good were life nets? The little ones went right through the life nets, and the pavement too. Nobody could hold a life net when those girls from the ninth floor came down."

The fire only lasted 10 minutes, but when it was over, 141 workers had died; 125 were women.

Nine months after the fire, Blanck and Harris were put on trial on manslaughter charges. However, the trial, like the earlier building inspections, was a farce. The judge was Thomas Crain, a Tammany Hall appointee, and he had little interest in justice for the dead workers. Judge Crain manipulated a trial where only an acquittal was possible. It took the jury just 100 minutes to render a verdict of not-guilty.

This did not go down too well with the victim's families. The day after the not-guilty verdicts, hundreds of despondent victim's relatives stood outside the Tombs Courthouse. Blanck and Harris, surrounded by five police officers, tried to slither out of the building through the Leonard Street exit. When the two men were spotted, they were quickly enveloped by an angry crowd.

David Weiner, whose sister had died in the fire, charged at the sweatshop bosses, swinging his fist in the air.

"Not Guilty? Not Guilty?" Weiner screamed. "It was murder! Murder!"

Weiner quickly was subdued by the police, but he was so distraught, he fainted and had to be rushed to the hospital.

In 1913, the victim's families won a lawsuit against Blanck and

Harris. The families were awarded a measly $75 per victim, whereas Blanck and Harris were paid by the insurance company $60,000 more than the total reported loss of life and property. Ironically, in late 1913, Blanck was arrested again, for locking the doors to his sweatshop.

The tragedy of the Triangle Shirtwaist Factory Fire did not go for naught.

The New York State Legislature - whose members included future Presidential candidate Al Smith, and Robert Wagner, the father of the future Mayor of New York City by the same name - forced the state to completely rewrite its labor laws. The State Legislature created the New York State Factory Investigating Committee, to "investigate factory conditions in this and other cities, and to report remedial measures of legislation to prevent hazard, or loss of life, among employees through fire, insanitary conditions, and occupational diseases."

As a direct result of the Triangle Shirtwaist Factory Fire, The American Society of Safety Engineers was founded on October 14, 1911.

Tweed, William (Boss)

William "Boss" Tweed, head crook at Tammany Hall, stole so much money from the New York City coffers, by 1870 Tweed had become the third largest land owner in the entire city.

Tweed, a third generation Scottish-Irishman, was born on April 3, 1823, at 24 Cherry Street on the Lower East Side of Manhattan. His father was a chair maker, and the young Tweed tried to follow in his father's footsteps, but the lure of the streets became too much for Tweed to overcome. Tweed ran with a motley crew of juvenile delinquents called the "Cherry Street Gang," who wreaked havoc on local merchants by stealing their wares and selling them on the street's black market.

Soon, Tweed became boss of the "Cherry Hill Gang," and he (as did most gang members of that era) joined various volunteer fire companies, which were a springboard for men with political ambitions. Tweed helped found American Fire Engine Company No. 6, which was called the "Big Six." During his time in the volunteer fire business, Tweed forged friendships with people of all ancestries: Irish, Scottish, Germans - anyone who could help him climb the ladder of public service, with only one thing in mind, steal big and steal often.

In 1850, Tweed ran unsuccessfully for assistant alderman on the Democratic ticket. However, a year later Tweed was elected alderman, a non-paying job, but with unlimited power for anyone smart enough, and crooked enough, to take advantage of its perks. Just scant weeks after he became an alderman, Tweed brokered a deal to buy land on Wards Island for a new potter's field. The asking price was $30,000, but Tweed paid $103,450 of the city's money for the land, then split the difference between himself and several other civic-minded officials.

In 1855, Tweed was elected to the New York City Board of Elections, which was another cash cow for the money-hungry Tweed. He sold city textbooks for his own profit, and he sold teachers' jobs to whomever had the money to buy one. In one instance, Tweed peddled a teachers' position to a crippled schoolmarm for $75, even though the job only paid $300 a year.

In 1857, Tweed was appointed to the New York County Board of Supervisors, which propelled Tweed into a much more profitable form of thievery. Tweed formed what was known as the "Tweed Ring," which was nothing more than Tweed and his buddies controlling every job and work permit in the entire city of New York. Every contractor, artisan, and merchant who wanted to do business with the city had to cough up the cash, and they coughed up plenty. It is estimated that Tweed's Board of Supervisors pocketed 15 percent of every dollar spent on construction in New York City.

Concerning Tweed and his cronies, American lawyer and diarist George Templeton Strong wrote in 1860, "Our city government is rotten to the core."

By 1865, Tweed's wealth had grown to impressive proportions and so did his girth. Standing 5-feet-11-inches, Tweed's weight ballooned to 320 pounds. His reputation for eating was legendary, and he consumed enormous amounts of the finest foods in the finest restaurants. Tweed floundered around town, like a whale out of water, with a huge diamond stuck right in the middle of his fancy shirt, flouting his tremendous wealth.

It is estimated, from 1865 to 1871, Tweed's gang stole as much as $200 million from the New York City Treasury. They did this by over-billing the city for everything imaginable. They paid out of the city's coffers $10,000 for $75 worth of pencils, $171,000 for $4,000 worth of tables and chairs, and $1,826,000 for the plastering of a municipal building, which actually cost only $50,000 to plaster. Tweed also gave citizenship to over 60,000 immigrants, none of whom could read or write, but who could vote for Tweed and his cohorts on election day.

Tweed's downfall began on December 25, 1869, when *Harper's Weekly* published a cartoon of Tweed and his gang breaking into a huge box, with the caption "Taxpayers' and Tenants' Hard Earned Cash."

Upon seeing the cartoon, Tweed said, "Stop them damned pictures. I don't care so much what the papers say about me. My constituents don't know how to read, but they can't help seeing them damned pictures!"

With the pressure mounting to unveil the extent of Tweed's corruption, a blue ribbon panel, headed by future Presidential candidate Samuel J. Tilden, was formed to investigate New York

City's financial documents. When the books were checked, it was discovered that money had gone directly from city contractors into Tweed's pocket. The next day, Boss Tweed was arrested.

His first trial, in January 1873, ended in a hung jury; a jury many people thought was bought with Tweed's money. However, in November of that same year, Tweed was convicted on 204 out of 220 counts and sentenced to 12 years in prison.

Tweed was incarcerated in the Ludlow Street Jail, but, for some unknown reason, he was allowed home visits. During one such visit, Tweed fled the country and traveled to Spain, where he worked as a seaman on a commercial ship. Because his picture had been seen frequently in the newspapers, Tweed was recognized and returned to America. Tweed again was imprisoned in the Ludlow Street Jail, but this time no home visits were allowed.

On April 12, 1878, Boss Tweed died in the Ludlow Street Jail from a severe case of pneumonia. He was buried in Brooklyn's Greenwood Cemetery, and due to Tweed's outlandish treachery, New York Mayor Smith Ely would not allow the City Hall flag to be flown at half-mast in Tweed's memory.

No one could account for what became of Boss Tweed's vast amounts of ill-gotten gains. And not surprisingly, there were no reports of a Wells Fargo stagecoach following his horse-drawn hearse.

Watchmen (Leatherheads) and Roundsmen

The first New York City police force was created in 1845, but before then the streets of New York city were "protected" by a motley crew of incompetents, called Watchmen and Roundsmen.

The Watchmen first came into existence in the late 1700's, when the Dutch ruled New York City. Their job was little more than patrolling the streets at night, looking for any possible disturbances, but mostly avoiding them. They would also call out the hours of the night with such inane declarations as, "By the grace of God, two o'clock in peace." Or, "By the grace of God, four o'clock and a cold, raw morning."

Except for a 33-inch club, the Watchmen carried no arms. And they wore no uniforms, except for a fireman's leather hat, which they varnished twice a year, which made the hat as hard as a rock; hence they received the name - "Leatherheads." They were also called "Old Charlies," which was also not a term of endearment.

Starting in 1829, Watchmen were required by New York City ordinance to call out fires. If they saw smoke, the Watchmen would scream out either the name of his post, or the street name of where the fire was located.

There was also a street curfew, which stated anyone seen outdoors after 9 p.m. was considered to be of "bad morals." It was the Watchmen's duty to arrest anyone they caught wandering the streets at night, and then bring them to the local jail to be locked up until daylight.

The Watchmen's pay was a mere $1 a night. They were also paid an additional fifty cents to attend as witnesses at Special Court Sessions. There, they would testify to the particulars of any crime they may have seen while on duty, which, because of their lack of energy, hardly ever happened.

The criminals and gangs of New York City had very little respect for the Watchmen, who numbered only 30-40 in the entire city. The Watchmen were considered not to be very bright, nor very ambitious and were known to be frequently drunk on duty.

Each Watchmen had a post, or watch-box, which consisted of an unanchored wooden shack, where they would frequently fall asleep on duty, usually after consuming large amounts of whiskey. A favorite activity of the young ruffians throughout the city was to catch a Watchmen sleeping in his watch-box, lasso the watch-box with a rope, and then drag it through the streets, whooping and hollering like banshees. The soon-to-be-famous writer Washington Irving was known to be one of these pranksters.

Whereas Watchmen patrolled New York City at night, the crime solvers, or Roundsmen, were the daytime duty men. Roundsmen were considered the plainclothesmen, or detectives of the era, but solving crimes was certainly not their strong suit. Roundsmen were usually common laborers, or stevedores, who could not find work in their chosen fields of endeavor. As a result, Roundsmen were not especially adept at solving crimes, or catching criminals

Roundsmen were paid no salary, and they derived their income solely by serving legal papers, or collecting rewards from citizens for returning stolen property. This led to some very enterprising Roundsmen forming alliances with groups of criminals. The crooks would steal the goods, and the victims would post a reward for the return of their property. The Roundsmen would then "find" the stolen property, collect the reward, and then split it with the crooks.

Solving murders was very low on the list of the Roundsmen's priorities, since there was usually no reward for finding killers. The only way a Roundsmen could make a profit going after murderers was if the family of the victim posted a reward. And if the Roundsmen was lucky enough to catch the killer, which was very unusual, he would collect the reward and a further stipend from the city for serving a legal summons on the perpetrator.

Because of their outright incompetence, the Roundsmen and Watchmen were fast becoming an endangered species. It was the 1841 murder of Mary Rogers that put the final nail in their coffin. With plenty of clues as to who the murderer was, the Roundsmen dragged their heels, long enough that Rogers's killer was never found.

In 1845, the public was fed up with the archaic system of Watchmen and Roundsmen acting as an incompetent and un-industrious quasi-police force. Spurred on by the fury of the press, New York City reformers disbanded the Watchmen and Roundsmen system, and they replaced it with a functional police department, which was then copied by many cities throughout the United States of America.

Weyer, John (Johnny Spanish)

Johnny Spanish, whose real name was John Weyer, was one of the most feared gangsters in the early part of the 20th century. Weyer took the name Johnny Spanish because he was half-Jewish and half-Spanish. On his Spanish side, Weyer claimed to be a descendant of Butcher Weyer, the last Governor of Cuba. Weyer figured "Johnny Spanish" had much more cache to it rather than plain old John Weyer the Jew, so he claimed the name Johnny Spanish as his very own.

Spanish was born on the Lower East Side of Manhattan, and he quickly immersed himself in various street crimes. The short, frail, and morose Spanish was a loner, whose specialty was robbing saloons. When robbing a dive, Spanish liked to throw in the twist of sending a message to the saloon owners first, telling them of his imminent arrival. Spanish's legend grew immensely, when he performed that feat in a joint on Norfolk Street owned by Mersher the Strong Arm.

On the morning of the robbery, Spanish gave Mersher notice that he would arrive at a certain time. And that he did, armed with his usual four guns and an accomplice lurking behind him. Spanish threw a couple of shots through the mirror behind the bar, and then he emptied the till. To add insult to injury, Spanish lined 10 customers against the wall, and he relieved them of all their cash and jewelry. Spanish's notoriety grew, and soon he was accepted into Paul Kelly's Five Points Gang where he continued his shenanigans.

As an addition to his saloon crimes, Spanish found it quite profitable to steal the proceeds from the lucrative stuss gambling games located throughout New York City (stuss was a game which was a variation of the popular faro). Spanish had his eye on one such game, operated by Kid Jigger on Forsyth Street. One day, Spanish approached Jigger, who was known to be a fierce gunfighter, and he demanded half the take from Jigger's stuss game.

"And why should I give you half my stuss graft?" Jigger inquired.

"Because I'll knock you off if you don't," Spanish said.

Jigger just laughed.

Spanish took offense and told him, "Alright then, I'll knock you off tomorrow night."

Sure enough, being a man of his word, on the following night, as Jigger strode from his stuss game on Forsyth Street, Spanish opened fire with two guns. Jigger ran back into the building to safety, but the bullets struck an 8-year-old girl who was playing in the streets, killing her on the spot.

This necessitated Spanish leaving New York city for several months, until the heat died down. When Spanish returned, he was alarmed to find out that his girlfriend (who happened to be pregnant by who-knows -who), had been stolen by fellow thug Kid Dropper, real name Nathan Kaplan.

Spanish figured he'd settle with his ex-girlfriend first. He grabbed her off the streets, threw her in a taxicab, and then he headed out to the marshes of Maspeth, Long Island. There, Spanish tied her to a tree, and then he emptied five bullets into her pregnant belly. Spanish left the woman there to die, but miraculously, she survived. However, her baby was subsequently born with three missing fingers.

For this atrocity, Spanish was arrested, tried, convicted, and sentenced to seven years in Sing Sing Prison. Upon his release in 1917, Paul Kelly's Five Points Gang had dissolved, so Spanish figured he would take over Kelly's former rackets. The only problem was, Kid Dropper had the same idea.

The two old foes battled over the union protection racket for more than two years. One day in early 1919, the bulkier Dropper cornered Spanish on the street, and he carved him up badly with a knife. Spanish survived, but not for long.

On July 29, 1919, Spanish was entering a restaurant at 19 Second Avenue, when Dropper and two accomplices opened fire, hitting Spanish several times in the chest.

Bullets working better than blades, Spanish died a few days later in Bellevue Hospital.

Wexler, Irving (Waxey Gordon)

In the 1920's, Waxey Gordon was one of the richest, most powerful gangsters in New York City. However, after he was set up by his enemies for a fall, Gordon was reduced to selling junk on the streets like a common two-bit criminal.

Waxey Gordon was born Irving Wexler in 1889 on the Lower East Side of Manhattan to Polish/Jewish parents. Not having a great fondness for the New York City school system, Wexler took to the streets, and he became the best pickpocket on the Lower East Side. Wexler was so good at his trade, he got the nickname "Waxey," because he was so "light fingered," he could pick someone's wallet, like his fingers and the wallet were coated with wax. Waxey Gordon sounded better than "Waxey Wexler," so Waxey Gordon it was, from that point on.

Gordon did what most tough Jewish criminals did in those days. He got involved in the labor rackets (with the Dopey Fein gang), and soon Gordon was "schlammin'," or breaking heads, with the best of them. To supplement his income, Gordon also did a little burglary and minor dope dealings on the side.

One of the men Gordon cracked heads for was the legendary gambler Arnold "The Brain" Rothstein, who was known to do a little investing in other people's illegal enterprises. It was the beginning of Prohibition, and Gordon hooked up with small-time hood, Max "Big Maxey" Greenberg, who had big ideas, but little cash. Greenberg had left his home in St. Louis for the bright lights of Manhattan, because he heard there were certain people who might bankroll his dream of owning his own bootlegging business. Greenberg needed $175,000 to get started, and through Gordon's connection to Rothstein, Maxey and Waxey approached "The Brain" (on a Central Park bench, no less), about loaning them the cash they needed in return for a piece of the action.

At first, Rothstein turned them down flat. Then, Rothstein had a change of heart, as well as a change of plans. Rothstein saw tremendous potential in the bootlegging business, but what Greenberg and Gordon were planning was strictly small-time. Rothstein said he would loan them the money, but with very specific conditions.

First, Rothstein would run the operation; no questions asked. Greenberg and Gordon would act as Rothstein's main men, using their street contacts as secondary employees, who were needed for such a big operation.

And second, instead of smuggling cheap hooch in boats from Canada, Rothstein saw more monetary potential in shipping in top-notch booze from England. Rothstein purchased six speedboats, and when the cargo ship he hired, carrying 20,000 cases of Scotch, arrived in American waters from England, it would stop several miles off the coast of Montauk, Long Island. There it would be met by the six Rothstein speedboats, each of which would carry nearly 1,000 cases of booze back to shore. After the speedboats made three or four trips from ship to shore, trucks would take the booze to a warehouse in Manhattan, where it would be stored, and then distributed to thousands of speakeasies throughout the city.

This continuing operation brought Gordon much wealth. It was estimated, Gordon earned between $1 and $2 million a year, pure profit for himself. With this dough, Gordon bought several office buildings in Manhattan, a string of speakeasies, and illegal gambling houses.

After Rothstein was killed over a bad gambling debt, Gordon purchased his own fleet of motor boats, to keep the illegal flow of booze coming from across the pond. Gordon also bought a townhouse in Manhattan on Central Park West and a castle in New Jersey, complete with its very own moat.

Gordon soon formed bootlegging partnerships with the Italian gangs, headed by Lucky Luciano, who was himself was partnered with Jewish kingpin Meyer Lansky. By this time, Luciano was in the process of organizing Italian gangs throughout the country under one umbrella, and Lansky was doing the same thing with Jewish gangs.

The only problem was, Lansky and Gordon, both Jews, couldn't stand each other and wouldn't even sit at the same table together. Both accused the other of hijacking their bootlegging trucks, and both were right in their assumptions.

What transpired next, was what was known in the press as "The War of the Jews." Lansky killed Gordon's men, and Gordon returned the favor. Luciano tried to step in to settle the dispute, but to no avail.

Gordon had now been declared "Public Enemy Number One" by the FBI, which put him right in the cross-hairs of Special Prosecutor Thomas E. Dewey. In 1930, it was Luciano's idea to feed Gordon to Dewey on an income tax rap, with Lansky's brother Jake leaking information to Dewey's investigators, about Gordon's financial operations. Gordon was arrested and indicted by Dewey.

At Gordon's trial, Dewey was able to show that Gordon lived high on the hog, raking in almost $2 million a year and only reporting an annual salary of $8,125. One hundred and fifty witnesses testified against Gordon, and they minutely explained to the jury Gordon's illegal moneymaking activities. As a result, the jury took only 51 minutes to come back with a guilty verdict, which sent Gordon to the slammer on a 10-year sentence.

In 1940, when Gordon was released from Leavenworth, all his properties had been seized by the government and his millions had somehow disappeared. He told reporters, "Waxey Gordon is dead. From now on it's Irving Wexler, salesman."

Gordon became a salesman alright, but not in the conventional manner. Gordon moved out to California, and he began peddling dope on the streets. In 1951, Gordon was arrested while delivering $6,300 of heroin to a federal narcotics informant. One of the cops who arrested Gordon was Sgt. John Cottone.

As Cottone was putting the cuffs on Gordon, Gordon started crying "Please Johnny, don't arrest me. Don't take me in for junk. Let me run, then shoot me."

In December of 1951, Gordon, now 63, was convicted of narcotics trafficking and sentenced to 25 years in Alcatraz Prison. Gordon, broke and a broken man, died in prison six months later of a heart attack.

Whyos Street Gang

The Whyos were a vicious Irish street gang which ruled Lower Manhattan, starting right after the Civil War and running through the 1890's. The Whyos started out as an offshoot of a pre-Civil War gang called the Chichesters. Their headquarters was in the 6th Ward on Baxter Street, formerly Orange Street, and named after Mexican War hero Lt. Col. Charles Baxter.

The Whyos got their name from the bird calls they made to each other to identify themselves as members of the gang. When they first appeared on the streets of Lower Manhattan, the Whyos cruised the area called Mulberry Bend, robbing, beating, and killing with ungodly gusto. Soon, they extended their domain to the Lower West Side, into Greenwich Village, and then further north.

Author Herbert Asbury said about the Whyos "The Whyos were the most ferocious criminals who ever stalked the streets of an American city."

The Whyos favorite hangout was a dive on the corner of Mulberry and Worth called "The Morgue"; an apt name, since it was estimated that over 100 murders took place on the premises. The bar owner boasted his booze was powerful and quite tasty but could also be used an excellent embalming fluid if necessary.

Myth had it, that in order to become a member of the Whyos, an aspiring member had to kill, or at least make an attempt to kill someone. One of the Whyos early leaders was Mike McCoin, who was hanged in the Tombs on March 8, 1883, for the slingshot murder of a saloon owner on West 26th Street named Louis Hanier. The day after he killed Hanier, McCoin announced to his gang, "A guy ain't tough until he's knocked his man out (killed)."

Some hard men took McCoin's remark to heart and a string of murders followed, precipitating new members being inducted into the gang.

In the 1880's, the Whyos reached the height of their power, when such miscreants as Big Jim Hines terrorized the city. Hines was the first person to hold up stuss games, which were then run by the Italian and Jewish gangs and a great source of revenue. The stuss games were played nightly at numerous locations, from east of the

Bowery, up to 14th Street, and then west to Broadway. Almost every night, Hines bounced from one stuss game to another, a huge gun in each hand. Using impending force, Hines extracted a fat percentage of each game, but he always left a substantial cut for the house.

Once, after he was arrested, Hines told a detective, "Them guys must be nuts. Don't I always leave 'em somethin'? All I want is me share."

In 1884, Whyos member Piker Ryan was arrested for one of his numerous crimes. The police found a book on him, containing prices for a laundry list of crimes the Whyos performed for monetary profit. The list read:

Punching -- $2,
Both eyes blacked -- $4
Nose and jaw broke -- $10
Jacked out - - $15
Ear chewed off -- $15
Leg or arm broke -- $19
Shot in the leg -- $25
Stab -- $25
Doing the big job (murder) -- $100 and up

Another prominent Whyos member was Dandy Johnny Dolan, who was fastidious in dress, with oiled and plastered hair, and a penchant for wearing only the finest shoe apparel available.

Dolan was also the inventor of two gruesome weapons. The first was sections of an ax blade, embedded in the sole of his "Fighting Shoes," which he used to stomp and stab a fallen foe. The other was an "eye gouger," made of brass and worn on Dolan's thumb.

On August 22, 1875, Dolan decided to rob a brush manufacturer at 275 Greenwich Street. On the premises, he confronted James H. Noe, and Dolan bashed Noe over the head with an iron crowbar. Then Dolan proceeded to rob Noe of money, a gold watch and chain, and Mr. Noe's walking stick, which had a metal handle formed into the shape of a monkey. However, before Dolan left, he gouged out both of Mr. Noe's eyes with his "eye gouger," and then he proudly showed Noe's eyeballs to his pals.

Mr. Noe died a few days later, and when Dolan was soon arrested, he was walking with Mr. Noe's distinctive cane and carrying Mr. Noe's eyeballs in his pocket. As a result, Dolan was tried and convicted of murder. He was hung in the courtyard of the Tombs Prison, on April 21, 1876.

The most famous of the Whyos leaders were a couple of Dannys; Messrs. Driscoll and Lyons, who co-ran the Whyos in the 1880's. In 1888, Driscoll became involved in a gunfight with Five Points gang member John McCarthy, over the affections of a prostitute named Beezy Garrity. Not being the greatest of gunslingers, Driscoll accidentally shot and killed Ms. Garrity instead.

At his trial, Driscoll swore it was a case of mistaken identity, and that John McCarty had fired the fatal shots at Ms. Garrity. However, Garrity's mother, Margaret Sullivan, said on the witness stand that as her daughter lay dying at St. Vincent Hospital, she whispered into her mother's ear, "Danny Driscoll shot me, mother."

Even though Driscoll was represented by famed trial attorney William Howe, as a result of Garrity's deathbed statement, on October 1, 1887, the jury took only 29 minutes to find Driscoll guilty of first degree murder. Seven days later, Judge Fredrick Smyth sentenced Driscoll to death.

On January 22, 1888, Driscoll was hanged in the Tombs Prison. At the gallows, after the black mask had been pulled over Driscoll's face, his last words reportedly were, "Jesus, have mercy on me!"

Danny Lyons was considered the most vicious gangster of the 1880's. Lyons's downfall was an argument over a young lady, too. It seemed Lyons snatched Pretty Kitty McGown from her paramour Joseph Quinn. Quinn vowed revenge, and on July 4, 1887, the two men squared off with guns, at Paradise Square in the Five Points area. Lyons was better with a gun than his pal Driscoll had been, and he shot Quinn right through the heart, killing him on the spot.

Lyons took it on the lam for a few months, but he was finally captured. Lyons was hung at the Tombs Prison on August 21, 1888, just seven months after Driscoll had met the same fate in the same place.

After the deaths of Lyons and Driscoll, the Whyos fell into disarray. In the late 1890's, Monk Eastman defeated what was left of the Whyos. For the next 20 years, Eastman battled with Paul Kelly, leader of the Five Points Gang, for control of all the rackets in Lower Manhattan.

Wood, Fernando, and the Police Riots of 1857

In 1857, it was chaotic times in New York City, as the city's two adversarial police forces battled over the right to arrest people, and to accept graft from anyone willing and able to pay.

In 1853, under Democratic Mayor Harper, the first uniformed police force in New York City was created. Their uniform consisted of a blue coat with brass buttons, a blue cap, and gray pants. Led by Police Chief George G. Matsell, the police were generally more crooked than the crooks, taking bribes not to arrest people and sometimes taking bribes *to* arrest people. The citizens of New York City complained that their police force, called the Municipal Police, was "the worse in the world."

By the age of 37, Fernando Wood was a millionaire in the real estate business. On January 1, 1855, after buying votes through his wealth, Wood was elected Mayor of New York City. Wood immediately inserted himself as head of the police graft-gravy-train; charging new police captains $200 a year for a promotion to their $1,000-a-year job. Of course, to make up for the shortfall, the police captains charged each patrolman under their command $40 a year. The policemen, in turn, shook down honest citizens and protected dishonest citizens for pay, so everyone on the public law enforcement dole was quite happy to keep things just the way they were.

However, the New York State Legislature would have none of that.

In 1857, the legislature passed an act creating a new Metropolitan Police Force, with Fredrick Tallmadge named as Superintendent of the Force. The legislature also ordered Wood to immediately disband his 1,100 member Municipal Police Force. Wood refused; saying the creation of the new police force was unconstitutional. Thus, the court battle began over which police force would be the one to patrol New York City.

The Supreme Court soon voted that the creation of the new police force was indeed constitutional. Yet Wood, with the backing of Police Chief Matsell, steadfastly refused to cooperate. Eight hundred men, all aligned with the Democratic Party, stayed with

Wood and Matsell. However, three hundred men, under respected Police Captain George W. Walling, defected and comprised the new Metropolitan Police Force, which was backed by the Republican Party.

On June 16, 1857, the issue came to a head. The street commissioner Joseph Taylor had died, and Wood, for the sum of $50,000, appointed Charles Devlin as the new street commissioner. On the same day, Republican Governor John A. King appointed Daniel Conover to the same position. As Conover entered City Hall to assume his new post, Wood had his Municipal Police throw Conover out of the building. Conover immediately went to a Republican judge, who swore out two warrants for Wood's arrest: one for assault and one for inciting to riot.

Captain Walling strode to City Hall to arrest Wood on the assault charge, but he was met by a contingent of five hundred Municipals. Captain Walling was allowed to enter the building and Wood's office. However, when Captain Walling told Wood he was under arrest for assault, Wood refused to recognize the legality of the arrest warrant.

Captain Walling grabbed Wood's arm to lead him out of the building, but he was immediately swarmed by 20 Municipals and thrown out of City Hall himself. Captain Walling repeatedly tried to go back up the steps of City Hall, but he was beaten back every time.

Suddenly, a contingent of one hundred Metropolitan Police, wearing their new uniforms of frock coats, and plug hats, arrived to serve the second arrest warrant on Wood. Instead of wearing the gold badges of the Municipals, the Mets wore copper badges, which gave birth to the term "coppers," and then "cops."

The motley Metropolitan Police were described by essayist G.T. Strong as, "a miscellaneous assortment of suckers, soaplocks, Irishmen and Plug-Uglies (an Irish Street Gang)."

Thus, began a horrendous half-hour battle between the two New York City Police Departments. The Mets were vastly outnumbered by the Municipals, and when the fight was over, some Mets were lucky enough to be able to flee unharmed. However, 53 Mets were injured, 12 hurt seriously, and one was crippled for life.

While the fighting was intensifying, Captain Walling rushed over the office of Sheriff J.J.V. Westervelt, and he implored the sheriff to arrest Mayor Wood. After consulting with a state attorney,

Captain Walling, Sheriff Westervelt, and the state attorney marched to City Hall, and they pushed their way into Wood's office.

When the three men informed Wood he was indeed under arrest, he shouted at them, "I will never let you arrest me!"

At the same time, a beaten contingent of Mets spotted the Seventh Regiment of the National Guard boarding a boat for Boston. The Mets convinced the National Guard that they were needed to police a state matter.

Recognizing the severity of the situation, Major General Charles Sandford marched his men to City Hall. As his troops stood guard, Sandford strode up the steps of City Hall and into Wood's office, where he announced to Wood that he was under arrest. Wood looked out the window and spotted the National Guard. Realizing his men were no match for the military troops, Wood finally submitted to the arrest.

Yet, this was only the beginning of a long strife. For the rest of the summer, the two police departments constantly conflicted. When a Met cop arrested a crook, a Municipal would step in and set the man free. And vice versa. On numerous occasions, contingents of policemen would raid the other department's station house and free all the prisoners.

In the meantime, the criminals of New York City were having a field day.

While the two police forces battled each other all hours of the day and night, honest citizens were being robbed while walking the streets. Murders were committed with impunity, and still, all the two police departments were interested in was fighting each other.

This total indifference by the two New York City police departments led to a two-day riot on July 4 and July 5, of 1857, when the Bowery Boys and the Dead Rabbits street gangs squared off with fists, knives, stones, and pistols. As many as a thousand gang members were involved. Hundreds were injured, and several gang members were killed. The riots also led to the indiscriminate looting of stores, in the Five Points and Bowery areas and as far north as 14th Street.

Finally, in the fall of 1857, the Court of Appeals upheld the Supreme Court's ruling, that the Metropolitan Police were the only legitimate police department in town. The Municipals were disbanded, and although Mayor Wood had been arrested, he was released on bond and never tried.

The Mets, who were injured in the June 16 fight, sued Mayor Wood for personal damages. They were awarded $250 apiece by the courts, but Mayor Wood refused to pay a dime. Finally, the city of New York was forced to pay the damages from the city treasury, including the injured Mets' legal costs.

Wood was defeated in the 1858 Mayoral race by Daniel F. Tiemann. Yet, in 1860, the rotten Wood was somehow re-elected mayor of New York City, until 1862.

After the Civil War started, Wood floated a trial balloon, whereby New York City would secede from the state of New York, which was run by Republicans, and therefore, become a free city. Wood's proposal was shot down, and *New York Tribune's* editor Horace Greeley, wrote in an editorial, "Fernando Wood evidently wants to be a traitor. It is lack of courage only that makes him content with being a blackguard."

In 1867, Wood found his true calling in the United States House of Representatives, where he served, not too admirably, until his death on February 14, 1881.

A year later, statesman and author John Bigelow, who knew Wood well, said that Wood was, "The most corrupt man who ever sat in the mayor's chair of New York City."

Yale (Uale), Frankie

Frankie Yale, real name Uale, was the number No. 1 mobster in Brooklyn for most of the Roaring 20's.

Yale was born in the Calabrian town of Longobucco, Italy, in 1893. In 1901, he emigrated to the United States, and soon Yale became immersed in a life of crime. Although his stomping grounds were in Brooklyn, Yale met fellow Brooklynite Johnny Torrio, and he became partners with Torrio in the Five Points Gang in Lower Manhattan, under the tutelage of mob boss Paul Kelly.

Torrio and Yale were involved in several illegal endeavors, but their biggest moneymaker was a version of the Black Hand extortion shakedown, in which they threatened to kill Italian immigrants unless the immigrants paid protection money. Most paid, but some didn't. It was reported that Yale had killed a dozen times before he reached the age of 21.

Yale and Torrio decided to split with the Five Points Gang, and they relocated to Brooklyn, where their base of operations was the Harvard Inn, a bar and brothel near the Brooklyn Navy Yard.

In 1919, Torrio moved to Chicago, to work for his uncle-through-marriage, mob boss Big Jim Colosimo. Yale filled Torrio's absence by hiring a friend of Torrio's, the 19-year-old Al Capone, as his main bouncer at the Harvard Inn. Soon afterwards, Torrio summoned Capone to work for him in Chicago, with the eventual intention of killing Colosimo and taking over his rackets.

In 1920, Torrio decided the time was ripe for Colosimo's death, so he asked his friend Frankie Yale if he could make the trip to Chicago to do the dirty deed. Torrio set Colosimo up by telling Colosimo to go to his cafe to receive an illegal shipment of booze. When Colosimo got to the cafe, instead of liquor, Colosimo was greeted by several rounds of hot lead supplied by the reliable Yale.

Torrio's Chicago empire was being threatened by Irish mob boss Dion O'Banion, who ran a flower shop on North State Street. Torrio decided O'Banion had to go, too and figuring his local shooters couldn't get close enough to O'Banion to kill him, he called on Yale again. The reason Torrio picked Yale for the hit was because O'Banion had never met Yale and wouldn't recognize him.

In November 1924, Yale entered O'Banion's flower shop, and he greeted O'Banion with a firm handshake. O'Banion tried to pull his hand free, but before he could extricate himself from Yale's death grip, two of Torrio's men, John Scalise and Albert Anselmi, busted into the shop and shot O'Banion to death. O'Banion had, up to that point, the biggest funeral in the history of Chicago; costing over $30,000, including a $10,000 coffin.

In 1925, Torrio was ambushed and shot several times in front of his apartment building. After he recovered from his wounds, Torrio decided to retire from the rackets, and he handed over his entire illegal empire to the 26-year old Capone.

Capone worked a deal with Yale, to import his illegal booze from Chicago to New York City, under Yale's protection. Soon, Capone's trucks were being hijacked before they got to New York City. Capone, suspecting Yale was the culprit, sent one his best men, James DeAmato, to survey the truck-hijacking situation in New York City. Soon, DeAmato sent word back to Capone that Yale was indeed hijacking Capone's trucks, and then selling the liquor back to Capone. Six days later, DeAmato was gunned down on a Brooklyn Street.

With Capone safely in Miami, Florida, he sent six of his best shooters to New York City by car. Yale was summoned from his home on a ruse, and while he was driving down 44th Street in Brooklyn, Yale was met with a deadly deluge of bullets fired from the new weapon of choice: a Thompson submachine gun.

Yale had always admired the grandeur of O'Banion's funeral, so he did O'Banion one better.

Yale's funeral procession attracted ten thousand mourners and his funeral cost $50,000, including a $15,000 nickel and silver coffin.

Take that, Dion O'Banion.

Zelig, Big Jack (Zelig Harry Lefkowitz)

Big Jack Zelig was born Zelig Harry Lefkowitz in New York City in 1888. Zelig started his criminal career at the age of nine. By the time Zelig had reached 13 and working for the Crazy Butch Gang on the Lower East Side, he became known as one of the best pickpockets in New York City. By the time he was 15, Zelig was a member of the feared Monk Eastman Gang. As an Eastman, Zelig was respected on the Lower East Side as a feared street fighter, who was especially adept at using a knife. Because of his roughhouse escapades, Zelig was dubbed by the police, "The Most Feared Man in New York City."

While Eastman was in jail for assault and robbery, the Eastman gang was headed by Max "Kid Twist" Zwerbach, who appointed Zelig his No. 1 lieutenant. When Zwerbach was killed in 1908 by a member of the rival Five Points Gang, Zelig took control of Zwerbach's gang.

Zelig's gang robbed casinos, banks and brothels, but their specialty was thuggery for hire. The Zelig gang even had a printed menu of the gang's services.

To have them slash the cheek of someone, it cost anywhere from $1 to $10, according to your ability to pay. A shot in the leg or arm cost $5 to $25. Tossing a live bomb to take down an establishment also cost $5 to $25. And to render someone dead, they charged anywhere from $10 to $100.

Zelig's capable men included such notables as Harry "Gyp the Blood" Horowitz, "Lefty" Louie Rosenberg, and "Dago Frank" Cirofisi.

Zelig's two chief nemeses, who were fighting with him behind the scenes for control of the former Eastman Gang, were gang members Chick Tricker and Jack Sirocco. Tricker and Sirocco tricked Zelig into going on a back robbery with them. After Tricker and Sirocco were in possession of the bank's cash, they left Zelig behind to take the rap. Zelig was arrested and none too happy with his pals.

To add insult to injury, Tricker and Sirocco refused to bail out Zelig; figuring with Zelig behind bars, they could assume control of his gang. However, Zelig had friends in high places in Tammany Hall, and soon he was set free. Thus commenced a war between Zelig, and Tricker and Sirocco.

On December 6, 1911, Zelig threw a shindig for his gang at Stuyvesant Hall. Tricker and Sirocco were not invited, but they sent their associate Jules Morello to the party, with the expressed intention of killing Zelig.

However, Morello had a few too many drinks at the bar, and he started yelling "Where's that Yid? I'm gonna kill that Yid."

Meaning Zelig.

Zelig heard the commotion, and before Morello could do him any damage, Zelig shot Morello four times, leaving him dead.

On October 15, 1912, Zelig was drinking at Segal's Cafe, at 76 Second Avenue, when he got a phone call from his girlfriend saying she needed company for the night. Delighted at his good fortune, Zelig hopped on the Second Avenue Street Car in front of Siegel's. When the street car reached 13th Street, a junkie thug named Red Davidson snuck up behind Zelig and shot him once behind the ear, killing him.

"The Most Feared Man in New York City" was now dead at the age of 24.

Davidson's motive was never ascertained, but it was reported Davidson killed Zelig because, a few days earlier, Zelig had beaten Davidson to a pulp over a monetary dispute.

Zwerbach, Maxwell (Kid Twist)

"Kid Twist," real name Maxwell Zwerbach, was a ruthless killer who rose up the ranks of the Monk Eastman mob, only to die because he decided to cheat on his wife.

Zwerbach was born in Austria in 1884. His Jewish father, Adolf, and half-Italian mother, Hanna, emigrated to New York City in 1886 to escape the anti-Semitic riots. The family took an apartment on Delancey Street, where Adolph opened a tailor shop. Adolph hoped his son would follow in his footsteps and alter clothes for a living. However, Zwerbach, who was now called Kid Twist on the mean streets of the Lower East Side, had other ideas.

Kid Twist started out as a petty thief. Soon, he hooked up with the famous Monk Eastman gang, made up of Jews who were constantly at war with Paul Kelly's (Paulo Vaccarelli) Italian Five Pointers over the Lower East Side rackets. Kid Twist killed his way up the ranks, until Eastman installed him as his top lieutenant, along with Richie Fitzpatrick, a Jewish killer who took on an Irish last name.

In early 1903, Eastman had the misfortune of getting himself locked up in a Freehold, New Jersey jail, after he beat up a potential witness against a friend of his on the courthouse steps. When Kid Twist heard of his bosses' predicament, he rounded up 50 of his best thugs, with the intention of driving to New Jersey to bust Eastman out of jail.

However, before their cars could leave their Christie Street headquarters, a battalion of policemen, led by Inspector McCluskey, descended upon them and beat them with nightsticks back into their club.

Kid Twist decided to change tactics, and he contacted Eastman's cronies in Tammany Hall. The crooked pols used their Jersey connections and Eastman was sprung the following day.

Eastman was not so lucky in 1904, when he was arrested near Times Square for assault and robbery. This time Tammany Hall refused to come to his rescue. Eastman was tried, convicted, and sentenced to 10 years in the slammer.

Kid Twist thought he was now the rightful heir to Eastman's

throne, but Fitzpatrick had the same idea. Both men argued over who was the new boss. Finally, Kid Twist told Fitzpatrick, he had a plan on how the rackets could be split down the middle with both men having separate but equal powers. Fitzpatrick thought Twist's idea sounded just swell, and he agreed to a meeting to work out the details.

On November 1, 1904, Kid Twist enticed Fitzpatrick into the back room of the Sheriff Street Saloon (which oddly enough, was located on Christie Street). As soon as Fitzpatrick arrived, the lights went out and so did Fitzpatrick. He was shot twice through the heart by Kid Dahl, real name Harris Stahl, thus installing Kid Twist as the No. 1 man in the Eastman Gang, all by himself.

As a result of Fitzpatrick's sudden demise, Kid Twist took over all of Eastman's operations, which included several brothels and stuss card games. In a show of bravado, Kid Twist announced to the world that "no Wop and no Mick would ever rule the Lower East Side of New York."

As a side moneymaker, Kid Twist championed his own brand of the popular "celery soda," which was the only brand of celery soda allowed to be sold on the entire Lower East Side of Manhattan.

Even though Kid Twist had several stuss games of his own, he coveted the one on Suffolk Street owned by the Bottler, which was under the protection of Paul Kelly's Five Pointers. First, Kid Twist approached the Bottler, and not in a very nice way, Kid Twist told him that he was now the Bottler's partner, not Paul Kelly. Before the ink was dry on Twist's verbal contract, he informed the Bottler that the Bottler was out completely, and that Kid Dahl was now Kid Twist's partner in the Suffolk Street stuss parlor.

This time the Bottler made a stand, and he refused to comply with Kid Twist's demands. As a result, Kid Twist imported Coney Islander Vach Lewis, known as Cyclone Louie, a professional circus strongman, who was famous for bending iron bars around his neck, and sometimes around other people's necks, too.

While Kid Twist was in the Delancey Street police station screaming at the desk sergeant over some trivial matter, and Kid Dahl was in a Houston Street restaurant arguing with the owner over what time of day it was, Cyclone Louie calmly walked into the Bottler's stuss parlor. As 20 customers looked on in shock, Cyclone Louie shot the Bottler twice in the chest, killing him instantly.

With Kid Twist and Kid Dahl eliminated as suspects because of their contrived alibis, a few days later Kid Dahl strode into the Suffolk Street stuss parlor and announced to all that the stuss parlor was now his and Kid Twist's possession. All this did not please Paul Kelly too much, and he waited for the right time to get back what was rightfully his.

On the night of May 14, 1908, Kid Twist and Cyclone Louie decided to travel to Coney Island, to visit the supposedly happily married Kid Twist's girlfriend, dancer Carroll Terry. The two men were sitting inside the dance hall Terry performed in, when a kid rushed inside and told them Terry wanted to see them outside.

As soon as their feet hit the pavement, Kid Twist and Cyclone Louie were blasted with bullets fired by Kelly henchman, Louie "The Lump" Pioggi and several other of Kelly's men. It took only one slug to the brain, shot by Pioggi, to finish Kid Twist, but Cyclone Louie, true to his reputation as a strong man, needed five bullets in his torso to render him deceased.

When Terry showed up seconds later, Pioggi, a jilted suitor of hers, whipped a slug into her hip. Terry fell face forward, and although she would survive, the unconscious Terry landed across the body of her lifeless boyfriend, Maxwell "Kid Twist" Zwerbach, thereby putting a dent in the premise that "true love never dies."

The End